# THE SPIRITUAL REAWAKENING OF THE GREAT SMOKY MOUNTAINS

## PAGE BRYANT

Page Bryant
1994

THE SPIRITUAL REAWAKENING OF THE GREAT
SMOKY MOUNTAINS

by Page Bryant
Copyright © July, 1994 by Page Bryant
All rights reserved. No part of this book may be reproduced in any form or by any means, except for the inclusion of brief quotations in a review, without permission in writing from the author and/or publisher.

Address all inquiries to Page Bryant
Mystic Mountain Center
707 Brunswick Drive
Waynesville, N.C. 28786

First Edition
Printed in the United States of America
ISBN 0-9641390-0-6
Library of Congress Catalog Card Number
94-94381

COVER AND INSIDE PHOTOS COURTESY OF
NORTH CAROLINA DIVISION
OF TRAVEL AND TOURISM
Ilustrations by Scott Guynup
Typesetting by Sam Godwin
Book design by Scott Guynup

This book is dedicated to the memory of **Sun Bear**....a true Earth Warrior and my friend.

# TABLE OF CONTENTS

INTRODUCTION

| | |
|---|---|
| Chapter One | THE BIRTH AND EVOLUTION OF THE SMOKIES |
| Chapter Two | MAN AND MOUNTAINS UNITE |
| Chapter Three | SACRED VOICES IN THE WILDERNESS |
| Chapter Four | THE SMOKIES AND THE BLUE RIDGE: ANCIENT SACRED LAND |
| Chapter Five | GRIDS AND LEY SYSTEMS |
| Chapter Six | THE SOUL OF THE GREAT SMOKY MOUNTAINS |
| Chapter Seven | PLANT KINGDOM: THE GREEN NATION |
| Chapter Eight | FOREVER FLOWS THE SACRED WATERS |
| Chapter Nine | CONCLUSION |

# ACKNOWLEDGEMENTS

Writing a book is a long process that never happens because one person has an idea and picks up a pen. Quite the contrary. The idea is just the beginning. In fact, the writing is the easy part that, oftentimes, goes rather fast. Much precedes the writing; the searching out of similar ideas from others so as to support the idea; the reading, the search for data, and, in the case of this book, the hours of driving throughout the Blue Ridge and the Smokies....down backroads, through valleys, up steep mountain grades, through beautiful green forests and breathtaking gorges.....all a pleasure. Aside from the people who help by sharing their knowledge and experiences through their books, there are also those who give of their time, knowledge, expertise, and support in so many ways. There are many such individuals whom I must thank for without them this book could not have become a reality.

I would first like to give a heart-felt thanks David Wheeler, a writer for the Katuah Journal. I met David when I first arrived in North Carolina when he interviewed me for an issue of *Katuah Journal* that was dedicated to earth energies. (Issue 31, Summer 1991) David's excitement about the project, his encouragement, and his kindness in providing me with all the back issues of Katuah Journal were a tremendous help. I also thank the staff of Katuah Journal for allowing me to quote ideas and information from Katuah Journal, which was, without question, the finest publication of its kind I have ever encountered. Heartfelt appreciation goes to the authors and publishers who granted permission to use various quotes and information from their books.

I thank Don O'Neal and Mark Stevens for reading the finished manuscript for me. I thank my brother, Brad Watts, for going on so many of those rides with me, and most of the time doing the driving, and for sharing the experience of these old mountains which, like myself, he loves deeply, so willingly and joyfully. I thank Fred Spinks for his support in the early days of this project, especially for providing for me several of the books I needed for research. Thanks goes to Lloyd Owle. Lloyd has been a loving friend and supporter to both my husband and myself, and it is because of him that we have had the opportunity to experience a part of the Cherokee spirituality that still lives in these ancient mountains.

I wish to honor the spirit of Sun Bear that inspired me throughout the unfoldment of this project. I often recall my last conversation with him.....when I telephoned him to let him know that I had just learned that the sacred fire, Ancient Red, had returned to the Great Smoky Mountains. Sun Bear deeply understood the symbolism involved with what he referred to as "a time of returning to the medicine wheel". He was quick to recognize those sometimes subtle, sometimes obvious conditions and events that testisfied to the revival of interest in Native American spirituality. Such only confirmed what he knew to be so.

Thanks much go to Zelda Fortner for her believing in my work and her role in making this book a reality. Thanks to Sam Godwin for his patience in typesetting the manuscript. In fact, patience is not the word; tolerance of my "computer stupidity" is probably more accurate. Thank you, Sam, for lugging your computer back and forth from your home to the office. We've both learned a new meaning for the word "serenity"! For encouragement and help, thanks must also go to Robin Dunn, Walker Calhoun, and especially to Rita Livingston who made Scott and I feel a part of the New Age community when we first arrived.

I am also extremely endebted to my husband and best friend, Scott, for his tireless hours of love and support, his ideas and suggestions, his illustrations, and his belief and commitment to the project........and for trusting my decision to move to the Smokies.

NOTE: Past issues of *Katuah Journal* are still available. A complete list is available through Rob Messick; P.O. Box 638, Leicester, N.C. 28748

# INTRODUCTION

This book was written for a number of reasons. One involves my concern for the overwhelming environmental issues with which we are currently faced. Slowly, we search for ways that we, as humans, can pull ourselves and our planet out of the effects of the ecological atrocities we have heaped upon both. Perhaps we are trying to make changes because we sense an impending environmental disaster. Out of our ecological concerns has arisen the "green movement" which, to many, is a collective voice being raised in defense of ecological values and tactics that allow, and often *cause*, environmental ruin. Along the way of our concern, we seem to have rediscovered something very important.....the way of life and spiritual values of the American Indians, particularly the part that involves their relationship with the Earth Mother. For many of us, as non-Indian people, as we continue to learn about their age-old Tradition, find it to be a "tool" that, when truly put into practice, can help save Mother Earth and ourselves.

Another purpose for this writing is that it gives this writer an opportunity to reflect upon and share my own personal interest in and experiences with Native American spirituality in general and, in this writing that of the early Cherokees; a tribe whose ancestral tradition is an integral thread in the tapestry of the indigenous peoples of Turtle Island. Though buried beneath the domination of modern society and Christianity for over a century, I feel that a new cycle of interest in Cherokee spiritual tradition, as well as the traditions of other tribes, is indeed being born. This "birth," perhaps better called a "rebirth", was predicted long ago by at least one native elder, the Holy Man of the Oglala Sioux, Black Elk. In his famous vision, Black Elk predicted the resurrection of the spiritual ways of his people. I see this happening and it is good. It is a process that is not occurring with all tribes simultaneously or to the same degree. But it is happening. As time goes on, I feel the Cherokees will be among those whose traditional ways will hold tremendous interest for all people, and that a revival of the sacred knowledge and rites of the Cherokees, the Indian mountaineers will continue to take place. I believe this has already begun; a rebirth that is taking place as their homeland, the Great Smoky Mountains, are being reborn to their full power. I think that one of the most significant points to be made about this current interest in Native American spirituality is that it is occurring within both natives and non-natives alike. This may be, in part, due to an innate awareness that the sacred Red Road may be the path that leads us back to a connection with Mother Earth and, ultimately, with the Universe as a whole.

I am not an expert on the Cherokee people nor Cherokee spirituality. What I know comes from research and study born from my sincere interest in the matter, conversations with many of the people, and from what I have intuited in my mind and feel in my heart. Throughout this writing, which has taken the better part of three years, I have taken the liberty of speaking from my heart......the only true and honest path open to me. I am aware of the ill feelings that are often stirred when a non-native person speaks, writes, or teaches about native people and their religious traditions. But I have chosen to look past the potentiality of such controversy and to go beyond the human-imposed boundaries of skin color and cultural differences and rely upon my thirteen years of knowledge and personal experiences with various native people and their ceremonial ways. When I have spoken from my intuition in this writing, it has been from a place of love and respect for my human ancestors who lived on this continent, from my relationship with many native elders and teachers, and from my understanding, albeit limited, of the Indian way of life. I believe their wisdom belongs to us all and that we all can learn from and make good use of it. If this book in any small way contributes to an increased awareness of and interest in the *whole* of Native American spirituality by its reflection upon the Cherokees, so be it.

Another purpose for this book regards my personal concern for what may very well be at the root of many, if not all, of the problems faced by our current society: *the broken ties between humans and our planet.* We seem to have forgotten the lyrics of the ancient Song of Creation. We have lost the melody. I think it is time we went in search for what we have lost. Time is running out for us to reconnect with all our relations on the planet and with the planet herself. This book is intended to give us *a way* that we can begin to do just that. Although this writing is about only one small part of the body of the Earth Mother, we can adopt the principles and techniques presented within these pages toward our getting to know the entire planet better.

The final reason for the existence of this book is that, for some time now, I have been keenly aware that something subtle, yet very powerful, is happening in these grandfather mountains that we call the Smokies. These old mountains are in the process of awakening from a long slumber. I believe they are "re-awakening", if you will, to their full physical and spiritual power. And I feel this surge of power is a direct result of the current cycle of planetary changes, a truly positive event being born out of a time which most view as negative and when we are likely to focus on the earthquakes, volcanic eruptions, and other geological upheavals and meteorological events that are feared because of their destructive consequences. We must keep in mind that when there is the negative, there must always be the positive to balance it out. Such is the nature of the universe. I sense that natural earth energy is intensifying right now in the southern Appalachians far beyond what has ever occurred during our lifetimes. And I feel that the current revival of interest in the spirituality of the Indian people who have known these old mountains as home for a millennia is but a facet of this awakening.

No doubt the road to regaining our lost relationship with Mother Earth is a long one. But the first steps must be taken and, for some, the first steps may be discovered in the chapters on geomancy in this book. For others who may have already taken these steps, it is my hope that this writing will offer additional knowledge and techniques or, at least, another perspective of what you already know, that will help refine your knowledge and enhance your experience of being a *conscious* part of and taking a *conscious* place within the great web of the life that is our planet.

I believe in a well-rounded way of thinking. It is not enough to seek to know the earth from a purely spiritual perspective. Rather, we must also know basic geology in order to learn how the planet was formed and the changes she has gone through over time. It helps to also know the fundamentals of meteorology which teaches us the dynamics of the aura of our living earth. Knowledge gleaned from both the physical and spiritual perspectives leads to a deeper, more valid understanding. And, without understanding, can we ever experience a relationship with our planetary mother or come to know true compassion for her and all our relations with whom we share our home? In this writing I have tried to present a broad view of each subject discussed so my readers will be betters equipped to view the Great Smoky Mountains with both their minds and hearts.

As is always the case, teachers learn from those they teach. I know I will learn much from those who read this book. I know there must be many sacred sites and power spots in these mountains of which I am not yet aware. I know I will learn much more, in time, about the Cherokees and their traditional wisdom from readers who have far more knowledge and experience with these people than I. What is presented on these pages reflects my own knowledge and experience of the land, the culture, the history, and Cherokee tradition gained over the past three plus years of my residency, as well as with my familiarity with the land gained during summers I spent here during my years of growing up in coastal South Carolina. Some might feel that this is not a long enough time to really know anything. But is time the important issue? I think not. The issue is what is being said and whether or not it can serve the purpose of opening doors within the minds of my readers that might not be opened otherwise. Perhaps there will be those who will be inspired to go further and learn about leys, sacred sites, and power spots that exist all over the globe.........and still others who will be led to find out more about the spirituality of the American Indians because of what they read about the Cherokees in the pages. Maybe some will become more sensitive to the living planetary forces, the devas, and the spirits and forces of nature from reading these words. It is my hope that there will be those who will never walk in these mountains and green forests again without perceiving the presence of the great Mountain Devas that reside here......or seeing the Little People.....or hearing the voices of the indwelling spirits of the waterfalls. Even though we often behave as if we are separate from all of these lives, or as if they do not exist at all, they do. We are all a part of the life of Mother Earth and are interdependent with one another. All good things in life come when we begin to live from from this perspective and in honor of this truth. Is this not what the term *spiritual* really means? Through conscious inter-relating, we not only acknowledge our kindredship with all that lives, but we also experience a true, living sense of brotherhood and sisterhood with all our relations.

Finally, this book is about *memory*. There is a perennial wisdom that has endured throughout human history; a wisdom whose very core states that the earth is alive. Most ancestral cultures have held and lived by this belief. I believe this ancient belief is in our genes! Somehow, someday, we have to *remember* the fact of the living earth so that our future actions and values will, once more, be governed by it. We must awaken from our amnesia. As stated, our ancestors have had such a deep awareness in the past and such an awareness leaves its tracks. Although the actual tracks may be long gone, there is still left the seed of its wisdom which, like a spore, awaits the time for its revival. "For our ancestors, landscapes were saturated with *memories* (italics mine) marking the places where significant interactions, confrontations, revelations, and emotions took place between people, spirits, deities, and the three kingdoms."[1]

Throughout this writing, direct quotes from other written sources have been properly footnoted. In addition, ideas that are my own and/or those that have been gleaned from various books, pamphlets, and articles I have noted in parentheses in the text. A complete bibliography appears in the back of the book.

These ancient mountains are a storehouse of the *memories* of planetary birth and evolution. They hold the *memories* of the sacred songs and rites that echoed across their canyons and peaks. They are home the spirits and forces of nature with whom we have lost touch; they are a part of the terrestrial stage upon which the drama of life continuously unfolds. And, yes, the mountains are a "book" that can, and will, reveal what they know. The time for that revelation is now. The mountains are our Elders; they are our teachers. And, for what they can and will reveal to us, I give thanks.

Page Bryant<br>Waynesville, N.C.<br>Spring, 1994

[1]Sacred Places by James Swan; Bear and Company Publishing; Santa Fe, New Mexico: 1990

# THE SPIRITUAL REAWAKENING OF THE GREAT SMOKY MOUNTAINS

## BIRTH AND EVOLUTION OF THE SMOKIES

### CHAPTER 1

The Great Smoky Mountains are the oldest mountains on Earth. They existed before humans walked upon their forested slopes, or drank from the crystal waters of their rivers, lakes, and streams. They existed before the bears, deer, and other animals, great and small, foraged for leaves and dined on their abundant succulent berries and nuts so abundant; before the first coyote pursued any prey, before the lonesome howl of the first red wolf echoed across their majestic peaks. They existed before the first ferns and mosses raised their heads above the virgin soil, and before the hardwoods, spruce, and firs towered above the woodland floors. So ancient are these Old Ones that they, alone and desolate, received the first gift of life from the primordial seas....the seas that "seeded" them with the first life forms born from the Earth Mother. Yes, these mountains witnessed the genesis of life itself. Imprints of these "first-born" lives still slumber in their silent tombs of ancient granite; fossils that bear mute witness to the incessant rhythm of Time. The watchful eyes of the Smokies peer out from behind the ever-present haze that gives the mountains their name; looking out of a long-gone past that saw the rock-building cycles expose the surface material of the earth, pushing it slowly upward, generating colossal geological events unimaginable to the human mind, yet inspiring and perplexing to the human spirit. These same watchful eyes also peer into a future that, to these old mountains is, paradoxically, both threatened and secure. Much of the drama of life has unfolded here. And, it continues to unfold, forever caught in the natural cycle of birth and death.....forever echoing the Song of Creation sung by the sons and daughters of the mountains who were, and are, the plants, animals, and indigenous peoples.

You see, there exists a legend among the Indians that tells of an ancient event.....an event that resulted in the birth and formation of the Great Smoky Mountains. Before the earth came into being, the animals, birds, and reptiles, and the people were still sky dwellers. They lived in a place they called Galun'lati. (Walker, 1991, pg.5) Below the sky world there was only ocean. Since all lived in the sky, things got very crowded. So it was decided that a tiny water beetle, Dayunisi, grandchild of Beaver, would be sent in search for land that might exist in the Great Sea. But the little beetle searched in vain. He could find no land. Not being one to give up, the tiny beetle finally dove to the ocean's bottom and brought a small piece of mud up to the surface. Soon, the mud began to grow and expand and form the planet Earth. The earth became a huge island afloat in the great waters, suspended at each of its four cardinal corners by solid rock ropes that hung down from the heavens. Someday, when the earth grows old, all will die. The rope will be broken and the earth will sink, once again, into the Great Abyss and there will be only water, everywhere, as before.

In the beginning of its life, the young planet was very soft and flat and wet. But with Sky Country becoming more crowded, the animals, became especially impatient, for the new land to dry so they could move there and spread out. Over time, buzzards were sent to the earth to see if it was dry. Time and again, they had to return to Sky Country because they could find no place to light. Finally, the chief buzzard reported that the earth was indeed dry enough to become their home. And so, after delivering the long-awaited message, Buzzard returned to Earth to prepare the new land for all the others. He soared over the entire planet until, finally, he flew over Cherokee country. By this time, Buzzard was very tired. His great wings began to drag the soft ground as he flew, forming a valley each time they touched the surface of the infant earth. And when he lifted his sweeping wings, the mountains were made. The home of the

Cherokee is mountains and valleys first formed by the Great Sky Buzzard.

The animals soon came down to Earth and began the task of settling into their new home. But they faced still another problem: their home was dark. They had no sun. So, they got Sun and, after a few adjustments so that the land would not be too cold or too hot, they set the sun on an east to west track above the land. This, so it is said, is how the land and the mountains were made. (Walker, 1991, pg. 10)

Much time passed until, some 1,000 years ago, the Cherokees arrived in the great mountains which they called "the place of blue haze".[2] This name obviously makes reference to the ever-present haze that lingers over the Smokies, the result of the processes of evaporation and transpiration, a process by which plant leaves emit moisture into the air and the forests below. By the time the Cherokees arrived, the mountains were already among the oldest on Earth, shaped by colossal terrestrial and atmospheric forces that have, to date, been going on for more than a half a billion years! (Moore, 1988, pg.5) The Smokies once stood much taller but have been gradually worn down by eons of erosion. What the Cherokees found here was one of the most remarkable and unique biospheres on the planet, complete with twenty majestic peaks that still towered more than 6,000 feet into the sky. They found a world that had received the myriads of animal and plant lives that had been pushed southward by the relentless creeping of the massive glaciers of the Pleistocene Age. Although the glaciers never actually reached the region of the Smokies, the mountains had, nonetheless, inherited a legacy from their close presence just to the north. The peaks had evolved into the splendid, beautiful terrain of flora and fauna which we still see today. (Walker, 1991)

The earliest time period, the Precambrian Age, spanned an incredible 4600 million years ago. That's a long time! Geologists tell us that most of the rocks in the Great Smoky Mountains are of the late Precambrian Age. (Moore, 1988, pg. 5) All three of the basic kinds of rocks....igneous, which come from the earth's molten core; sedimentary, formed from sediments deposited on land and water; and metamorphic, which are either igneous or sedimentary that have been changed by heat, pressure, and/or chemicals....are found in the Smokies. Of these, is of the metamorphic sedimentary type. (Moore, 1988, pg. 17) Like all life forms....though most of us are not accustomed to thinking of mountains as living beings....the rocks that make up the Smokies were "born" in the sea that lay between several drifting continents. The land that is Shaconage, "the land of the blue haze",[3] is indeed some of the most prolific land on our planet. Today, the Smokies are home to 1,500 species of flowering plants, some 150 of which are rare, and over 4,000 non-flowering ones. (Walker, 1991, pg.5) Species of trees, usually found only in the far-north territory, such as spruce and fir, flourish in the higher elevations. There are also over a hundred kinds of trees here, making the land home to the largest virgin hardwood forests in the eastern United States. If you stroll through the Smokies at the lowest levels, you will find stands of yellow poplars, cove hardwoods, maples, and a variety of oaks. Up higher live the eastern hemlocks, northern hardwood, and yellow birch. In between the tree groves lie grasses and heath balds that give the area yet another stroke from the brush of uniqueness. The present-day cove hardwood stands are what is left of an ancient forest that once covered the entire U.S., Europe, and Asia! (Walker, 1991, pg.19) The remainder of the arcane woods contains some 80 types of trees, many of which grow to tremendous sizes.

    Climbing even higher, a hiker can see the forest of northern hardwoods composed mainly of birch and beech. Still higher, are the spruce-fir woods, thriving over a thousand miles south of their natural domain, thanks to the glaciers and the whims of Mother Nature! Often hidden by the misty veils of the mountains and buffetted annually by the icy winds and snows, these spruce-fir forests play an important role in the delicate ecosystem that is the Smokies. A tree falls and decays, forming the foundation for new life to evolve. Wood ferns and other plants growing alongside a fallen log, a common sight throughout the region, adds a sort of "gnomeland" effect, making one wonder what eyes are peeping out from behind the trees and shrubs; what fairies and elves dwell deep within these fragrant, damp woods?

The forests of the Great Smoky Mountains are home to many of the animal and bird creatures whose ancestors first descended the rock ropes that dropped from Sky Country. These include over 200 types of birds, some 50 kinds of fishes, and 60 different mammals. There are also 73 species of reptiles and amphibians. (Walker, 1991, pg. 25) None, however, have captured the attention of humans or has actually become the living symbol, the archetype, of the Smokies more so than the black bear. The only type of bear living in the east, these wonderful and powerful animals are popular with tourists and Natives alike.

In the earliest days, the Cherokees made no real distinction between animals and humans. They believed that each formed a society, complete with specific rules, tribes, and games each played with their own kind. But things changed. All the kingdoms lived in harmony, so it seems, until humans became overly aggressive and began to pay little or no attention to the rights of the others; an act perceived as one of aggression and that provoked the ire of the animals, insects, birds, reptiles, and fishes. So it became the task of the people to find ways to, once again, come into balance with the animal kingdom. And they did. Although humans remained the paramount power in the wild and continued to hunt game and birds, their general attitude took a positive turn. They began to *give thanks* to the animal and birds who gave their lives for food and shelter. They also placated the survivors of their prey by offering gifts to the living relatives of the kill. This has remained an accepted practice not just with the Cherokees but with all tribes of Indian peoples. (Mooney, 1982)

An interesting point, perhaps unique among the Cherokees, involves a belief taught by their shamans that animals have a definite amount of time allotted to live. So if an animal's life was/is ended prematurely through violence such as that suffered by being killed in the hunt, the death was believed to be only temporary and the prey quickly reincarnated, in the same form, from drops of its own spilled blood. The animal or bird was then free to live out its allotted time. (Mooney, 1982) When humans died, however, their fate was different. Humans were believed to go into the *Land of Darkening* (Mooney, 1982); a sort of "other world". This, of course, is not an uncommon belief among ancient and modern cultures worldwide.

Aside from the black bear, whom the Cherokees called *Yonah*, the Great Smoky Mountains are home to white tail deer, coyotes, raccoons, rabbits, beavers, bobcats, squirrels, red foxes, marmots, cougars, river otters, and wild boars of the European variety. Sculpturesque red tail hawks are often seen soaring on windswept wings over and across the lofty forested peaks, while owls, five species in all, claim their reputation as the vigilous hunters of the night. Wild turkeys and grouse, loons, quail, several varieties of ducks and geese, kingfishers, gulls, terns, and woodpeckers all share the bounty of the thick green forests. Jays, crows, and ravens dance on the mighty wind currents . Bright red cardinals, orioles, finches, nuthatches, and chickadees are among those who raise their sweet voices throughout the mountains. Turtles, snakes, and the most diverse population of salamanders also call the Smokies and the Blue Ridge home. (Walker, 1991, pg. 25)

Plants and trees, animals, birds, reptiles, and humans all combine with the mountains, soil, and sky to form the unique ecosystem that is the Great Smoky Mountains; both a part of the ancient Appalachians which span the eastern United States from Maine to Georgia. When viewed in segments, the Appalachians form the higher peaks of Maine, the White Mountains of New Hampshire, the Green Mountains of Vermont, the mountains of Connecticut and New York, the Berkshires of Massachusetts, the Catskills, the ridges of Pennsylvania and Virginia, the Alleghenies, the Cumberlands, the Blue

Ridge and the Smokies; some 2,000 miles of beauty that soars as high as 6,500 feet above sea level and adorns 14 states.

The air in the Smokies is currently being tainted by pollution from various sources, is usually crisp and clear. Fire from Father Sun warms the land and its life forms. The earth, in her enduring path around the sun, exposes her children to four full seasons, each magnificent and challenging in its own way. Mother Nature's presence becomes most evident perhaps in the autumn when the changing leaves set the woodlands and peaks ablaze with splendid colors of red, yellow, and gold. The once soft virgin earth is now hardened and fragrant and fertile; empowering the endless cycles of life.

Water, the last of the four ingredients of the physical world, is no stranger to this thriving land. Nestled among the forests, streams and rivers serve as life-nurturing veins that run over 600 miles throughout the Smokies. Streambeds dressed in emerald mosses paint living masterpieces on terrestrial canvases fed by abundant rainfalls and mists that average about 80 inches annually on the peaks, and some 50 inches that soak the verde valleys with its life-sustaining nectar. (Walker, 1991; pg. 39) Seasons change like a kaleidoscope, bringing temperatures that range, in the extremes, from the high 80s to 12 below zero. Soft snows can grace the higher summits and sometimes blanket the entire region in a quiet, peaceful cloak of white. In this time of reawakening, however, I sense that the Snow Mother will return in full force to take up residence in these old mountains and, as a result, the amount of annual snowfall will steadily increase from what it has been over the past 30-50 years. Water, as it has done for millions of years, continues to erode, shape, and nourish the old mountains. Whether as snow, sleet, or rain, and whether it is enjoyed in the rushing streams or seen thundering over the rocks and precipices as a magnificent waterfall, or lazing sleepily in a still mountain lake, water is here......lovely, nourishing, cleansing, mountain water.

In 1934, the Great Smoky Mountains National Park was born,

creating one of the largest environmentally protected areas in the eastern U.S. The area comprises some 800 square miles that straddle the states of eastern Tennessee and western North Carolina. From east to west, the Park measures 54 miles, and about 15 miles from north to south. In total, the park covers 520,004 acres. Hailed as the most popular of all national parks, the Smokies host between eight to ten million visitors each year. Aside from the obvious reason of physical beauty, there is also the matter of the Park's being convenient to two-thirds of the population of America. (Walker, 1991; pg. 62)

The Great Smoky Mountain National Park is recognized as one of the most diverse biological regions in the U.S. due to its rich variety of plant and animal life. It comes as no surprise, what with the current threatened ecological condition of Mother Earth, that the flora and fauna of these mountains are in danger. Thankfully, this has led to the Smokies being declared, in 1976, an International Biosphere Reserve, one of only 43 so designated sites in the country. Sadly, this has not solved the problem of the rapidly diminishing abundance and diversity of life. Environmental threats, most of which have their origin far outside the Park's boundaries, continue to prove that no place on earth is immune to human industrialization and its destructive by-products. No one can control the flow of the air patterns that expose the Smokies (and every other region) to a life-threatening variety of air pollutants. No one can cleanse the rain that falls on these ancient peaks and valleys. Automobile exhaust, coal and oil burning wastes and agricultural chemicals are increasingly affecting the Park's inhabitants. Surely the Earth Mother weeps salty tears for the life blood being drained from one of her most beautiful facial features. I hear her sobs here as clearly as I heard them echo softly across the spanse of the Grand Canyon.....soft, silent sobs that invade every corner and crevice throughout the most awesome chasm on the planet. The damage is clearly apparent. The tear in the ozone layer of the planetary aura is known to be damaging the red spruce in the Smokies. In fact, over 50 species of plant life are currently (1993) teetering on the brink of extinction! The American chestnut is completely gone. The Frazier fir and dogwood are being severely threatened by exotic insects and diseases that are not native to the area but which have been brought here by humans. Alien exotic plants, fungus, honeysuckle, and cudzu, along with animals such as wild hogs and rainbow trout, are all evidence of human interference and ignorance, intentional or not, that upsets the balance of Nature in the Smokies. This area will not escape the inevitable unless our present understanding of and relationship with Mother Earth improves. We must cease our reckless determination to dominate and control nature.

One of the few occasions where humans attempted to right the wrongs against the balance of nature occurred in the Smokies in November of 1991, when, for the first time, "a major predator was returned to the wilds of a national park. On that day, two adult red wolves and two female pups were released to roam the slopes and hollows of Cades Cove."[4] It is my understanding that the wolves are being closely monitored to determine if the experiment can rescue this animal's population from the brink of extinction.

Clearly, each of us must do what we can to protect the diversity of life on our planet. And we must begin now. We must not only change our damaging habits, we must change our values. We have to take the responsibility of educating ourselves about the harmful things that are going on, and make every effort to support legislation designed to eradicate pollution and conserve energy. I do not believe it is too late. Not yet, at least. Each of us, individually, can do our part to protect the Smokies and the Blue Ridge mountains and, collectively, we *can* save our beautiful home and ultimately, the entire planet.

There is no question of the uniqueness of the Great Smoky Mountains, both in their physical splendor and in their rugged, yet fragile, ecosystem. Such a place was surely destined to give rise to a human culture that would be equally unique. In the next chapter, let us explore the appearance of humans on the scene and re-trace the rise of civilization and culture in the area. In doing so, we will see successes and tragedies that have unfolded on the stage that is Shaconage....."the land of the blue haze". We will see what has influenced the ups and downs humanity has experienced, and is still experiencing, in their lives upon this ancient land.

## ECOLOGICAL UPDATE OF THE GREAT SMOKY MOUNTAINS

Astonishingly, while at this stage in this writing (Spring, 1992), I came across some information that brought a rude awakening concerning the current ecological condition of the specific area that is designated as the Great Smoky Mountain National Park. Katuah Journal reprinted a news bulletin from the Natural World News Service that stated that the area that is the Park itself (though massive surrounding areas are obviously affected)....."the Park ecosystem is deteriorating from pervasive pollution that drops from the skies. Because of the high altitude of the Park's highest ridges, clouds carrying contaminants gather at their crests and drop their deadly burdens. Thus, atmospheric pollutions that affects the *whole region* (italics mine) tends to be concentrated at high altitude sites such as those in the Great Smoky Mountains National Park."[5] This deterioration is occurring in spite of provisions stated in the Clean Air Act to provide protection for most of our national parks and some of the larger wilderness areas! The culprits are industrial development and wastes, auto exhaust, and other air polluting conditions. The article goes further to state that......"NPS (National Park Service) researchers also point out that since 1950 visibility in the Park has declined 40%, and the famous blue haze from which the Great Smoky Mountains derived their name has turned into a sickly gray or a poisonous looking yellowish white pall, depending on the season."[6] Plant life is already showing damage with some 95 species being considered in danger due to ozone contamination. Thankfully, the director of NPS, James M. Ridenour, banned any expansion of the Eastman Chemicals Company out of Kingsport, Tennessee, a company that wished to install a new coal-fired boiler that would spew over 1,500 tons of nitrogen oxide into the atmosphere annually.

When reading this report, my suspicions and fears became reality. Having been born and raised in coastal South Carolina, I spent time during my childhood in the Smokies. Coming here now, over thirty years later, I thought that I detected a negative difference in the quality of the air and in the healthy appearance of the forests. Upon my arrival, I heard several newscasts regarding the deterioration of the forests around Mt. Mitchell due to acid rain, as well as of the pollution of the French Broad and Pigeon rivers. I also found out through articles in the Katuah Journal that aquatic life is being threatened and that the beautiful Cullasaja River's life is in danger of becoming contaminated by 500,000 gallons of treated sewage water daily. (At the time of this writing, 1993, permission has been granted to the town of Highlands to go ahead with this contamination of the Cullasaja) The cove areas of the Pisgah National Forest are also teetering on ecological disaster! And I am sure there is more.

When will it all end? Will it end? The answers to these questions are simple: it won't end unless we change our values and do something *now* as individual and collective citizens of Planet Earth. And we can and must do something through and with the power of our *vote*. The bottom line is ....."The Great Smokies Park [also] stands as the ecological standard by which we judge the health of the rest of the forest."[7] And....."The Park acts as a barometer for the ecological health of the region as a whole." These are the facts and, sadly, they are terribly disturbing facts. We have to change our values and we have to change them now. It is my hope that this writing will serve, in some small way, to help human beings to look beyond the physical beauty of the earth and see the life force that flows through the souls that dwell within the myriad of forms in Nature and I dedicate it to that purpose. We can, and we must, gain a greater awareness of the "crown jewel" of the Southern Appalachians and, ultimately, of the whole Earth.

[1] Walker, Steven L.; <u>Great Smoky Mountains: The Splendor Of The Southern Appalachians</u>.
[2] <u>Smokies Guide</u> (Spring 1992); pg. 4.
[3] <u>Smokies Guide</u> (Spring 1992); pg. 4.
[4] <u>Katuan Journal</u>, Spring 1992; pg. 24.
[5] Ibid
[6] Ibid

# THE SPIRITUAL REAWAKENING OF THE GREAT SMOKY MOUNTAINS

## MAN AND MOUNTAINS UNITE

### CHAPTER 2

"The Cherokees in their disposition and manner are grave and steady; dignified and circumspect in the deportment; rather slow and reserved in conversation; yet frank, cheerful and humane; tenacious of their liberties and natural rights of men; secret, deliberate and determined in their councils; honest, just and liberal, and are ready always to defend their territory and maintain their rights."
William Bartram
Naturalist and social historian

We know, primarily due to the modern-day environmental difficulties we now face, that when humans move into and settle an area, they cannot do so without having a profound effect upon the land and to all the living creatures that inhabit the land. The same is true in reverse; the land and its minerals, plants, and animals also affect people. However, the latter's affect is usually a much more positive one than the former. To be sure, the relationship the early Native Americans had with the earth and the other life kingdoms was far more sane and gentle and reflected greater values than those of our present-day. Still their presence changed these old mountains forever.

When the Cherokee Indians migrated to the Great Smoky Mountains over a thousand years ago, they soon realized that they were not the first people to arrive. (Mooney, 1982; pg.22) Who the earliest inhabitants were is not known for sure, but it is possible they were among primitive Asian tribes who crossed the Bering Strait into North America over 11,000 years ago. However, it is uncertain whether the Bering Strait theory is as cut and dry an explanation as it once was believed to be. I know that many Native American peoples dispute it. An example is the Hopi of northeastern Arizona who say their ancestors came from the west from a place they call "Pacifica", which is, perhaps, the same place others call Lemuria. This creates an interesting challenge to most anthropologists and suggests a kindredship between the Hopi, and perhaps other southewestern peoples, and the Polynesians. I must say that while in Hawaii in 1989, I was struck by the physical similarities between many of the Hawaiian people and the Hopi. I also encountered a Hawaiian kahuna (shaman/medicine person), Makua, who spoke openly about his people and the Hopi (and other Indian tribal people) sharing a common ancestry. Intuitively, I accepted Makua's views on the subject and believe his beliefs have merit. I also noticed a striking likeness of my Hawaiian friend, Pua, when I took her for a visit to the Hopi reservation some years ago. Pua's features were very Hopi-like and she easily blended into the pack!

The Cherokee hold onto strange and persistent legends that tell of the people they found already living in the Smokies. "There is a dim but persistent tradition of a strange white race preceding the Cherokee, some of the stories even going so far as to locate their former ancient works found in the country."[1] The "ancient works" being referred to are undoubtedly the petroglyphs that were drawn upon and etched into the rocks long before the appearance of the Cherokees. "The Cherokee tell us that when they first arrived in the country, which they still inhabit, they found it possessed by certain 'moon-eyed' people who could not see in the day time. These wretches they expelled."[2] Some suggest that these people constituted an albino race. Regretfully, whoever they were, the moon-eyed ones must forever remain a mystery that allows speculation to be the only satisfying, albeit frustrating, exercise. Perhaps my own speculation may shed some light on the identity of these curious primitive settlers. The following is a part of a channeling given by my Spirit Teacher, Albion, in the summer of 1990, just prior to our relocation to western North Carolina. A complete account of the information will be given in another part of this writing.

"Since the last major cycle of earth changes, some ten thousand years ago, these great mountains (the Smokies) have been 'asleep', their energy dormant, their life force but a shallow breath. It was during those ancient times of upheaval when these mountains were first inhabited by Atlantean migrants who spread throughout the world seeking refuge and new beginnings. To this day, there are arcane rock and bark scrolls, cave drawings and rock etchings that are Atlantean in their origin and that still exist within various parts of these mountain peaks."

"This place (the Smokies) has long been the site of sacred ceremonies. Although many of the mountain peaks have, over time, been worn down considerably from their original heights (the Smokies were once higher than the Himalayas) there were once seven summits that were considered to be sacred and that were used throughout the centuries as ceremonial and pilgrimage sites. The areas around them still conceal remnants and artifacts of the Old Ways. Some of those you call Native Americans were born from these Atlantean ancestors, while other peoples migrated and settled here from other continents." Whether these Atlantean migrants that Albion spoke about and the "moon-eyed" people referred to by Cherokee legends are the same, I do not know. But it is certainly possible.

The Cherokees of a millennium ago were not exactly "primitive". They lived in log houses and farmed the fertile lands, including the land that is now called the Smokies, the Blue Ridge mountains of western Virginia, the Great Valley (also of eastern Tennessee), and the Appalachian highlands of South Carolina. In addition, they moved into areas as far south as the northern part of what is now Alabama. The land was a bountiful paradise. Seemingly endless streams were filled with fishes which they speared with blowguns or trapped with natural skill. They grew several crops that included squash, corn, melons, sunflowers, pumpkins, gourds, beans, and tobacco, which they used for pleasure, healing, and ceremonial purposes. Feathers from wild turkeys, eagles, hawks, and other birds were used for making headdresses and for decorating clothing worn for sacred rituals and other special occasions. They were excellent basket makers and potters; crafts that are still produced today. Unique baskets were, and still are, fashioned from river cane, white oak, and honeysuckle, and dyed with natural dyes made from roots and barks such as black walnut and yellow root. Cherokee pottery, which dates back 2000 years was formed from clay, crushed quartz and sand, which was dried and fired. Their primary methods of travel was by foot, dugout canoes, and horses. (Walker, 1991)

In some of the earliest Cherokee villages, a curiously imposing mound was constructed in or near the center. Atop the mounds there was erected a ceremonial building called the "council house." (Mooney, 1982; pg. 396) It was here where guests were received and entertained and where ceremonies and dances took place. It was also the place where tribal bards retold stories that told of their ancestors and of the mythic monsters and many animals the people held in esteem.

It was in 1540 when the Europeans first encountered the Cherokees. (Walker, 1991) DeSoto, hearing of the Indians using implements and jewelry made from copper, thought they might also have gold. That first contact with whites began what was to become a long, often tragic, history between the two races. Mooney's history tells us that because of the various wars waged against neighboring Indian tribes and the Colonists, the Cherokees found themselves engaged in many conflicts. Try as they would to resist the relentless encroachment of white society, the Cherokees were fighting, for all practical purposes, a losing battle. Making matters worse, in 1738 the dreaded "white man's disease," smallpox, spread like wildfire through Cherokee towns, killing over half of the entire population!

Sadly, smallpox was not the only nor the greatest tragedy to befall the Cherokee people. By 1828 the mood of the entire country was anti-Indian due, in part, to the personal views of then-President,

Andrew Jackson. Ten years later, after much protest by the Indians and their few white supporters, the removal of the Cherokees from their land took place, an event that was to widen the gap of hatred and distrust that had been building between the Indians and whites for more than a century. Even now, little or no healing or end is in sight. Aside from the few Indians who were allowed to stay in their mountain homeland, many others fled into the refuge of the mountains and remained fugitives for some time. Several thousand (some say 17,000) natives were forcibly evicted and doomed to relocate, on foot, to "Indian Territory" in Oklahoma. This dark event became known as the Trail of Tears and was without doubt one of the most infamous events in American history. Along the way, it resulted in the death of some 4.000 Cherokee people, mostly elders, women, and children. The "walk" took until the following Spring to complete.

Of those who gained freedom by escaping into the mountains, one stood out as their champion. His name was Tsali. When the soldiers could not capture the Indian renegades, they made a deal with Tsali, who had been wrongfully accused of murdering a white woman. He was promised that if he and his two sons surrendered, all the other fugitive Cherokees would be unharmed and be allowed to remain on their land in peace. Tsali agreed. But, in but one of many broken promises and treaties that litter the history between Indians and whites, Tsali and one of his sons were shot to death! And, to make matters worse, the dreadful murders were carried out by his own people who were forced to do so by the white soldiers. The Indians who had fled into the mountains became the root population of what is now known as the Eastern Band of the Cherokees. The survivors of the Trail of Tears became the Western Band.

Though Tsali was a beloved man of the Cherokee people, it was Junaluska who was their most influential patriarch. (Sakowski, 1990) It was he who tried to convince his people not to fight in the war between the Americans and the British. Ultimately, however, the Cherokee did side with the Americans and, at the Battle of Horseshoe Bend in 1814, "it was the Cherokees who saved the day."[3] It was also Junaluska who vowed to exterminate all of the Creek Indians, the bitter enemies of the Cherokees, whose barriers the white soldiers could not penetrate. But Junaluska could not kill them all. From then on, he was given the name Junaluska, which means "he tried repeatedly but failed."[4] Ironically, it was Junaluska who once saved the life of Indian-hater, Andrew Jackson! Perhaps he would have not done so had he known what the future held.

Junaluska and his family were part of the forced march to Oklahoma. His wife and other members of his family died along the way. Upon his return to the Smokies from the west, (he walked all the way) understandably harboring intense bitterness, that Junaluska discovered that Jackson had become President. In light of Jackson's prejudice against Native Americans, it is said that Junaluska did indeed regret saving Jackson's life. Although Junaluska tried to reclaim his land, it was forbidden by the government. The Indians were, in fact, only allowed to settle in certain unoccupied places. Author Carolun Sakowski tells us that in 1847, the state made a tardy retribution by awarding Junaluska 337 acres of land, the sum of one hundred dollars, and made him a citizen of North Carolina. He was 71 years old at the time. Junaluska died in November, 1858. He was over a hundred years old. Sadly, the Trail of Tears did not begin or end the Cherokee's problems with the white or with the U.S. government. Constant disputes over land rights and boundaries and other political and social problems continue to dog them to this day.

Though not remembered for military or political matters, no pursuit of knowledge of Cherokee luminaries would be complete without mention of Sequoya. Crippled for life by an unfortunate hunting accident, Sequoya was born of a Cherokee mother and a white father around the year 1760. (Mooney, 1982; pg.109) A hunter and fur trader, there is evidence that the young man had never learned to read or write the English language. After his accident Sequoya, having a lot of time on his hands, thought of how the whites could communicate by means of writing. So he began to envision something of the same for his people. He worked for years, undaunted, before finally producing the Cherokee syllabary and presented it to his people. This was a leap in evolution, to be sure. The people now had a way to read and write in their own language. A newspaper, the <u>Cherokee Phoenix</u>, followed soon thereafter. In the eyes of many, the Cherokees had become civilized!

The first European settlers began moving into the Great Smoky Mountains in the late 1700s, where they busily set about clearing the land, building log houses, growing crops, and raising livestock. (Walker, 1991) This put a human imprint upon the pristine wilderness that would change its face forever. The white settlers who came to be known as "mountain people" were forced to eke out a life and living by totally relying upon the land and its resources that their descendents still call home today. They came to depend upon roots, herbs, and other plants for their medicinal needs. They constructed dwellings from trees and raised sheep and spun wool for clothing and other essentials. Their primary crop was corn which they ate as food and drank in the form of "moonshine" whiskey.

Mountain folks were, and still are, a tight-knit bunch; existing in a "clan-like" consciousness. Being good neighbors to each other was an essential part of survival. Barn raisings, quilting bees, cornshuckings, and harvests were not only times when neighbor helped neighbor, but were social times as well. But the mountain folks began to see their isolation end with the outbreak of the Civil War, the building of roads and railways, and the arrival of the mail service in the mid-1800s. All these linked the people and the mountains, forever, with the outside world.

Perhaps the first activity that started what was to become a serious and damaging threat to the delicate ecological balance of the Smokies was the wholesale cutting of the pristine forests and wooded slopes by the white settlers. It did provide a good and steady income and many settlers sold their land and their crops to the influx of lumbermen. Sadly, like today, money dominated common sense and any real concern for the land's future. By the 1920s, two-thirds of the wilderness had been logged or burned! Some of the ongoing damage was thankfully ended by the acquisition of land that was subsequently set aside as the present Great Smoky Mountain National Park. Slowly, life began to recover. Today, descendents of the mountain people and the Cherokees still reside in the areas, carrying on legacies that embody two of the most unique human cultures in America.

[1] <u>Myths Of The Cherokees/Sacred Formulas Of The Cherokees</u>; Mooney, James; Charles and Randy Elder-Booksellers, Nashville, Tennessee: 1982.
[2] Ibid
[3] <u>Touring The Western North Carolina Backroads</u>; Sakowski, Carolyn; John F. Blair Publisher, Winston-Salem, North Carolina: 1990.
[4] Ibid

# THE SPIRITUAL REAWAKENING OF THE GREAT SMOKY MOUNTAINS

## SACRED VOICES IN THE WILDERNESS

### CHAPTER 3

"The sacred myths were not for everyone, but only those might hear who observed the proper form and ceremony."

James Mooney

Native Americans across Turtle Island (North America) have not found it easy to maintain their culture or the practice of their religious and spiritual traditions. Most have tried; few have totally succeeded. Even with the passing in 1979 of the American Indian Religious Freedom Act, which was suppose to free native peoples to practice their traditional ceremonies, the road has not been without severe bumps. But right now it is apparent that native peoples across North America have come to a real turning point that has the potential of pulling them and their sacred ways back from the very brink of extinction. There is, and I believe there will continue to be, a renewed awareness and practice of the various American Indian tribal cultures, languages, medicine (both sacred and medicinal), and religion. Many native peoples had foreseen this happening and in many ways it is beginning. But the struggle towards "awakening" has really just begun and the road is likely to be a long and steep one. In her book Voices Of Our Ancestors, noted Cherokee teacher and author Dhyani Ywahoo's words are all too clear: "In these times Native American people are confronted daily with cultural and physical genocide. In this very moment the Native people of this hemisphere are pawns in the multinational cooperations' concept of progress and profits."[1] The author goes on to describe being taught as a child that the "Native religion is a whole way of life, based on everything being in relationship. The sacred rituals are to maintain harmonious balance of the energy of sun, moon, earth, indeed the entire universe, so that the seed's bounty can be brought forth."[2] It is my feeling that the sacred rituals slumber safely within the minds and hearts of the living descendents of the ancestral people. They are a part of the people's archetypal existence. The wisdom has not died. It but sleeps. As these old mountains reawaken, I believe the tradition will awaken with them into a new and different cycle of life. When that time comes, and the process has already begun, perhaps the sacred voices will speak to all people of all colors as loudly and clearly as they once spoke to the early people of Katuah. A new day....a new Age....can and will dawn. The holy places will come alive again. It is my prayer that the Old Truths will be rediscovered and made known so that the Earth Mother might be healed and that all may live in the beauty of harmony, trust, health, and peace.

Like all Native Americans, the Cherokees have always possessed their own unique sacred ways. They say they were placed on Earth by a Great Power From Above, which they know as the Great Spirit. (Walker, 1991) But their "national legend" that once embodied the tales of their origin, has been all but completely lost or, some might say, ignored. Any secret medicine societies or priesthoods which may have once existed are now either gone or what of it is left is in the safe hands of a few individuals who work independently according to the specific knowledge and spiritual gifts they inherited from religious elders who lived before them. What we can find out about Cherokee spiritual lore from the few written sources speaks of hero-gods, ancient monsters, the creation of the earth, the nature of the elemental and celestial forces, a secret knowledge of plants and animals, and a strange and powerful world of spirits. It is likely, as is common with all tribal peoples, that the most sacred of the myths were known only by the keepers of the secrets, while other more basic spiritual knowledge was probably known by the whole population. The holy myths provided the foundation for Cherokee ceremonials and calendar observations. It is also likely that the same or similar legends were held in common amongst other Indian tribes of the area, namely the Creeks, Tuscarora, and the others of the numerous tribes such as the Catawba and the Cheraw who comprised the Eastern Sioux. (Mooney, 1982)

An intriguing concept found within early Cherokee spirituality tells of another "world" down under; a world like our own in every way, with the exception of its climate and seasons. "The streams that come down from the mountains are the trails by which we reach this underworld, and the springs at their heads are the doorways by which we enter it."[14] It is said that before one can enter this "Otherworld", one must first fast for a time and enlist one of the "underground people" as a guide. What humans found in the other dimension is not known. It is only from what they knew and thought about the everyday world around them we can learn. (Mooney, 1982)

It is known that the earliest Cherokees believed their physical world to be endowed with a powerful spiritual essence. The special energy inherent in plants and animals was determined long ago, perhaps at the very beginning of time, the result of an intriguing "initiation", the outcome of which was that, of all the animals and birds, it was only the owl and the panther who passed. To them was given the powers to see in the dark for capturing prey. Of all the trees and plants, it was the holly, spruce, pine, cedar, and laurel who passed the test, resulting in their being given the special powers of being green year round and the energy to heal. (Mooney, 1982)

"The animals of the Cherokee myths, like the traditional herogods, were larger and of a more perfect type than the present-day representatives. Like humans, they had chiefs, councils, and even townhouses. They mingled with human beings with an attitude of perfect equality and spoke the same language. In some explained manner, they left their abode in the lower world and ascended to Galun'lati, The World Above, where they still exist. The removal was not simultaneous, but each animal chose his own time to ascend. The animals we know, small in size and poor in intellect, came upon the earth later, and are not the descendents of the mythic animals, but weak limitations.[4] This quote from the classic work, <u>Myths Of The Cherokee/Sacred Formulas Of The Cherokee</u> by James Mooney, gives clear indication of the Cherokee perspective of the plant and animal kingdoms, mythic and living creatures alike. Plants and trees were likewise considered to be alive and possess the ability to communicate with humans.

From all accounts it seems that among the animals, the frog, rabbit, and bear figured most prominently in Cherokee lore. It is at this point of our learning that we have to rely almost totally on James Mooney, whose monumental work I have relied upon for the remainder of this part of this chapter. The Frog is the council leader, while the Rabbit is the messenger to the people and the leader of the sacred dances. Rabbit also fills the role of "Trickster", not unlike the infamous Heyokah who often takes the form of the coyote among the Plains people. The Trickster employs stretching the truth, talking in riddles or backwards, and even scare tactics to accomplish their goal of "tricking" humans into learning some of life's most valuable lessons. The Cherokees thought of the Bear, who was depicted as having a human form, as the possessor of special healing powers. (Mooney, 1982)

Earth was not the only place of importance in Cherokee spirituality. The Sun, Moon, individual stars, and constellations such as the Pleiades and the Thunder and Lightning Spirits, all played a role in the legends and were the source of all spiritual powers. (Mooney, 1982) There exist stories which tell of these things. For example, as with all ancient cultures, the Sun and Moon held special positions and powers. Contrary to most Native American mythology however, the Cherokees thought of the Sun as a feminine being who had a human form. It seems that the Sun did not like humans very much and they had to go to great lengths to gain peace with her. Legends tell of a time when the Sun bore her heat down unmercifully upon the earth people, causing them tremendous misery. Another tells of a time when upon the death of her daughter, the Sun cried so many tears that the whole world was flooded! Isn't it interesting that so many primitive cultures have legends of a global flood that surely was one of the most memorable of all past earth change events? To this day, the Cherokees say that the cardinal (redbird) is the embodiment of the beloved daughter of the Sun. The Sun is a young woman who lives in the East, the Moon is a male, her brother, who lives in the West.

Let me digress here and consider an interesting comment I recently came across in my studies of Jungian psychology regarding this reversal of the masculine/feminine energies of the sun and moon which constitutes a departure from that which is generally held to be true. In his book <u>Jung And The Story Of Our Time</u>, Laurens Van Der Post, commenting about the feminine sun and masculine moon subscribed to in German and Japanese mythology. ......"the sun, which is the image of the light of reason in man and walks as a god tall in most highly differentiated mythologies, was for the Japanese the same feminine phenomenon that it was for the Germans. Yet the infinitely renewing and renewable moon that swings the sea of change and symbolizes all that is eternally feminine in the spirit of man, by some ominous perversity of the aboriginal urgings of both Germans and Japanese, was rendered into a fixed and immutable masculinity."[5] Van Der Post's interpretations of this reversal of masculine/feminine energies leads him to draw conclusions about the general archetypal make-up of these two cultures regarding their approach to war, aggression, and other attitudes displayed in their interaction with other countries and cultures. While this mythological reversal is rather unusual to most cultures, it was true with the early Cherokees. Could this have in any way contributed to the Cherokees being more aggressive and/or caused them to be motivated on the deepest levels as a collective people into excessive or exceptional conflicts which brought difficulties upon them and that would eventually result in their having to struggle harder to overcome many setbacks, any one of which might have destroyed them. A glance at Cherokee history might very well shed some light on this possibility.

Other celestial phenomenon also played a role in Cherokee mythology. For example, eclipses were caused when a frog tried to swallow the Sun and Moon. (Mooney, 1982) During these occasions the people got together to beat drums and make as much noise as possible in order to scare the frog away. It always worked!

Stars were also important, although there is some disagreement regarding their physical forms. Some believed they, like the Sun and Moon, have human bodies, while others saw them as balls of light or as "living creatures with luminous fur or feathers."[6] Other parts of the sky were also recognized in Cherokee myth. The Milky Way, called by a name that means "where the dog ran", was/is believed to be a trail of cornmeal that dropped from the mouth of a running dog. And the seven stars of the Pleiades were said to be a group of Indian boys who had risen into the sky because they were angry at their mothers who had incessantly scolded them for playing ball instead of tending to their chores. (Mooney, 1982)

While I find all myths of interest, the most intriguing of the Cherokee myths and spiritual beliefs I have come across are those about the "Little People". I find these to be unique among Native American beliefs and stories that I have encountered in my studies and experience to date. Called the *Yunwi Tsundi*, these entities are loosely defined by James Mooney, one of the few definitive sources of information available on the subject. Most of the accounts I have come across are based upon and/or are quoted heavily from his book. Few are based upon the personal experiences of the authors. Generally, the Yunwi Tsundi are described as being very short in statue, barely coming up to the knees of a human being. They have very long hair that often reaches to the ground, are well-built physically, and are quite handsome to look at. Mooney tells us that, even though the Little People are great lovers of music and dancing, and are, generally, delightfully good natured folks, they do possess negative qualities. They are fiercely protective of their privacy and have been known to cast evil spells on humans who seek them out or otherwise disturb them. Their dwellings range from those that are subterranean, to those located in caves, under the water, and in rocky places along streambanks. Some stories tell of Little People who lived beneath the sacred mounds like the huge earthworks known as Nikawsi located in what is now the town of Franklin.

Whether the Yunwi Tsundi are real and akin to the mythological beings like the "fairy folk" so common in Irish and British folklore or, as some say, purely imaginary, is truly difficult to determine and is perhaps best left to the individual to decide. Some have offered opinions and/or drawn conclusions, however, like in the booklet compiled in 1991 by a group of students in a University of Western North Carolina English class. "Perhaps the Little People are not *merely* (italics mine) subjects of myths and legends or even another dimension of reality. Perhaps recognizing them and learning from their lessons are steps in the process toward understanding *our* (italics mine) spirituality as well."[7] I, for one, could not agree more.

The Little People, at least those that still remain, can be divided into three different types: the Laurel People, the Rock People, and the Dogwood People. (Reed; Western Carolina University; 1991) The Rock People are reported to be mean-spirited, whereas the Laurel People are benignly mischievous. The Dogwood People are "good Samaritans" who do nice things for humans and their own kind. From each of these folks there are lessons to be learned......lessons that have to do with the true nature of joy and compassion and of reaping what we have sown. Real or imagined, the Cherokees believed the Little People could speak their language and served as powerful allies who protected the humans whom they looked upon as friends. They also knew they would harass those humans whom they felt were harmful enemies. Their harassment, more often than not, took the form of simple rock-throwing but perhaps their wrath should not be underestimated! Although I am relating this information in the past tense, I do not intend for that to suggest that a belief in the Little People is completely lost to today's Cherokees because I seriously doubt if this is the case. What is more likely is that the stories of the Yunwi Tsundi have become just that; stories rather than remaining a living tradition.

## A THOUSAND EYES IN THE FOREST LOOKING BACK AT YOU!

I have actively pursued my own experience with the Little People. I am of the opinion that rather than deliberately seeking out and thereby forcing personal encounters with invisible entities and forces, that we simply need to become "open" to the possibility of their existence and *allow* our imagination to provide empirical data that will serve to prove or disprove the reality of the entities, forces, or dimensions. This is a much better approach and is more likely to provide a truer sense of satisfaction and conviction regarding their reality. By taking this approach, revealing experiences can occur when we least expect them.

My own experiences have lead me to believe in the existence of several different kinds of entities that fit comfortably into the general category of the Cherokee Little People; the Nune'hi. Since my arrival in western North Carolina I have spent a lot of time in the Great Smoky Mountain National Park. Though the entire area is beautiful and helps to put me in a calm and open state of mind, I am particularly drawn to the beautiful little roadside waterfalls found throughout the area. These wonderful moist, green spots are delightfully fragrant with the smells of the rich soil, the moss-covered fallen trees, and the negative ions that seem to reach inside and caress the soul. The first time I visited such a site I was almost instantly propelled into an altered state of what I call pure "nature consciousness".....that precious frame of mind and heart that stirs and opens my deepest senses and emotions in complete safety and compassion for all that lives; the state that brings my "connection" with all that lives to full consciousness. Being in this precise frame of mind, which over the years has become so welcome and familiar, occurred during a visit to the Park. I walked into a lush green site in the forest framed by overhanging tree branches, where the water zigzagged between and poured over rocks of various sizes and colors, singing its song of life and nourishment. After but a few moments it seemed as if a sort "nighttime" descended. The entire scene became transformed as if bathed in soft, surreal moonlight. All around me, from behind every branch and tree, from beneath the dried leaves, and from behind every rock, I could *feel* what seemed like a thousand pairs of eyes watching me; big, bright yellow-white eyes. I immediately related these "eyes" to what I call "nature spirits," which I have experienced in numerous forms and ways at many places, especially at sacred sites. Most are human-like in form, although I have perceived some who are winged; the ones I think of as fairies. When I sought to perceive the form of those whose eyes now watched me so intensely, I "saw" them as tiny ones about 6" in height, with heads a bit large for their body size. Their facial features resembled elves or Irish leprechauns. I felt these little ones to be very shy and beings who rarely interact with humans, choosing, rather, to observe us at a safe distance. I also suspect they are nocturnal, thus the "night" occurring in my psychic sight. While, in retrospect, I feel these beings I experienced that day are not the same as the Little People who are usually spoken of in most Cherokee legends, I have in fact come to believe that the Nune'hi, in general, are but one of several kinds of nature spirits, little people, and fairy folk who have resided within the Appalachians for eons of time, pre-dating humans by many ages. These are earth beings or spirits, if you will, who have varying tasks, all of which are involved with the maintenance in the balance of the planet and nature. The little ones I "saw" at the waterfall fit aptly into the category of what Clyde Hollifield (Keeper of the Fire) says are found near streams and creeks and who work closely with the spirits of the water. (Katuah Journal; Hollifield; Spring 1984) I feel their work, in part at least, involves determining what courses the water will take. These creatures know when floods are coming and perhaps are acutely aware of and responsible for all matters that concern water in these ancient mountains. Some have heard them making "pounding" noises beneath the water and say they are notorious for fouling up fishermen by tripping them and stealing their lures. These supernaturals also care for all plants that grow in or near the water.

Most descriptions and discussions of the Little People offers little or no distinction as to there being different types who have different forms. An exception is found in the writings of Clyde Hollifield, whose information I learned of through reading the Katuah Journal. Like Hollifield, I too feel the need to make such a distinction whenever possible as I have done in this writing and in my teachings on the subject. Although my "distinctions" may differ somewhat from Hollifield's, I respect what of his work I have read. I also feel that making physical form distinctions can help readers to better visualize the various entities that exist as well as demonstrate how each type has its own tasks within its own life and nature which distinguishes it from all others. Sometimes it is difficult, if not impossible, to do so because the story being told is based upon the subjective experience of another person. A case in point concerns an intriguing article written by an anonymous author about the Little People that appeared in the Winter 1985 issue of the Katuah Journal. The writer says......."The Little People are the spirits of things. They were not always little, and they were not always like people." The following is the lovely story which the author tells and which I retell in my own words, of the time when the Little People came into the world.

They lived under the stars. Starlight nourished them and cast its gentle, glowing light upon the water and everything in the forest, causing the mountains and trees to sparkle with a mysterious beauty. Translucent rocks reflected the starlight back into the heavens; all shone with stellar radiance. During these times each star emitted its own audible sound; sounds that changed as the stars changed position in the sky. Together, all resided in a glorious terra-celestial harmony. During this time the Little People had no defined shapes, although once in a while they would partially manifest out of the shadows allowing a hand, an arm, or eyes to take shape and be seen. All the time there was laughter....joyous laughter....that echoed endlessly through the forests and valleys and high mountain slopes into the timeless world of the little ones.

Deciding there was a need for light and time, the Little People met in council to address that need. Suddenly they saw a glow on the horizon! Spellbound, they watched as the light brightened and spread into a perfect circle that slowly rose above the mountain. Now they had light. They called it Moon; the first thing to have a name. The moonlight also gave the light needed to define the shapes of the Little People. But things soon changed and happiness turned to despair. The first time the moonlight waned the Little Ones were perplexed and fearful about where the Moon had gone and along with it their beautiful creation. But at the new moon they again rejoiced. Unfortunately it didn't take long for the Little People to come to take the moon for granted.

Next, through the power of their collective wishes, they created the Sun, which cast a different and new harsh, bright light upon everything. It was then when the Little People first noticed that their bodies were short and "squatty". The sun's light brought new growth of vegetation and the appearance of trees. Day by day, the sun grew hotter, oppressing the Little People. They could not see the stars anymore. And, even though they succeeded in causing the sun to set, it rose again and again, seven times. Finally, as the Sun set the Moon rose, revealing the barren, dry landscape. It seemed as if everything was deadened by the sun's light except for the tiny mushrooms who hid beneath the leaves and twigs on the forest floor. The mushrooms' silvery bodies bore mute evidence of when everything shone with the soft light of the moon, resulting in the mushrooms becoming a reminder of what it was like before incessant daylight prevailed.

Today, both the sun and moon shine alternately in the heavens. The Little People still shun the hottest solar hours. They come out at night and they always rejoice and give thanks at the time of the Full Moon. And they still possess their magical powers. It is said they still have much of the "shadow" left in them and that they can still change their shape at will. They still dance in the moonlight within the fairy rings of mushrooms deep within the forests and alongside the rippling streams; they still live and dance by the cycles of their beloved moon. The End.

Stories such as this always serve to tune me in to the Little People and their world. But I must say that in my pursuit of knowledge regarding them, none has intrigued me more or rang more true to my own feelings and experiences than that of Clyde Hollifield. In the Spring Issue of the 1984 Katuah Journal, Hollifield reveals his acute sensitivity to what he simply calls the Little People and makes some definite distinctions regarding their appearance and the tasks they perform. He acknowledges, and I feel quite correctly, that the Little People of which he speaks can, and do, take on animal and bird forms and are adept at and delight in tricking humans! A word to the wise from Hollifield states that when one's motives for contacting the Little People is not good or out of line, they can be treacherous in their retaliation!

Hollifield divides the Little People into some six categories. One lives in the laurel thickets and are not known for their friendliness to humans. They can cause humans to lose their way and are not generally trustworthy. There are also those found on dry ridges and serve as "lookouts" to warn their kind of impending dangers or intruders. Then there are those I described earlier who dwell near the streams and who work with the water and the springs. Remember the "eyes" I felt watching me? Still others are found on craggy balds at the higher elevations like Grandfather Mountain and Shining Rock. Hollifield calls these the "heath" types which make moss and rock gardens and are perfect bonsai-makers. The ones Hollifield describes as found on farms and in the fields seem to be like the ones I have named the Underground People. There are also those who live in the rich cove areas where wildflowers are so plentiful. He says these work closely with the plant spirits such as ginseng and oversee all who pass through the woods. Hollifield's knowledge and intuition is further evidenced by his interesting description of a "control room" wherein the Little People monitor all activities that occur above ground. Hollifield also says that there are Little People who live underground and only come out at night! The "control room" is set up to receive quite literal impressions, he says, of humans when they step on strategically-placed stones, or when they leave their facial imprint upon walking into a spider's web! (Katuah Journal; Spring, 1984; pg. 18-19) How absolutely delightful this information is! It is surely sufficient to inspire anyone to learn more about the Little People and to learn with right motive and due caution. Hollifield's love for the Little People and his sensitivity to the land and the mountains comes through very clearly when he shares his belief that the magnificent Grandfather Mountain is the seat of all the nature spirits and their activities for this entire region. I simply do not feel any knowledge or experience of the profane or sacred ecology of these ancient grandfather/grandmother mountains would be complete without one's being aware of the existence of Nature's ambassadors: the Little People.

Whereas the indigenous people of the area have generations of myths and accounts of personal experiences handed down orally for generations to rely upon as "proof" of the existence and presence of the Nune'hi, others of us must simply accept their stories as truth and/or depend solely upon our individual intuitive insight for our experience with them, except perhaps upon the rare event of a personal physical "sighting" of them. On numerous occasions, particularly in areas such as Big Cove and other parts of the Qualla Reservation, areas around Bryson City, in the Nantahala Gorge, in Cades Cove, and on farmlands throughout western North Carolina and eastern Tennessee, I have "seen" and "felt" in my mind the presence of a kind of little person-and in this case the word "person" should be taken quite literally-who is a perfect duplicate of a human but who stands only about one to one and a half feet in height. The males are usually heavily bearded, their hair and beards grey and very coarse. The women have been clad in long pioneer-type cotton-like dresses and some wear bibbed apron-like garments over the outer garment. The men's clothing look as if they too have been woven from heavy cotton, although some did look like they were fashioned from thick wool. Both the males and females wear leather boots similar to hearty high-top hiking boots. The aura put off by these entities always gives me the impression that they are not fairies or elves of any sort. Quite the contrary. I feel they are a "race" of small humans who, although they may possess spiritual "powers", do not pass from one dimension into another. Rather, they live underground in the physical world and have since the appearance of human and human settlements in these mountains. I did find it interesting and must note that the Cherokees do say that the Nune'hi live underground and specify some of the locations of their dwellings as Pilot Mountain, Shining Rock, the Nikawsi Mound in Franklin, and Blood Mountain. (Katuah Journal; Winter 1985-6) I also believe it is highly likely that these same type of entities exist underground in various places worldwide. From this point on in this writing I shall refer to these little humans as the "Underground People". These are different from what others have called gnomes or brownies or from those Hollifield calls the Little People.

    The Underground People are like humans in every way except for their dwelling place. Like humans they live off the land, their diet consisting mostly of the leaves and roots of plants, berries, forest fruits and nuts, herbal teas, small birds and rodents, and of course water. All of these, with the exception of some moles and rodents, are gathered from above ground. I have sensed their villages as being "clustered" in certain areas, many in close proximity to human rural towns and particularly near farms. I suspect that the Underground People are another kind of human being that have never lost their connection to the earth and the natural elements; those who never evolved, if you will, into above ground humans such as ourselves. I am sure there were times, long past, when the Underground People encountered people like us. Such encounters are a matter of the oral record of the Cherokees. But as the human world progressed and became more complex it also became more dangerous. So these small humans retreated totally into the safety and sanctity of the underground where they remain and thrive until this day in a world far different from our own. As we threaten our world, we threaten theirs. Sadly, the time could come when the Underground People will become extinct, ending one of the most well-guarded secrets that is one of the little-known treasures of these ancient mountains......that being the fact of their existence. I do not expect my readers to rely solely upon my having "seen" these little ones nor have you rely upon my truth as your own. I encourage you to open your mind to the possibility of their existence and allow your own experience of them if they exist, and I for one believe they do, to unfold.

Another interesting perspective of the Little People is offered by Lloyd Owle, noted artist and Cultural Specialist in Cherokee, N.C. Lloyd, himself a Cherokee born on the Qualla Reservation, tells a story of the Little People being representative of different dimensions of the [human] mind. (Katuah Journal; Winter l986-87; pg. l) "All the dimensions are here, and sometimes we slip into another time or another phase of the mind, and we find ourselves seeing things in a different way. It feels strange to us only because we have become separated from ourselves." Owle says he often thinks those we call the Little People are, in actuality, a *sense* that is given to humans to help us protect ourselves and, ultimately, to survive. He also acknowledges the fact that Native American people have always listened to that "other voice" which he says may be ESP or intuition or simple good judgement. According to Lloyd, such involves both a manner of thinking and a method of communication. He speaks of experiencing these moments of precious insight when he is engrossed in doing his stone carvings; how the images seem to appear out of the rock, suggesting that as one touches into these altered mental states, creativity flows freely so that the eyes and heart are able to perceive and create that which one could not and would not have "seen" otherwise. Owle's opinion is worth careful consideration. Being married to an artist, and being a writer, I am familiar with the "worlds" into which creative people must journey in order to get in touch with images hidden from our normal sight, and of going to the fountain of love energy and power that so often deludes the average waking state, Psychically, I have experienced the landscapes of these "worlds" many times. I have retrieved their bounty; tasted of their sweet nectar, and experienced their spiritual intoxication.

In keeping with our investigation and discussion regarding the Little People I am reminded that, once in a while, Nature throws us a curve! One such curve is found in the unusually exquisite stones known as the *fairy crosses*. No one knows exactly how these natural mineral crosses are formed though they appear to have been purposely shaped by man. No! They are truly gifts from the Earth Mother. The Cherokees, and others, have long valued these wonderful stones. Cherokee legends say the crosses come from benevolent Little People who possessed special supernatural powers which included helping lost humans to find their way home and assisting fishermen in a good catch. These mysterious little folk could, at will, change from being visible to invisible but usually remained invisible when humans were around.

On the package of a fairy cross I purchased in the town of Cherokee, I learned that the Cherokees say that when the crucifixion of

Christ occurred the Little People were greatly saddened. Their tears fell onto the earth and were immediately transformed into tiny crosses. The crosses are abundant (at least they were at one time) in the area around Brasstown, near Murphy, in Cherokee County. They may also be purchased in mineral and gift shops throughout the area and are sometimes found in stores far and wide. These delightful natural treasures are believed to bring good fortune to their owners. I suggest that to those fortunate enough to have one might carry it on their person in a medicine pouch. It should be considered to be a powerful amulet; a "link" with all nature spirits and especially to the Little People. Hold it in your hand while calling upon the fairy folks for guidance and blessings. Being in conscious contact with the nature spirits can go far in helping one expand their ability to "see" into other dimensions of Time/Space and gives one a greater sense of truly belonging to the earth and of being related to our siblings which are her children in all kingdoms.

Of course all sorts of claims have been made over the years by those who say they have encountered the Little People in one form or another. Some even say they will drive a human crazy who dares to talk to them! Others warn humans never to challenge them less we risk the danger of unpleasant consequences. With all the changes that have taken place in the Great Smoky Mountains, what with the progress/development, tourism and the toll it has and continues to take, as well as the current ecological problems we face, is it any wonder why the Little People are all but gone? Perhaps they have retreated, forever, into a world invisible to our eyes. Maybe the loss of a harmonious relationship with our Earth Mother by humans has rendered a relationship with the little folk and the fairies impossible. In any case, it is certain that when our eyes and hearts are open to nature and when we are truly aware of her delicate balance, we can see, hear, and know, intuitively, things that we cannot otherwise know or experience.

In addition to a knowledge of the Little People the Cherokees also had a belief in another type of fairy folk or supernaturals whom they called the *Immortals*. As well as I can determine these entities were associated with sacred ceremonial sites and were the keepers of the sacred ceremonial fire. There were also the *Thunders* or *Thunderers*, as well as a spirit called *"The Fire Carrier"*, who the people feared and who went around at night carrying a "light". And there are the elementals or undines called *"The Water Dwellers"*, some of whom assist fishermen with a good catch; and others who live in people's houses and protect the residents from black witchcraft.

As I read what I could find about the Little People and other of the fairy folk and spirit beings known to the Cherokees, I was struck by the numerous tales, particularly those related in Mooney's book, that tell of "monsters" of various sorts who were once residents of the Smokies. Most of them were depicted as overgrown animals or insects who varied not only in size, but in the roles they played in the lives of the Earth's inhabitants, including the ancestral peoples of the area. At the time I came across this information I was already keenly aware of the existence of similar monsters known to other Indian tribes, ranging from Uncegila, the great water monster of the Sioux, the Achiyalatopa of the Zuni, a peculiar being who had knives for a tail, and the various ogres of the Hopi who fulfilled various roles within Hopi mythology. However, I found the *sheer number* of the monster tales related by the Cherokees absolutely astounding! In reading Mooney's accounts one learns, for example, of a great huge fish named Dakwa'; the mythic hawk called Tla'nuwa'; the eerie serpents Ustu'tli, and Uktena; Great Buzzard who formed the Smokies with his wings, and even huge insects like the Great Yellow Jacket, and of giant rabbits, and other monster fishes. In addition there were those such as Tsul'kala or Judaculla the Slant-Eyed Giant, and the Water Cannibals who lived at the bottom of the deep streams and rivers and who dined off human flesh! These were monsters alright, but they had human bodies! Some were benevolent; some were not.

To me the most intriguing of all the monsters in Cherokee mythology as related by James Mooney is Uktena....."a great snake, as large around as a tree trunk, with horns on its head, and a bright, blazing crest like a diamond upon its forehead, and scales glittering like sparks of fire. It has rings or spots of color along its whole length, and can not be wounded except by shooting in the seventh spot from the head, because under this spot are its heart and its life."[8]

It was the diamond in Uktena's brow that caught my attention. Described as transparent the diamond possessed great powers that could work wonders for the human fortunate enough to own it. But capturing it was no small task for Uktena's blazing light easily blinded a would-be conqueror, causing him to run headlong into the serpent's deadly gaze! The Cherokees say only one warrior was successful. He secured the diamond, a treasure said to still be in the possession of the people. (Mooney, 1982)

In light of the current revival of interest in the powers inherent within crystals and other minerals, I found it very interesting that the "diamond" taken from Uktena is actually described as being a large transparent crystal which is shaped like a bullet with a vertical red streak running through its center. (Mooney, 1982) Legend has it that the crystal requires its owner to "feed" it every seven days with blood from a small animal. Twice a year, though some say only once every seven years, the treasure is rubbed with the blood of a large animal such as a deer or bear. I was particularly intrigued by the crystal's similarity to the one described by the famous psychic Edgar Cayce in his readings about Atlantis. According to Cayce, the Atlantean crystal also possessed great and wonderful supramundane powers. Cayce suggests that human misuse of the crystal's power was actually at least a contributing factor to the now-lost continent's succumbing to destruction during a previous period of planetary upheaval. While I know of no stories that suggest Uktena's crystal had any such negative influence on the fate of the land or the people, it did have powers that were perhaps oriented more toward personal and individual human needs, including the guarantee of a successful hunt, the finding of true love, the gift of prophecy, and rain-making. Whether or not the Cherokee crystal actually exists now or ever did is, I suppose, a matter of opinion. Perhaps Uktena's crystal and its Atlantean ancestor may have been the prototype or symbol for all quartz and its inherent powers. Or maybe we should take the legend literally. Maybe Uktena's crystal was very real and embodied great powers, but has long since been lost. Perhaps it was hidden away somewhere in these mountains and will, someday, be found again. No one can say. But it is sure fun to speculate!

Whether we should take the existence of Uktena and other monsters literally or symbolically now is a matter addressed aptly by author, teacher, and Cherokee lineage-holder Dhyani Ywahoo. In her book *Voices Of Our Ancestors*, Ywahoo refers to Uktena (Ukdena) as....."the great dragons that used to protect this land, and who have now moved into another dimension." Ywahoo, *Voices Of Our Ancestors,* pg.16) Ywahoo goes further to suggest that the dragon is the "unconscious" nature of the land that faded into obscurity. She says that the last of the dragons was seen in the Smokies in the 1700s. Ywahoo's wonderful definition of *the supposed evil* inherent within dragons such as Uktena comes from our own ignorance in our minds and hearts, and our misunderstanding of the reciprocal relationship between the earth and humans. I agree. Ywahoo also relates much information about quartz and other stones, giving teachings about the ten sacred minerals of her people. She also stresses the absolute necessity of having the proper knowledge of how to work with crystals, citing that "misuse of crystal energy can be as destructive to the physical and light bodies as the use of drugs".....and....."...crystal energy is as volatile as the atom bomb, and when you work with the crystal whatever is going on in your mind is going to be amplified." (*Voices Of Our Ancestors;* pg.236) In light of the renewed interest in crystals and crystal power I think that these warnings are well-taken. Anyone interested in more detailed information specifically regarding Cherokee views about the use of quartz and other minerals, I recommend Ywahoo's book. I also have two books on the general subject of crystals and their use which the reader may find informative. These are *Crystals And Their Use* and *The Magic Of Minerals* (Sun Publishing; Santa Fe, New Mexico)

Not all of the monsters or dragons that appear in Cherokee mythology are animals or gigantic insects. Some are humans. An example is seen in the tales of Utlun ta or Spear Finger, a female ogre who fed on human beings. There was also The Stone Man and The Ice Man. (Mooney, 1982) Certainly one has the choice whether to accept these seemingly outrageous creatures as actually having once existed physically, or whether to consider them as being purely mythological, which surely seems to make more sense. But if the latter is true then we must consider the possible reasons for the appearance and prominence of such incredible beings throughout Cherokee lore.

Aside from the obvious reasons that such stories surely made for darn good entertainment around village campfires, there is probably something much more important involved. Certainly Dhyani Ywahoo's explanation of them being protectors of the land is an interesting and probable one that surely allows for their literal existence. However, upon reading the monster accounts, three things became apparent to me that may result in the reader looking at these monster figures from other perspectives. The first came when I realized how frightening they were and the terrible dangers they posed to human life. Could the stories have been a tool of discipline? More than one Indian parent has used, perhaps even created, such stories to help discipline unruly children, literally scaring them into good behavior! While this may not be a good disciplinary method, it is nonetheless quite effective! I know this is a common practice among the Hopi and other Pueblo peoples in the Southwest. For example, at Hopiland there is the annual appearance of a giant ogress who comes in the middle of the night and disciplines bad children with a yucca whip, while the parents look on without interference. Secondly, are not such creatures reminiscent of the giant animals and birds that once roamed the planet during the age of the dinosaurs? Could the legends be *archetypal remembrances* of such giant creatures? And thirdly, could not such "unworldly" creatures embody the *power of and personify the Great Unknown* and the myriad of archetypal, supernatural entities and forces that the human psyche has always perceived as existing beyond the physical dimension? And do not such archetypes reside within the deepest, most primordial recesses of individual selves; the part of self that Jung named the collective unconscious? Any of these could be true. Something which seems highly likely occurred to me while reading Mooney's accounts of these incredible creatures and the human exploits required to conquer and/or control them and obtain their powers or magical objects: could the legends embody or even camouflage highly esoteric *initiation processes* undertaken by apprentice shamans? The possibility got me to thinking. Most, if not all of the various monsters seemed to possess certain supernatural powers that, if they could be obtained by humans, would bestow superhuman knowledge and skills. Human beings have always sought such powers. We see clear evidence of this with Uktena in whose brow was the coveted diamond. Also keep in mind that before a human could obtain the "power" held and/or guarded by a given monster or supernatural, he or she must go through certain prescribed procedures which ranged from the seeker displaying an immense degree of courage, to knowing certain magic words designed to mesmerize the creature so that the object or the body-part that had the "power(s)" could be secured. Such ideas are clearly portrayed, for instance, in Mooney's account of Uktena. The winner in the encounter automatically became a hero. This and other similar tales are curiously reminiscent of the Grail Quest embarked upon by the famous Knights of the Round Table in the legends of King Arthur. The knights faced many such perils during their search for the sacred cup which possessed the power of enlightenment and immortality. It does not take stretching the imagination to see that the Cherokee myths are quite similar. Agan uni'tsi, the brave warrior who won Uktena's diamond, is portrayed as having gone through the same types of dangers as Arthur's knights, overcoming them one by one. The story is filled with clever tactics dreamed up by Agan uni'tsi to defeat Uktena and the three other serpents he encountered prior to his meeting the dreaded Great One. And each of the three serpents represented certain dangers. In the end the warrior conquered all the obstacles and overcame all his fears and life-threatening dangers, including surviving a deadly poison spewed out by Uktena and getting caught up in the great serpent's deadly gaze. After winning the diamond Agan uni'tsi returned to the people, like a knight coming home from his quest, and was proclaimed as the most powerful medicine man in the world! The hero archetype embodies the powers of one who has met the challenge........one who has fought for the "cause" and has emerged victorious. A hero represents the best of the best, the cream of the crop. Such adoration serves to further empower the hero and provides the people with a role model and, sometimes, a messiah. So who is to say that hidden within the context of the Cherokee monster legends lies a complete body of spiritual knowledge, an esoteric formula if you will, that contains the most sacred and powerful of all medicine knowledge held within Cherokee religion. If this is true, the myths definitely serve an extremely useful and spiritual purpose. Furthermore, heroes do a lot toward assuring the continuity of a given society. Through them the people are linked to their own unique past and to the past in general. Stories which tell of heroes live long after they are gone. Because heroes serve as role models for the young men and women coming along, the future seems somehow more secure. When viewed in this way it seems clear that the early Cherokees, like all ancient peoples and cultures, devised a clever and enthralling mythology that personified places, animals, and people of great powers and provided, in a profound way, an explanation for the unexplained.

After reading about Cherokee legends and religion, primarily through Mooney's account, I could not help but wonder just *how much*, if any, of the ancient tales and spiritual practices related continue to survive today. When I posed this question to several Cherokee people I found that the validity of Mooney's material was questionable to some of them. They seemed to view it with the belief or attitude that it was mostly "made up" or that those who had told Mooney the things he wrote about simply lied or deliberately misled the author. In a conversation with one native woman I was told that most Cherokees have long since converted to Christianity and lost touch with the old religion. Few have any desire to even know of, much less practice the traditional ways. The woman also implied that the only *true* teachings were never written down anyway and were only passed on orally, suggesting to me at least, her disregard for Mooney's accounts. One must wonder how many Cherokees there are today who really *know* the traditional myths, sacred ceremonies, and general spirituality/spiritual philosophy. And how many of them actively practice the old songs, dances, and ceremonies? Surely there must be precious few but thankfully a few is all it takes for the ancient wisdom to survive! It is obvious to me that Mooney was told of the things he wrote and that he accepted them in good faith. It seems highly doubtful that anyone would have or could have gone to the trouble to make up such information just to fool one writer. For what purpose? Besides, Mooney's sources were numerous, making it unlikely, if not impossible, for an orchestrated conspiracy to take place. I think something else is going on here. The outside, modern, non-Indian world has encroached upon Cherokee life just as it has upon virtually every Native American tribe to one degree or another. As a result, regretfully, many traditions and sacred rites are dying and others are completely lost. This seems to be true to a much greater degree with the eastern and southeastern tribes than with the people that make up the northern Great Plains and the northwestern and southwestern tribes. Throughout the eleven years I lived in the American Southwest (Arizona and Colorado) I spent many Saturday and

Sunday afternoons attending the sacred dances on the three Hopi mesas in northeastern Arizona; ancient dances/rites that have been done continuously for centuries. This does not seem to be the case with most of the eastern tribes, as many, though not all, their ceremonies and religious practices have been discontinued or lost. It would appear to me that Mooney has chronicled Cherokee history and spiritual and cultural lore as accurately as one could hope to do through hearing it second hand (though he is reported to have witnessed some of the sacred rites) and that, in doing so, has done a true service for future generations, Indian and non-Indian alike.

Over the course of writing this book I had the opportunity to speak to my friend, Lloyd Owle, on several occasions. My husband and I met Lloyd at a Sweat we attended when we first moved to the area. I learned that through his mother's side of the family, Lloyd is a descendant of Drowning Bear, the chief of the Cherokees during the difficult times of the Removal (Trail of Tears). I asked Lloyd if he thought that the spiritual tradition of his people was all but dead and whether he felt there was any chance that it will survive. After what seemed to be careful thought, Lloyd replied that, considering all the "set backs" the people have suffered, he feels that quite a bit of the old knowledge and ways are still very much alive. "Much of it is underground. You know....it goes back to when the government outlawed other religions. So many bad things have happened. During the Removal time, pipes were broken, the mounds were covered with dirt....the Stomp dances stopped." He said that it is because of some of the "old timers" like Walker Calhoun, Will West Long, and Lloyd Sequoyah that much of the knowledge has survived. "Over the last thirty years.....it has been slowly coming back....the tradition.....the dances....are returning." These statements gave me hope and some small insight as to the plight the tradition has already undergone and quite possibly might yet undergo in the future before it comes back into the light. And Lloyd's final words gave me a feeling for how the Cherokees, like other Native people, must live and think today: "We must walk with a moccasin on one foot and a shoe on the other. We must stay, some how, in the middle of the road within society. We really cannot go completely over to either side." Such an attitude does not demand that Indians practice their spiritual/religious traditions exclusively, but it does insure the survival of the Old Ways for those, natives and non-natives alike who wish to know their wisdom and learn from the old ways.

Thankfully the lack of interest or apathy among the Cherokees to carry on their cultural and spiritual traditions may be slowly changing. Pride is returning. Or perhaps it has been there all along and is simply re-emerging. In either case, this is positive. For the first time in many years an inter-tribal Pow Wow was held in 1991 in Asheville, and it is my understanding that future gatherings are planned for every year from now on. Many Indian tribes from all over the country were represented. Some performed sacred and social dances, while others told stories and displayed various examples of their traditional arts and crafts. It is my understanding that some of the traditional members of the Western Band of the Cherokees have come to the Eastern Band people in order to rekindle an interest in and to teach of their religious and spiritual heritage, and to reinstate the performance of some of the sacred rites. Another Cherokee woman told me that, for the past three years, some Cherokees have come together to perform the Green Corn ceremony. This is good news. Again, perhaps the current interest in the traditional ways by both Indians and non-Indians, will serve to enhance the chances of its survival. If this happens we will all be the beneficiaries of the powers and knowledge inherent within these precious indigenous cultures, and of a spiritual tradition that links humankind with the old gods and goddesses and with the Earth Mother unlike none other in this land. Ultimately, our individual relationship with the Earth Mother is a personal matter. Each of us must accept the responsibility of learning all we can of the traditional ways of the Native people of Turtle Island and seek, in turn, to *apply* that knowledge and awareness toward re-establishing our relationship with nature. Only this will change our values. Only this will guarantee the continuity, indeed the very survival, of the sacred ways.

Aside from the legends which are a part of the ancient Cherokee spiritual tradition, there is that which is a demonstration of the principles and beliefs. Of these, the dances and the songs that went with them were, and are, an integral part of the heart and soul of the people. There were dances and songs for the assurance of good health, good harvests, good hunting, war, peace, victory, and for giving thanks. (French and Hornbuckle; 1981) The Cherokees had three instruments that were used during the sacred dances; a hollowed-out water drum made from the trunk of a buckeye tree and covered with woodchuck hide; gourd rattles; and rattles made from box turtle shells.

In addition to the Green Corn Ceremony there was once a time when many other dances and songs echoed through these ancient valleys. Of these perhaps none other was more mysterious or more complex than the *Booger Dance*. Though this may not have been the original name (Fogelson and Walker; 1980) the Booger Dance, in the earliest days, is thought to have been a ceremonial opportunity for the elder men and young boys to come together to "act out the basic tension between the two."[9] This forum also provided an opportunity for one group of males to participate in and experience certain qualities, both positive and negative, of the other; a way of showcasing problems of every Cherokee life. The Booger Dance was done in wintertime after the first frost. The dancers wore carved wooden masks that were painted red, white, or black (some say to represent human races) (Fogelson and Walker; Vol.V. Fall, 1980) Some of the masks were harsh and scowling, while other were more pleasant. During the dance, which had non-so-subtle sexual overtones, the participants were called by obscene names that described dirty acts. The dancers, each taking his own solo turn, behaved in a rather barbarian-like manner.

Next, as requested by the Boogers, a Bear or Eagle Dance was performed. The entire evening was climaxed by mixed social dances that gave the people an additional opportunity to celebrate. Some say the Booger masks represented disease and that the dance was for the purpose of driving out evil. However, many say that the dance was meant to mimic, negatively, people of other races, particularly the whites and blacks. If this is so, it must have been incorporated after the Cherokees came into contact with these races and provided the Indians with a way of showing disdain for them and gave recognition to the insecurities the invaders brought into Cherokee life.

Masks were also used in other sacred dances. These included the warrior, medicine, and magical masks. (King; 1988) The warrior mask had one or two feathers in the front. The medicine mask, used to frighten away disease, had ears and horns, while the magical masks were carved with rattlesnake effigies on the forehead. Magical masks, though not used for medicine purposes, were said to be extremely powerful. They could kill or cure. (King; 1988) Most dance masks represented humans and were made from gourds, buckeye, or basswood, but there were some that represented animals such as the bear and deer.

In addition to war and victory dances there was the Beaver Dance; a line dance performed by dancers who carried a peeled sumac stick and who danced around a stuffed beaver or pile of rags made to represent a beaver. (King; 1988) The dance is the pantomime of a beaver hunt. My husband and I had the opportunity to watch respected Cherokee elder, Walker Calhoun, teach some youngsters how to perform the Beaver Dance, and we were allowed to participate as well. It was great fun and before the dance was over everyone was laughing heartily!

Like the Beaver Dance is a hunting dance, so is the Bear Dance a significant prelude to a bear hunt. In this dance the participants circle, counterclockwise, around a mortar in the center of a room or outdoor life. (King; 1988) In step with a beating drum and the sound of a gourd rattle, the dancers shuffle and sway like a real bear, complete with the imitating growls. Eventually, women entered the dance and, facing the men, danced backwards, perhaps lending some sexual significance to the rite. Another, the Eagle Dance was once done to prevent bad medicine men from using eagle feathers to cause evil and sickness. (King; 1988) The dance was performed with each dancer carrying a 20" eagle feather wand of sourwood, the feathers spreading out like a huge fan. Male and female dancers, facing each other, formed a line, keeping time to the beat of drums and rattles. Incidentally, a dance that is called The Eagle Dance is a part of the outdoor drama *Unto These Hills* and one can only assume that it is an accurate reflection of a sacred dance of the early Cherokees. In addition, there were similar buffalo and horse dances. And then there was the Corn Dance held to give thanks for abundant corn crops.

When I began my study of Native American spirituality and religion in the early 1980s I, early on, became aware of and had opportunities to participate in a powerful sacred rite called the "Sweat." The Sweat Lodge is quite common among Native tribes, although most of my personal experiences have been with Lakota and Chippewa people. The Sweat is a cleansing rite undertaken for healing, as a prelude to a vision quest, or other significant events. In earlier days the Cherokees had a sacred rite they called the "Sweat Bath", which was practiced due to its incredible invigorating and healing qualities. I am not certain that this particular rite is practiced today in exactly the same way. The sweats I have attended on the Cherokee reservation have been the same as those done by the Sioux and other tribes. It is my understanding that while the Sweat Lodge of other tribes is constructed of willow branches into an igloo or dome-like structure, the original Cherokee lodge was/is a small, earth-covered log house that one cannot stand up in due to its short height which is built only to accommodate sitting. Heated stones are placed inside and then dowsed with a concoction of water and wild parsnip. This mixture, if indeed the report is accurate, is unique to my knowledge and experience. I did attend a Sweat in northern California several years ago that was led by a Shasta medicine man named Charlie Thom. who used a large wild celery root to "bless" the hot rocks as they were brought into the Lodge. It is also my understanding that, in the old days, the Cherokees used a form of massage known as "rubbing", as well as "bleeding", bathings, and sometimes medicine dances as additional methods of curing and healing. I do not know if any of these methods are still in use, but I suspect they are, if only in secret among the elders and/or traditional people.

Further investigation of Cherokee spirituality reveals their views regarding certain colors with which they symbolized their world. (Mooney; 1982) The designations and meanings were no doubt determined in the earliest times by tribal shamans. It is a common practice among Native Americans to assign specific "powers" and esoteric meanings to certain colors. With the Cherokees each of the four cardinal directions is represented by a color: red for East; blue for North; black for West; white for South. Each color has both a symbolic meaning and a corresponding spirit(s). Red is the color of power and success. Blue is symbolic of trouble and defeat. The West is the abode of death and black is death's color, while white is the color of peace and happiness. Tribal shamans manipulated the powers of the various colors and the places and spirits connected with them. The Cherokees, like some other tribes, also have a designation for an upper world or "Above", and a "Below", a lower domain. The color brown is associated with Above, described by Mooney as a "propitious place," but yet an unknown location. Yellow is given to an unnamed place I am calling "Below" and is defined as the color of troubles. These are not unlike the Christian Heaven and Hell.

Also holding true to other ancient Wisdom Traditions, the number 7 is sacred to the Cherokees. (Mooney; 1982) The reader will recall the great serpent Uktena from whom Agan uni'tsi successfully captured the brow crystal which had to be fed every *seven days* and, in some cases, every *seven* years. We also see that in relation to the Green Corn Ceremony, *seven* ears of corn from the crop of the previous year were set aside for the purpose of attracting more corn until the new crop was ready to be eaten. When it was time for the sacred dance that was an integral part of this ceremony the *seven* ears of the old corn were eaten along with the new. Likewise, *seven* corn kernels were placed on each dirt hill at the time of planting. Cherokee cosmology also tells that the Great Spirit created *seven* "heavens" which seem to represent *seven* successive worlds, ranging from the lowest to the highest, it being in the highest or *seventh* "heaven" within which the Creator dwelled.

Because there are few definitive works on Cherokee mythology or their spiritual and/or religious beliefs and practices, it is difficult for non-Indians and Indians alike to gain any knowledge that one can be sure is truly authentic. The few books that do exist are all we have. So there is a problem. More than one Indian tribe will tell you that published works on their religious beliefs and sacred rites are, at best, incomplete or out and out incorrect. A case in point is the well-known *Book Of The Hopi* by Frank Waters. Though not all, I know many Hopis feel Waters' information is inaccurate. But I know from my own personal experiences and simple observations over a decade of time that this criticism for Waters' book is unfounded. I have witnessed many of the dances Waters describes and found his descriptions to be accurate. I have watched the ceremonial year unfold according to his description. This leads me to doubt that such books, including Mooney's *Myths Of The Cherokee/Sacred Formulas Of The Cherokee*, can simply be systematically cast aside as having little or no value. They are, after all, published and respected accounts claimed by their authors to contain valid information told to them by traditional people who had nothing to gain by deception. And unless some things change drastically, such publications may very well be *all* that ever will be left to attest to the traditions of the Native Americans of our continent. Too many unfortunate circumstances threaten to prevent the survival of the Old Ways, or render them unavailable to us who are alive now on the planet, or preserve them for future generations. If it isn't the myriad of problems such as those of poverty and social disintegration currently being faced by so many Indian peoples today, the widespread empathy, and in some cases the *unwillingness* of tribal members to share their spiritual and religious traditions with non-Native people, that threatens the survival of the traditions, it is the non-Natives who engage in "playing Indian" and who often change traditional teachings and ceremonies to suit their own purposes and/ or to exploit them for profit. These and other problems can, and will if they are not stopped, lead the tradition to extinction. The truth is that something very precious is in danger of being lost forever. Regardless of skin color or creed, it is now up to us, Natives and non-Natives alike, to revive and hopefully preserve the ancient earth religions that comprise the foundation of the spiritual heritage of our human ancestors of North America. And, for whites in particular, this may be one way the negative karma existing between the two races, white and red, can be ended. Can non-Indians not help carry on the Indian tradition with our sincere interest and participation in tribal ways? And by doing so can we not gain knowledge that will help to insure our individual and collective spiritual awareness and growth? One thing seems certain: if the hatred and distrust between the races continues, the apathy of the majority of the present-day Native Americans, and the encroachment of modern society insists, the days of the Old Ways are numbered.

The argument that non-Indians should be freely given the knowledge of the religious tradition of the native people poses questions that are difficult to answer. On the one hand, in light of the environmental difficulties we now face and our need to re-establish our relationship with Mother Earth, and the problems currently being faced by Native Americans that seem to threaten the very survival of their culture and religious traditions and practices, it would seem that the more people who find value in the Old Ways the better chance it will have to live on. I, for one, have met many people of all races who have genuinely embraced the Indian cultural and spiritual *values* and who seek to live them on a daily basis. Many of these same people are sincerely interested in being of service to various Native American "causes" which include both social and political issues. But whether or not this interest and concern warrants non-Indians being privileged to learn from native teachers and elders and be accepted into the sacred rites and practices is not altogether clear. When people outside of any culture or religion come into the fold, so to speak, it will inevitably bring change. So perhaps the real question must be *what* those changes will involve and are they more positive than negative in nature. As always there are two sides to the coin.

During my recent studies of the works of noted psychiatrist, C.G. Jung, I came across a passage that gave me pause and that may very well shed some light on the question of non-Indians being privileged to knowledge of Native American religion and sacred rites. During a trip to the Taos Pueblo, Jung observed the reluctancy of the Pueblo Indians to talk about anything concerning their religion. And when they did speak about such things, Jung made the following comment:....."It was astonishing to me to see how the Indian's emotions change when he speaks of his religious ideas." (*Memories, Dreams, and Reflections*; Jung, C.G.; pg. 250) The insightful psychiatrist recognized early on that their religious conceptions were not mere theories. To the Indians they were unquestionable facts! This realization led Jung to some conclusions about the close-mouthed policy of the Pueblo peoples that surely applies to any and all tribal cultures. "Never before had I run into such an atmosphere of secrecy; the religions of civilized nations today are all *accessible* (italics mine); their sacraments have long ago ceased to be mysteries." And...."This was not mystification, but a vital mystery whose betrayal might bring about the downfall of the community as well as of the individual. Preservation of the secret gives the Pueblo Indian pride and the power to resist the dominant whites. It gives him cohesion and unity; and I feel sure that the Pueblos as an individual community will continue as long as their mysteries are not desecrated." (*Memories, Dreams, and Reflections*; Jung, C.G.; pg 250) Not only are Jung's insights food for thought for any non-Indian person who is interested in learning of the traditional ways, but also makes one wonder if the current surge of interest has the potential of doing more harm than good. When there is the potential of damage, though it be absolutely unintentional, do we not have to pause to consciously reflect upon the entire matter. Perhaps the only real answer as to what attitude and action to be taken must lie totally in the hands of the native people themselves. Maybe instead of closing the door of knowledge and participation to non-Indians period, it might be best to take each individual in or keep he or she out depending solely upon their individual merit and what is "felt" from and/or about that person. At the very least I think that each of us who has an interest in knowing about Native American religion and practices must give the issue and our own motives some careful thought.

When I began writing this book I wished to speak personally to a particular Cherokee elder, Walker Calhoun, whom I had heard a lot about since my arrival in western North Carolina. I first learned of Walker through an interview in the Katuah Journal (Issue 32; Fall 1991) Referring to his people as *Katuah,* the elder spoke of the relationship between them and the land. Deep-rooted feelings for the old ways came through very clearly in the old man's words as he told of the "stomp (ceremonial) grounds", namely the one in his neighborhood, Big Cove, which he called The Raven Rock Nighthawk Ceremonial Grounds. He spoke of how each of the ceremonial grounds "has a mound where the spirit is."[10] Atop the mound, a fire was built; a fire that could only be kindled from a spark from a rock. "The Spirit of Fire is in that mound."[11] In the old ceremonies the fire was called "Ancient Red," and it was around the spiritual fire the dances were/are held. Dance is a method of praying, and the smoke from the fire takes the prayers to the Great Spirit. It was from Clingman's Dome, the highest peak in what is now the Great Smoky Mountain National Park, where the wisest men of the Cherokees held their meetings. It was also from there they got the dirt that was used to build the ceremonial mounds. It was there where they talked to the Creator.

At the time of the Removal Ancient Red was taken with the people to Indian Territory in Oklahoma, where it was kept, so it is said, in the Redbird Community. This left the mountains, in the sacred sense of the word, dark. But on September 29, 1989 the sacred fire was brought back to the eastern Cherokees; brought by a man named Hickory Star. Yes, the fire had returned to its ancient mountain home. Mission accomplished. And what a powerful and symbolic, mission it was. Hickory Star returned to Oklahoma where he died less than six months later! The article in the *Katuah Journal* whetted my appetite and some six months later I met Walker Calhoun.

During Cultural Heritage Week in the town of Cherokee in May, 1992 my husband Scott and I attended the afternoon activities. We felt privileged to witness performances given mostly by children from kindergarten through grade school ages of the Hoop Dance, Fancy Feather Dance, and the Peace Pipe and Quail Dances, for which Walker rattled and sang while the kids did the steps. As I sat there my eye caught the image of the Seal Of The Cherokee Nation that hung over the stage area; a seven-pointed gold star with another smaller star outlined in black inside. The date on the seal read September 6, 1839; the date of the official birth (?) of the Cherokee Nation. But I knew in my heart that the Cherokee nation was much older. As I sat and watched the children dance to the tune of the elder's chants, I saw a culture struggling desperately and proudly to hold onto a way of life....a custom....an identity....a pride....an integrity....while, at the same time, having to live in another, modern world. These were people, like all their Native American fellows, who have had to learn to live in two worlds. I felt I was in a room that was filled with energies and "ghosts" of the past, the now, and the uncertain future. I heard the teachers and leaders telling the children that they should know and be proud of who they are even though, at the same time, realizing that life and reality is relentlessly leading them somewhere different; somewhere away from their true identity.

When the dances ended I sat down for a talk with Walker Calhoun. I was immediately struck by his simplicity; there were no "airs", no pretensions. He was safe and secure in who and what he is, a fact that was gently evident. I liked him for him for there was nothing more to like him for. My mind and heart was filled with questions, most of which concerned the sacred ceremonies of his people, the "old times", and of what is still left of the "old ways". I first asked him to tell me about himself. I realized as he spoke that he, a man in his middle seventies, related himself and events in his life to the days before and after the Removal. When he was born he told me that his people (the Eastern Cherokees) had already lost the Stomp Dance. "The Booger Dance went too". When he spoke of the loss of the ceremonials and the Removal I could hear the quietness in his voice and a sadness that was old and deep. I knew the feelings had been with him throughout his life. "It's been fifty years since it (Booger Dance) was done. All disappeared." There was a long pause and then he continued. "Some of us....we still do it...." And the old man's eyes lit up when he told me that his son is one of the firekeepers. Then he told me the story of Hickory Star and the day the sacred fire returned to the eastern mountains and to his people here.

Knowing that Christianity had long since come to the Cherokees, I asked Walker if he felt that religion had helped him and his people survive. My question seemed to invoke deep thought for he got a far-off look in his eyes. When he did begin to speak he spoke ever so slowly about how 1600 missionaries had gone to Chief Bob Thoms (spelling ?) and told him to build a church, and how the Cherokees had translated the Bible. He said that most Cherokees now believe strongly in the Old Testament. But it was clear that for himself he was happy that the sacred fire had come back to the people and that the Eastern Cherokees were now showing renewed interest in working to bring their culture back. "Twenty years ago we were losing our language. But now it is being taught in our schools. When I was a boy we only talked Cherokee in our home."

After some further chit-chat I asked Walker a question I felt would not only give me some insight into the Cherokees of the past, but would also give me some indication as to what he felt personally for the land and for the mountains. I suppose I expected some philosophical dissertation but that was not what I got. What I did get were wandering words that told the simple truth of physical survival and human pain. "The mountains are the source of food. We get wild salads....wild meat....bear......squirrel. All we need we can get right here.....except for seasonings. We eat ramps (a type of strong, wild onion) in the Spring....other greens....jillico (I am not sure I heard this word correctly as Walker's voice was very soft).....bear grass....we gather them in the early Spring. During the Removal the people survived in the mountains....they hid out." When he stopped, again as if his mind was back in a time long past, I asked if he thought the mountains were dying. He replied, "Well.....the trees are dying....the deer left, the bears....the ravens left where they used to roost....where Ravens Roost in Big Cove, you know." "There was a lot of logging. But the deer and the bears, they are coming back." He seemed deep in thought. And, with a quick nod of his head as if to shake his thoughts and bring himself back into the "now", he said that the mountains were/are the place for gathering food and for practicing the religion. I clearly understood that the land had both physical and spiritual value to Walker Calhoun, and no doubt to others like him who have known these old mountains as home.

My final question seemed to puzzle him a bit. I asked if he knew why there seems to be so much interest today among non-native people in the traditional ways and spirituality of his and other

Indian peoples. Again there was a long pause. I wasn't even sure he had understood or whether he even intended to answer my question. After a while he began a very quiet and slow reply. "The way I think......since I teach the Old Ways sometimes they (people) come to me. They want to know about Cherokees. Maybe Native Americans have something they would like to have....." That was all he said. It was all he really needed to say. And with that we parted company. I was left with the feeling that Walker Calhoun was someone I wanted to know better. And thankfully our paths have crossed many times since that day.

Like all Native Americans the Cherokees had a close connection to the Earth. They called her "Mother". But they also recognized the "Father" in Nature; Father Sky. These, together, were Creation; they were the Great Polarities. When we search for knowledge and understanding of the Cherokee perspective of Father Sky we are once more indebted to James Moody. The Cherokees thought of the Sun as a young woman who lived in the East. The Moon was believed to be "a ball which was thrown up against the sky in a game a long time ago."[12] They named both the sun and moon Nunda; Nunda that lives in the day and Nunda of the night. (Mooney; 1982, pg. 257) There were times when the people had need to influence the weather, and would pray to the Moon not to let it rain or snow. The enigmatic eclipses occurred when a frog swallowed the sun or moon! And when an eclipse happened the people would come together and fire guns and beat drums to scare the frog away so everything would be normal again. Needless to say it worked every time!

Above the sky vault in the West lived Great Thunder and his sons. "The lightning and rainbow are their beautiful dress. The priests pray to the Thunder and call him the Red Man, because that is the brightest color of his dress."[13] Other Thunders are reported to live on the lower cliffs and in the valleys and under the waterfalls on the earth. They were believed to travel on "invisible bridges from one high peak to another where they have their townhouses."[14] The sky Thunders were considered beneficial, while the lower ones are quite mischievous. And one old, unwritten law stated that one must never point a finger at a rainbow for it will cause the finger to swell at the lower joint. (Mooney; 1982)

To some Cherokees the stars were balls of light, but others said they (stars) were humans. Still others saw them as "living creatures covered with luminous fur or feathers."[15] Sparks of light flew from them when they were rustled by the wind! I have heard it said that the Cherokees say they came from the stars, some say from beyond the Pleiades. Surely this suggests a strong connection between these people, Father Sky, and his celestial inhabitants. Evidence of this connection may be found in the fact that there are numerous power spots and sacred sites located throughout the Smokies that are associated with the Thunders or some other aspect of the sky. The location of some of these sites, along with the two special types of "beacon" vortexes, will be pointed out in a later chapter. Visiting such celestially-oriented sites helps us to connect with the sun and moon, as well as with other members of the Star Nation. These are places to perform star-related ceremonies or other rites associated with the sun, moon, and constellations.

In a channeling given some time ago, Albion once proffered some information that I have not found the likes of in any written or verbal source. It concerned three constellations which he said were directing and pouring their energy upon the Great Smoky Mountains. He told how these stellar forces were assisting in the process of the mountains' awakening to their full power. The constellations discussed were: Ursa Major (the Big Dipper), Orion (specifically the great star Sirius), and the Pleiades (this was, incidentally, prior to my hearing that the Cherokees believe they came from this constellation). Based upon my seventeen years of study in astronomy, and the ten years I spent studying the astronomy of the ancient peoples (archeoastronomy), I knew this information had powerful esoteric implications. Aside from Ursa Major being symbolized by the Great Bear, Yonah to the Cherokees, the power inherent within this constellation has made it sacred to numerous Native American tribes and other ancient cultures including the Celts. I recognize Ursa Major as a source of spiritual power, and the constellation is often regarded as a "protector". To the Native people the bear was, and is, a very special animal. "In most legends of the animal world, it is acknowledged that the bear is the head of the council of the animals, because of his fairness, his strength, and his courage."[16] Fairness, courage, and strength, as well as protection and spiritual power are therefore the qualities that Ursa Major bring into the vibrations of the Great Smoky Mountains.

The star Sirius is the brightest star that can be seen from the Earth. Since ancient times it has been heralded as the greatest of the stellar bodies. It was called the "Leader" star by many cultures. This great stellar luminary was frequently related to weather phenomena and considered the "cause" of meteorological events and, in that way, was also a major calendar star. (Allen; 1963) Furthermore, in some esoteric teachings, Sirius is called "The Central Sun" and is the location of....I prefer the term *embodiment* of......the great Hall of Records. (Bailey; *Treatise On Cosmic Fire)* Albion has also identified Sirius as a stellar source of prosperity.

If we consider the weather energies as proclaimed to be a part of Sirius' force, it is reasonable to relate the star to the changing climatic conditions with which we are currently being faced. I feel that Sirius' energy will help to "regulate" the weather in the area of the southern Appalachians. It is my feeling that the summers in the region will become much warmer, with moisture less frequent, though not to the point of dangerous or negative extremes. I also feel that the winters will vacillate between being longer and colder, with *more* precipitation, to being longer but warmer with *less* precipitation. I also feel that the snows will return, making the winters here whiter and colder. And I feel there will be more frequent episodes of flooding during the wetter times of each season.

Next, when we consider Sirius from the perspective of its being linked to the Akashic Records, we must take into account that *memory* is involved. I think if Albion and I are correct and these old mountains are indeed awakening to their full power, and since everything in nature is *cyclic*, there must surely have been times in the past when the Smokies have been in and emitted precisely that: *full power.* So the process of reawakening is following a sort of ecological, planetary genetic code or pattern. This places Sirius' in-coming power and its influence upon the Great Smoky Mountains on the archetypal level; the most ancient level of being. This implies that much of the "past" will be reborn; past climatic, cultural, social, and spiritual traditions, if you will. That Sirius is a star of prosperity is good news, but not only in the financial sense. When one looks beyond the material and considers prosperity as simple *abundance*, this is even more fortuitous for the region.

The Pleiades, already a prominent constellation in the Cherokee legends, reminds me of its importance as a calendar star of native peoples all across Turtle Island. It told of the time to plant and to reap. I feel that the focusing of Pleiadian energies upon the Smokies will have a definite and positive effect on the crop yields and the plant kingdom in general. This is in keeping with Albion's words in his initial channeling about the region that specifically regarded the increased potency of plants, which he said would increase in both their nutritional and medicinal values. Also, the Pleiades, according to Cherokee mythology, was formed by seven children (Mooney; 1982), linking this constellation, albeit indirectly, with the Cherokee lineage. I feel this constellation's energy will play a role in strengthening and giving longevity to the Cherokee nation and their spiritual tradition which I have been saying all along will be reborn. This strengthening could very well be a factor in the continuing resurgence of interest in the Old Ways and Indian life in general which has already begun.

With these three constellations pouring star power down upon the Smokies there will be a renewed "link" between Father Sky and the Mother Earth in this area. Such a renewal cannot help but generate an extremely powerful and positive "marriage" of the mountains' masculine and feminine forces. Such speaks of balance and harmony and a balance of natural qualities of this magnitude can, and does, equal the coming of peace. However, when we view the union of these qualities being achieved, we must also realize that the balance will not occur overnight. It is a process....a process I have labeled and described as the Process of the Spiritual Reawakening of the Great Smoky Mountains.

In considering the spiritual traditions and symbols of the Cherokee people and the land here, I cannot help but be reminded of the black bear, the most recognized animal of the Smokies and one who is the symbol of the Smokies; one who is not only the living symbol or totem of these old mountains, but perhaps the *archetype* as well. I feel the time will come, primarily due to Albion's teachings regarding the reawakening process that is currently taking place in this area, when the Smokies will be the most powerful and sacred of "light centers" on Turtle Island (North America). Teaching and retreat and healing centers will be established here in greater numbers than ever before. These light centers, some of which have already had their birth, will open the door to those who wish to come here to study, to go on vision quests, do ceremony, and otherwise advance themselves along their life's path. Teachers will come here. Journals, books, and other types of publications will originate from here. Medicine talk will be spoken freely here; sacred songs sung and dances danced. I believe this is the place that will become the spiritual hub for the next millennia. Time will tell.

Past tragedies and current problems aside, there exist Native Americans in the Great Smoky and Blue Ridge Mountains who possess an intriguing and powerful spiritual heritage; a people who, when asked about from where they came, told of their origin having been no less than the stars themselves! Yes, the Cherokees say they came to the Earth from the Pleiades! Superstition, you say? Foolish beliefs of a people who count little in today's sophisticated world? Maybe so, maybe not. But will we ever know, or care, if their religious tradition and ceremonialism dies out? Of this we can be sure. What did these ancestral people know that led them to believe what they did? What experiences and visions led them to devise a system of legends about fantastic creatures both delightful and horrible to behold? Through our gaining knowledge of their old ways can we not gradually regain our lost inner sense of being connected with our Mother the Earth? I for one believe strongly that this re-connection is imperative as we go through these challenging and sometimes perilous times of planetary change. Time may be running out for us, as humans, to regain the knowing and the link to our planet and her life forms from which we have severed ourselves. The main purposes of this book are to, first, offer the sincere seeker a way to gain knowledge about the Earth and, second, to serve as a guidebook for obtaining personal experience with her. Both will go far in helping us to re-connect with Nature. We must, if we and our planet are to survive, return to a remembrance that the Earth is alive! And we must live with this as a clear fact in our lives. We must, once again, armed with a knowledge of the sacred dances and songs, lift ourselves out of the mire of apathetic materialism into re-acquainting ourselves with the Old Ways that have been tried and proven so that we might heal ourselves from the ecological and spiritual tragedies which have resulted from our almost total reliance upon our intellect. I take nothing away from the value of logic and reason and feel it to be a necessary part of our approach to knowledge and understanding. But omitting intuition and by not bringing our intuitive faculties to bear upon whatever knowledge we gain, we run the risk of the precise one-sidedness of materialism so apparent within society today. Science and the lifeless mechanical world it permits to exist is not all there is. We can appreciate and seek to follow in the footsteps of those few modern scientists who are boldly utilizing the rationale of science to prove what shamans have always known: the earth is alive.....a departure from the orthodox scientific thinking that, ironically, offers "scientific evidence of the life and consciousness of the world that these old ones felt so clearly, so long ago."[17] There is still time for us to become aware of and to gain knowledge of the many mysteries of our beautiful blue planet and of the universe within which we live. The following chapter invites the reader to embark upon just such a journey; an exciting and sacred journey. For this journey to be successful we must carry with us the tool of *willingness*; a willingness to open our bodies and minds and hearts in exploration of the terrain of the Great Smoky and Blue Ridge Mountains. Each of us must have a honest sense of desire and expectation in order to become aware of the earth's living energies, and the mind to think of the world as a whole being that is held together by a real, living, unifying energy which links us all; every place to every other place, every soul to all other souls, and, ultimately, the Earth and her children to the stars. The reader must bring along the tool of your intuition and be willing to use it in conjunction with your intellect. You must bring your love of the Earth's beauty and be willing to peer beneath the physical grandeur into the very soul of the mountains, rivers, lakes, valleys, and forests. You must find the fragrance of the woods a life-restoring, healing tonic. You must have the desire to seek out and experience a real and true sense of at-one-ment with all that lives. And above all we must each have the desire to discover our true and whole Self and our place and role within Nature. Nothing less will do. So let us depart upon a journey into one of the most remarkably beautiful regions on Earth. Let us go willingly and unafraid, free from the limits of materialism, technology, and the fear of opening ourselves completely to the sights and sounds and fragrances that is Earth; to the world, visible and invisible, that is our home.

    The Cherokees referred to themselves as the "principal people". (Ywahoo; *Voices Of Our Ancestors*; 1987) Similar to the people of other tribes, they believed their land was the center of the earth and that all else radiated out from here. As we have seen, the Cherokees truly possessed their own unique sacred ways. Like most of us they believed they were placed on Earth by a Power From Above.......a Power they simply called the Great Spirit. May we take the essence of the power of their holy ways into the mountains as we go. And may we go shining.

[1] Voices OF Our Ancestors, Ywahoo, Dhyani; Boston, Massachusetts; 1987.
[2] Ibid
[3] Myths Of The Cherokees/Sacred Formulas Of The Cherokees, Mooney, James; Charles and Randy Elder-Booksellers; Nashville, Tennessee: 1982.
[4] Ibid
[5] Jung And The Story of Our Time, Van Der Post, Laurens; Penguin Books; London, England: 1976; pages 23-24.
[6] Myths Of The Cherokees/Sacred Formulas Of The Cherokees, Mooney, James; Charles and Randy Elder-Booksellers; Nashville, Tennessee: 1982.
[7] Stories Of The Yunwi Tsundi: The Cherokee Little People; edited by Jeannie Reed; Western Carolina University English 102 Class Project: 1991.
[8] Myths Of The Cherokees/Sacred Formulas Of The Cherokees; Mooney, James: Charles and RandyElder-Booksellers, Nashville, Tennessee: 1982.
[9] Journal Of Cherokee Studies; R.D. Fogelson and A.B. Walker; Vol. V, Number 2; pg. 88.
[10] Katuah Journal; Issue 32; Fall 1991.
[11] Ibid
[12] Myths Of The Cherokees/Sacred Formulas Of The

<u>Cherokees</u>; Mooney, James; Charles and Randy Elder-Booksellers; Nashville, Tennessee: 1982.
[13] Ibid
[14] Ibid
[15] Ibid
[16] Ibid
[17] <u>Katuah Journal</u>; Issue 32; Fall 1991; pg.31.

# THE SPIRITUAL REAWAKENING OF THE GREAT SMOKY MOUNTAINS

## THE SMOKIES AND THE BLUE RIDGE: ANCIENT SACRED LAND

### CHAPTER 4

"The idea of a sacred place........is apparently as old as life itself."

Joseph Campbell

I have long had an interest in and have written three books and many articles about sacred sites, natural power spots, and vortexes. Over time I have learned about places throughout the world that strike a deep, stirring chord within the human psyche.......Stonehenge, the Great Pyramid, the Sphinx, Avalon, Iona, Machu Picchu, Lourdes, and Mecca. (Swan: 1992) Each of them holds a great mystery. They draw us to them like magnets. Built by ancient hands each, some for reasons unknown, represents a place where the human spirit and the special power that permeates the whole universe come together in a symphony of raw energies that humbles the human nature. Whether natural and man-made, these places stand as silent sentinels of people and times so long past we can only speculate as to who they were and the reasons why they built their intriguing monuments. Some ancient sites seemed to have been erected for the purpose of linking their builders with the heavens. Others were not structures at all, but were sacred groves of trees, caves, mountains, valleys, and even volcanos; all natural planetary temples rooted deeply in the consciousness of our ancestors whose religion was Nature herself. From the earliest times there have been places set aside, seemingly not arbitrarily, from all others in a given area. Such places were proclaimed to have some special spiritual quality and significance, ranging from the power to heal to helping humans communicate with the Creator.

To a large number of the indigenous peoples of what is now the eastern United States, the Smokies and the Blue Ridge are the location of many sacred places. These mountains have been and still are home to many elders who have sat around campfires telling stories about these places and their importance down through time. They have no doubt spoken of the spirit essences that manifest at a given sacred site, and of the natural powers that are amplified there. But before I attempt to define even more precisely what is meant by the term *sacred site*, I feel it best to present a clear understanding of what just the word *sacred* involves.

In the first place *sacred* is a descriptive word for something, someone, or some place associated with God or a god, resulting in its being regarded with reverence. This definition does not take the beauty or any of the other physical attributes of a place into consideration. P*hysical* features are not important because sacred goes *beyond* the physical. It also goes beyond religion, beyond historical significance. (Swan; 1992) As pointed out by author James A. Swan in his book *Sacred Places: How The Living Earth Seeks Our Friendship*, in a quote taken from a work done in 1917 by Rudolph Otto....."true spiritual power includes both the light and the dark."[1] Otto claims that anything that is truly sacred involves a raw power that contains both positive and negative elements. A sacred place can strike a sense of wonder within us and, at the same time, invoke fear. (Swan: 1990) Awe, in fact, is an emotion that comes from a combination of both fear and wonder. Sacred sites are awesome for they do indeed contain natural elements that are both good and bad, safe and dangerous. A case in point is the Mt. St. Helens volcano. It is a beautiful mountain that is sacred to the indigenous people who know it to be the home of powerful ancient spirit forces. But the mountain can and did kill during one of its eruptive episodes in 1981. The same applies to Mt. Kilauea on the big island of Hawaii. It is home to Pele, the fire goddess, the most respected and feared of the Hawaiian deities. During a recent eruption, hot creeping lava claimed a massive amount of land, homes, and businesses, and even sacred heiaus (ancient temples), greatly upsetting human lives in the area.

Traditional people the world over have a definite understanding about what designates a place as sacred. Sometimes the place has some religious significance or it may be a burial ground, a mound, or ceremonial site. Other places might be considered special due to their having been home to an ancient monster, giant, or other mythological creature. (Mooney: 1982) It might also be a place where a particular Supernatural resides for such places, as we saw with the Cherokee legends, were often deified. In addition, sacred sites may be so designated because of the presence of a special stand of trees or particular plants, usually those that have medicinal or hallucinogenic qualities. Native Americans, for example, have been known to travel great distances to gather sacred herbs or plants from a particular sacred site. Regarding special trees, the once great cedars of Lebanon, the sacred groves of the Celtic Druids, and the gigantic Tule tree in Mexico are but a few examples. Sacred sites can also be the locations of specially-respected waters; waters that are usually the home of a powerful benign or destructive spirit or creature, or springs and wells that possess some inherent healing or magical quality.

Certain minerals have also been considered sacred by various cultures, including the Native Americans. Quartz and turquoise are an example, as are the unique fairy crosses found in western North Carolina. The special quality of some minerals have resulted in their quarries being designated as sacred sites. This is true with the Pipestone National Monument in Montana, where only Indians are allowed to quarry catlinite used to carve ceremonial pipes.

All over the earth there are sacred places that are the locations of incredible earthworks and shrines, some of which are extremely ancient. Some of the best known of this type of site in North America include the Great Serpent Mound in Ohio and the various mound sites sprinkled throughout the eastern part of the U.S., as well as the Big Horn Medicine Wheel in Wyoming. Occasionally, places where historical events, like a famous battle, have taken place are also considered sacred. Still others commemorate a famous person. But these are exceptions and do not necessarily involve the presence of any natural energy or spirit force. Such sites merely represent some event and in that way *embodies* the energy of it, but is not, of course, the event itself. More about these sorts of energy vortexes and worldwide vortex sites may be obtained from reading my book*s: The Earth Changes Survival Handbook* (Sun Publishing Company; Santa Fe, New Mexico) and *Terravision: A Travel Guide To The Living Planet Earth* (Ballantine Books; New York) I also highly recommend James Swan's book *Sacred Places* (Bear and Company; 1990) and Paul Devereux's *Earth Memory: Sacred Sites-Doorways Into Earth's Mysteries* (Llewellyn Publications; 1992).

As we shall see, the Great Smoky and the Blue Ridge Mountains contain virtually *all* of the aforementioned types of sacred sites. In the first chapter I sought to acquaint readers with these mountains from the physical point of view for without question they are among the most beautiful in the world. But now it is time to look beyond the beauty; beyond the physical. One way to do this is by once again looking at them through the eyes of the Cherokee myths. By doing so we find that many of the Cherokee sacred places found throughout western North Carolina, eastern Tennessee, and northern Georgia are of the type associated with mythic animals of varying kinds. These include the Thunders, the Nuhnehi (water dwellers/spirits), the Little People, the Immortals, and various monsters such as Uktena and Spearfinger. In the interest of space, the interested reader is advised to obtain a copy of *Where Legends Live* by Douglas A. Rossman and discover this information in more detail for yourself for Rossman has done a good job in providing a definitive guidebook to many Cherokee mythic sites.

Another approach to gaining an awareness and understanding of the sacred energy of the Smokies and the Blue Ridge, and the method I have employed during more than a decade of personal experience, is through the ancient system of *geomancy*. Technically, geomancy is defined as a system of *divination* by which the proper sites for ancient temples were once located. But this definition does not tell us *how* the sites were actually chosen, other than suggesting that it was done by some method of divination, which could be dowsing, or even through dreams and visions. As a result, some ten years ago, I chose to expand upon the definition and use of the term geomancy to include a way of determining the presence and precise location of natural earth energies and the *patterns* formed by their flow through the body of our planet. In early 1981, based on information given to me by my Spirit Teacher Albion, and through my independent studies and research, I devised a complete and simple system of knowledge by which one can open their intuitive faculties to the power of the living Earth. The following is a capsuled version of this system and should be of use in helping one to experience the energy inherent in sacred sites and, in fact in all the land that comprises the body of Mother Earth. This information is taken from two of my earlier books mentioned previously which offer the information in some greater detail.

Science tells us that *all is energy*. Energy is but the material matter of the universe. Since everything in the macrocosm is material, no matter what its form, this statement therefore suggests that energy is the *animating power* of the Cosmos. Our planet is an organism of energy, a unit complete and whole. A desirable goal is for us, as humans, to learn to see beyond the earth's physical attributes so as to be able to detect her energies; the energies the Ancients knew and sought out for various reasons. Because I have often become weary of teachers and writers who stress the value of our being able to sense the planet's living forces and our need to re-connect ourselves with Nature, but who fail to provide any real, workable system or method by which this may be accomplished, I felt a need to devise just such a step-by-step process by and through which this may be done. This desire led me to come up with the term *Life*

*Energies;* a theory within which lies its practical application. I have been working with and teaching this system for thirteen years.

*Life Energy* is simply the living, natural life force of the earth. However, I have divided the *one force* into three categories for the purpose of defining its multiple characteristics as it manifests in the physical world. I call these Life Energies *electricity, magnetism, and electromagnetism.* Remember: *collectively these three form the one life force or "breath" of our planet.* Likewise, these energies are manifest within every form in nature's kingdoms. Most do not realize that when we say the Earth is alive, it is not just the physical body of the planet that is being described. Rather, our whole planet is comprised of its own physical body, as well as all of the bodies of the four life kingdoms *and* the planetary aura which is the multi-layered atmosphere that extends some 20,000+ miles in all directions of Space. Each of the Life Energies, the names of which I chose arbitrarily, has its own specific quality of energy and, therefore, a specific *effect* on the human body and consciousness. This effect can be both positive and negative.

Let us begin with a brief discussion of *electricity* which is basically the male force in Nature. Electricity possesses attributes that result in greater physical vitality, emotional aggressiveness, re-birth, and renewal. Its element is fire. Electricity animates all forms or bodies that exist no matter what kingdom they belong to. When we apply the definition and attributes of electricity to the earth's terrain, we find that typically electrical land and environments have sandy soil, deserts, mountains, active volcanos, and volcanic landscapes. Man-made, therefore unnatural, electrical environments are created by the presence of large cities. This is due to their being highly populated and continually active places. There are also electrical climates. These are hot and arid and have frequent hot dry winds and are prone to intense lightning storms, sometimes in the form of dry lightning. In its effect upon the human physical body, electricity elevates the blood pressure and increases the heart's rate. It also increases and intensifies one's degree of vitality on all levels; physically, emotionally, mentally, and spiritually. It amplifies all emotions, be they positive or negative. Exposure to too much electricity over prolonged periods of time can result in a tendency to experience elevated body temperature, skin rashes, fevers, and extreme nervousness which can lead to various anxiety-related conditions. It is upon the human consciousness and soul-level however that I feel that electricity has its most positive and powerful effect. Spiritually, it can *awaken* the soul. Electricity also stimulates the intellect, making one quick to learn and grasp new concepts.

*Magnetism*, on the other hand, is the exact *opposite* of electricity. It is the feminine force in nature and is of the elements of earth and water. Whereas electricity uplifts and animates, magnetism calms and renders all things passive. Typical magnetic terrains include most bodies of water (the Pacific Ocean is an exception; it is electrical due to the presence of the Ring of Fire which is the site of over 78% of the world's active volcanos), swamps, marshes, wetlands, the tropics, some rain forests (depending upon location and altitude), most beaches and coastal areas, and many of the islands of the world. Magnetic climates are quite humid and rainy. Clouds are frequent. So magnetic climates are generally tropical.

On the human body, magnetism slows down the pulse rate, digestion and circulation. It also lowers the body's temperature and blood pressure. These effects, as with electricity, are of course subtle and, as a rule, slight except in unusual cases of prolonged or extremely intense exposure. Upon human consciousness magnetism helps one to turn within. Magnetism awakens psychic sensitivity, promotes vivid dreams and visions, and generally enhances all other subjective faculties and activities. Magnetic places usually provide a good environment for meditation, prayer, and ceremonies that require contact with ones deepest inner self, spirit forces and beings, and other dimensions of reality.

*Electromagnetism* is a balanced, harmonious combination of

*electricity* and *magnetism.* Typical electromagnetic terrains receive a moderate to heavy annual rainfall, have a varied and plentiful flora and fauna, hills, and/or mountains. Waterfalls are also a common feature in electromagnetic areas and often constitute powerful electromagnetic vortexes. The electromagnetic climate consist of four full seasons. Electromagnetism can brings balance to the human body and health on all levels, making it the *healing* energy in nature; the great *"equalizer".*

The area of the Great Smoky and Blue Ridge Mountains is generally electromagnetic, though there are isolated pockets of electricity and magnetism sprinkled throughout the entire region. Based upon my definition of electromagnetism, this makes the Smokies and the Blue Ridge and the vast areas around them one of the most powerful healing/balancing places on Earth. Prior to my re-locating to western North Carolina in late 1990 I received some intuitive information from Albion regarding the life energy of these mountains. The information addressed the mountains' past and their future from a unique and revealing perspective. It is appropriate to share these thoughts with my readers at this point in the writing. I have entitled this information *The Call Of The Ancient Ones.* It was this information that not only inspired my move to the Smokies, but that also prompted and formed the very foundation of and purpose of this book.

I must state emphatically my belief that there is a powerful *spiritual* reawakening occurring right now in the Great Smoky Mountains. And furthermore I believe this awakening is happening exclusively in this one particular part of the Appalachian range. My Spirit Teacher Albion was the sole source of this information and in order to portray the "feelings" he emitted as he spoke, I have used the Teacher's exact words. He began: "The Great Smoky Mountains are the Elders.....the Ancient Ones....whose voices have sung the Song of Creation on the North American continent longer than the voices of any other mountain range on Earth. They are so very, very powerful and that power may be explained in three ways."

"First, because of their particular geology and the powerful influence of the nearby sea (Atlantic Ocean), many of these mountains are *magnetic* in their charge of life force."

I must pause here to address the curiosity of Albion labeling some of the peaks in the Smokies and Blue Ridge as being *magnetic*, for this is highly irregular and contradicts the usual electrical charge of most other mountains in the world. When questioned about this the Teacher explained that the general area is purely electromagnetic. That many of the mountains are magnetic is due, in part, to the amount of annual rainfall and the number of natural water sources in the form of rivers, lakes, streams, and springs in this part of the Appalachians, as well as to the process of mountain-building that was involved with the mountains birth. Unlike the Cascades and other ranges these mountains are not volcanic. While it is true that millions of years ago, at great depths inside the earth, extreme pressures and temperatures developed, the Smokies were actually created by the tectonic power of continents colliding. The mountains we see today were sculptured later by the relentless forces of erosion by wind, water, rain, and freezing and thawing. (Walker; 1982) So all of this aquatic and geological energy makes many of these great peaks magnetic because they have retained much of the original natural magnetism. Magnetism holds the "memory" of a place, and these old mountains hold the most ancient of geological memories on the planet.

The Teacher continued: "Magnetism is of the elements of water and earth. Magnetism is conducive to helping one to turn within to tap [their own] subconscious and [be in touch with] the Collective Unconscious. Magnetism promotes sensitivity and awakens the psychic and intuitive faculties within the human mind and consciousness. It is the feminine force in Nature. These mountains are filled with natural springs and underground rivers and caves that have a subterranean water source."

"Secondly, because we are labeling some of them as 'magnetic mountains', we want you to understand that this means that they are especially conducive to the energies necessary to assist spiritual seekers with their vision quests and search for spirituality more so than any other mountains in the world at this time."

"Thirdly, these old mountains hold the *memory* of the breaking up of the continents during previous periods of major planetary changes and of the ancient mountain-building processes. They have 'recorded' the arcane voices of Nature unmatched on your continent. For a long time, about 10,000 years, these mountains have been 'asleep', their energy but a shallow breath. It was also during those ancient earth change times that these mountains were first inhabited by humans. The first were Atlantean migrants who spread throughout the world seeking refuge and new beginnings. To this day, there are ancient rock and bark scrolls and some cave drawings that are Atlantean in their origin and that still exist in various parts of the region."

"This place has long been the site of ancient religious ceremonies. Although the mountain peaks have been worn down by time, there were once seven summits in the Smokies and the Blue Ridge that were held to be sacred and that were used down through the ages as ceremonial sites. The areas around them still contain artifacts of the Old Ways. (Albion later identified a few of those seven summits as the ones we now know as Grandfather Mountain, Black Dome, Mt. Pisgah, Clingman's Dome, LeConte, Looking Glass Rock, and Chimney Rock) Some of those whom you call Native Americans were born from the Atlantean ancestors, while others (Indians) migrated from other continents and settled this land. For a short time, the mountains remained awake and emitted their full energy potential before gradually slipping into an introverted 'slumber'. Once, during the intervening centuries, the mountains' full natural power awakened, for a short time, to embrace and protect the Native people who fled into their midsts for safety so that they and their tradition could survive the threat of the invaders." This passage is an obvious reference to those Cherokees who hid in the mountains in order to escape the Removal to Indian Territory. That means that it has been approximately 162 years since the Smokies (or the Blue Ridge) have been "awake" and at full power, and that was only for a short time.

"Beginning in the middle of the decade of the 1980s, the Great Smoky Mountains began the process of reawakening to their full power. This process will reach its peak by the end of 1995 and be complete by the turn of the century. Between now and then, many people, like yourselves, will be drawn to this area. They will come to live and study and to connect themselves to Mother Earth. Many of them will be Light Workers. Many teachers will come and some will establish 'light centers'. Ancient ceremonies will be performed again on these mountain slopes and in the fertile valleys, by natives and non-natives alike. The Indian people and their spiritual tradition will become stronger and more important to all here. Sites such as Chimney Rock, Blowing Rock, Grandfather Mountain, Mt. Mitchell, Flat Rock, Table Rock, Clingman's Dome, and Looking Glass Rock, to name but a few, will once more embrace spiritual seekers and emit their most potent power. The waters will become more potent and can be used for healing the body. They will be rich for growth and fertility. The plants will increase in their power so that their medicinal value will be greatly enhanced. The formation of 'brotherhoods' and 'sisterhoods' will have their birth in these mountains once more."

Upon hearing Albion's words I knew beyond doubt where I had to relocate. I knew what the next step on my life's path would be and where it would take place. I knew what my future as a teacher must be. It is here in the Great Smoky Mountains where I now live and where I will work and savor the experience of the reawakening of the Ancient Ones. It is here I will listen to the Voice of the Earth Mother sing the precious Song of Creation....the melody of Wholeness....and of Rebirth. It is here I will add my "light" to the "lights" that are already here and to those yet to come.....in peace and in harmony with the Spirit Forces and the Great Devas of the mountains.

With these thoughts clearly in mind let us turn our attention to some additional information that might help the reader in the quest to gain a better understanding of the ancient principles of geomancy. These concern the existence of *ley lines, vortexes,* and *grids.* A brief definition of each of these terms is imperative toward having a closer, more conscious relationship with the Earth Mother, and to our being able to psychically detect the natural energies which are invisible to our physical eyes. When we think of the earth as being a living organism, the terms ley lines, grids, and vortexes then come to literally define the circulation system, organs, and the nervous system, respectively, of our planet.

The theory of the existence of *ley lines* dates back into antiquity, perhaps originating with the Chinese who called them "dragon lines". I personally perceive a ley (pronounced lay) as an invisible, thin, hollow "tube" through which natural planetary energy is conducted like electricity through an electrical cord. Some leys run just above the earth's surface, while others lie just below the ground. Because these lines of force are quite numerous, they *cross* or *intersect* at various points on the planet. I call these intersections *conjunction points* or *ley terminals.* Ley lines transport electricity, magnetism, and electromagnetism, the earth's life force or blood, throughout her body.

A *vortex* is a high energy place where natural planetary power has coagulated into an intensely powerful mass or cone of energy. The energy of a vortex moves in a rotary or whirling, spiral motion which results in there being a depression or vacuum at its center. Vortexes are found all over the body of the earth. Some are electrical, some are magnetic, and some are electromagnetic. Mount Shasta in California, Mt. Everest, and the sacred San Francisco Peaks in Flagstaff, Arizona are prime examples of electrical vortexes. Magnetic vortexes include the sacred lake at the Karnak Temple in Egypt, the Bottomless Pools in Hickory Nut Gap in western North Carolina, and the island of Bimini (and the other islands) in the Bahamas. Yellowstone and Niagra Falls are examples of electromagnetic vortexes. I believe that the existence and locations of all kinds of vortexes were known by the ancient peoples of the world and that, for the most part, they held them in esteem as sacred sites. Keep in mind that a vortex, no matter what its energy charge, may be a sacred site. But not all sacred sites are vortexes. Vortexes are like mini-earth *chakras*, not unlike the so-called acupuncture points in the human etheric body. I think of vortexes as acupuncture points in the Earth. When we remember that, for ages, the Chinese acupuncturists have used these tiny energy openings to tap into the flow of ch'i (life force) in the human body to unlock the flow for the purpose of maintaining and/or restoring better health, we can apply this same theory and practice to the planet. Vortexes are "openings" or meridians where the natural earth energy is extremely potent and where that power may be tapped. However, rather than acupuncture needles, the tools used are the human mind, prayer, and ceremony. I also believe there were occasions when a single or a collection of standing stones was used by the ancient people to tap the earth's power as evidenced all over the British Isles; the stones serving like acupuncture needles by the shamans. The Life Energy tapped into, in turn, has a definite influence that can have either a positive or negative effect on our lives, consciousness, bodies, and general well-being. I think the ancient people also knew this to be true. While they would surely have called the energies by different names than I have or even explained it all differently, the basis remains the same. (Information regarding a type of special vortex will appear in a later part of this work)

A *grid* is a power spot but it is not a vortex. Grids involve a much larger area than a vortex and its energy is somewhat less potent. Magnetic grids include the Everglades, the huge Okeefeenokee Swamp, Cape Cod, and the Great Barrier Reef. On the other hand, the Cascade mountain range is an example of an electrical grid, while the Linville, Nantahala, and the Cullasaja River gorges, all in western North Carolina, are electromagnetic ones. Vortexes can be present within grid areas and can at times possess a different charge than the grid within which they reside. This is common throughout the Smokies and the Blue Ridge region, which also contains ley lines, ley terminals, and vortexes.

For the purpose of this writing I have confined the majority of my identifications of leys, vortexes, and grids to the areas of the Smokies and the Blue Ridge. In doing so I have sought to provide clear directions as to how one can get to a given site. I have chosen to use the Great Smoky Mountains National Park as the major point of reference, as I feel that this electromagnetic grid comprises the heart of the entire southern Appalachians.

So let us embark on a wonderful scenic and spiritual journey. Keep in mind that when you visit in the forests, valleys, mountains, and riverlands, you should make every effort to leave things as you found them....or better. Should you see trash at the sites you visit, pick it up and dispose of it in a proper manner. Do not take any plants or stone away. (see next chapter). Be aware of the lives....in all the kingdoms.....that live in these areas. Take the necessary precautions to protect yourself from any life forms that might be harmful. Also be aware of the dangers involved with climbing, hiking, and with the elements, and make certain you are prepared in every way to venture into the wilderness as some of the sites listed here are remote. Leave nothing behind you but your footprints, your prayers, and the energy of your love for Nature and her wonders. Enjoy the scenery. Enjoy your communication with all your relations in the other kingdoms of life. And most of all, as you go along your way, let your actions, words, thoughts, and experiences be a celebration of the living Earth Mother.

[1] Sacred Places: How The Living Earth Seeks Our Friendship; Swan, James A.; Bear and Company Publishing; Santa Fe, New Mexico: 1990.

# THE SPIRITUAL REAWAKENING OF THE GREAT SMOKY MOUNTAINS

## GRIDS AND LEY LINE SYSTEMS

## CHAPTER 5

The land of the Cherokee is as powerful and beautiful as any on Earth. The land is a living entity that has no visible boundaries. It stretches in total freedom; reaching out in all four directions, unheeded by anything or anyone, except by the invisible lines imposed upon it by human territorialism. Like all humans the Cherokees often drew boundaries to serve as warnings to neighboring tribes, which included the Powhatan and the Monacan, the Cheraw, the Creeks, the Chickasaw, the Shawano, and the powerful Iroquois who were the virtually unchallenged claimants of all the land between the Ottawa river of Canada in the north to the Kentucky river in the south. Though the man-set boundaries and the natural terrain have changed over the centuries, it is still possible to determine the *sacredness* of the land and to once more come to view it and to live upon it in a sacred manner.

Our ancestors lived close to the earth. They knew the earth as a living entity; a being with a heart; their Mother who provided for all their needs. The heart of the land, like the heart of a human being, is the epicenter of life itself.....the distributor, if you will, of life force....the breath. The earliest Cherokees knew the heart of their land. They called it (and themselves) *Kitu'hwa*; an ancient settlement on the Tuckasegee river. (Katuah Journal; Issue 31, Summer 1991) It was Katuah (accepted spelling) that was the apparent original nucleus of the tribe. "Here, in the Katuah Province of the ancient Appalachian mountains....where once the Cherokee Nation lived in freedom between the Tennessee River Valley and the Eastern Piedmont...between the Valley of the Roanoke and the South Plain....on this Turtle Island of Mother Ela, the Earth."[1] Although the present-day Katuah village, though once the center of Cherokee life, is in ruins, it is still the invisible, spiritual heart of Cherokee land. And I sense that its power still pulsates and radiates power in all directions. When a tribe of people designated a certain place as the "heart" of the land they respected it as a sacred place; a place that nourished the people in every way. When I first viewed this old site clairvoyantly the residual life force that was once at its fullest power appeared in my mind's eye like a great luminous wheel whose spokes extended out from the center where stood a sacred mound. The "light wheel", as it spun slowly, seemed to generate a spiralling power which formed a double helix-like energy pattern that thrust skyward. As my vision unfolded I could feel the intense drawing power of the place and I knew that it had always drawn people to it. I knew that when the people were in Katuah they got recharged. I also felt that it was here where the people felt secure and where they most deeply and clearly experienced their being a part of the Whole; the whole tribe, the whole Earth, and ultimately the whole Universe. I always find it to be true that when I have become aware of the location of the "heart" of a particular region or people, I find that the current state of the heart chakra tells a lot about the overall condition of both the land and the people who still live in the area, an insight I gained from my studies of the Arthurian legends, specifically in the story of the Fisher King. The sorry condition of the lame and ailing king was directly reflected in the state of overall deterioration and barrenness of the land, as the land and the sovereign are one and the same. Based on the truth and logic of this perspective, then the traditional way of life and the sacred knowledge of the Cherokees is in ruins....left alone and all but forgotten; living only in the legends and in the minds and hearts of the elders, and in the memory of the land itself.

    History tells us that Katuah was the central town of the Old Nation. It is said to have formed the nucleus of the most conservative element of the tribe and sometimes gave a name to the nation itself. (Mooney; 1982) As these old mountains reawaken I feel that the heartbeat of Katuah will get stronger. Though its future will no doubt be different from its past, its role will, for it must, remain the same. It holds the memory of the spiritual life blood of the people, and to that and for that the people will go again, if only symbolically, drawn like a moth to a flame. Perhaps the Stomp Dance will be danced there again, who knows. Maybe the sacred songs will be sung. Katuah could be the site of some new spiritual or social center; a center erected for modern people for no less than sacred reasons. Only time will tell. But I do believe this place still possesses and guards the ancient, but vital, power of the Cherokee tradition...the ancient knowledge. If only on the astral plane, it still reeks of the smoke of the ancient fires. The day may very well come when Katuah will rise like the Phoenix from its own ruins to once more serve an important role in the future of the people and the land. So with the knowledge and recognition of Katuah, located just outside of Bryson City in western North Carolina, as the spiritual heart of the entire area, we can venture out and discover other of the energy patterns, leys, vortexes, power and sacred sites that comprise the living force of this incredible land.

Let us begin with the identification of the seven major *grids* located in the Great Smoky Mountains and their surrounding regions, including the Blue Ridge range. It must be kept in mind that all of these grids are formed by the presence of the natural, potent planetary energy within them. However, the boundaries that I will respect are of course man-created and in no way determines the exact extent of the actual grid areas and the general extent, area-wise, of their power. Therefore I identify the seven grids as the Great Smoky Mountain National Park; Shining Rock Wilderness; Linville Gorge Wilderness; Slickrock Wilderness; Upper Nantahala Wilderness; Ellicott Rock Wilderness; and the immediate area surrounding Mt. Mitchell. There are also several man-made grids (in this case meaning they are not natural but formed by some form of land engineering projects such as dams) that are magnetic and in the form of large lakes. Remember, a grid is usually a rather large land area, and occasionally water, that is charged with a more intense degree of living earth energy than other areas. All grids in the Great Smoky and Blue Ridge Mountains are *electromagnetic* in their natural energy charge. This results in their having the power to bring balance to the human mind, body, and consciousness. The energy here can heal. In fact, I believe this to be one of the most intense and potent healing areas on the entire planet. Food grown in these areas has strong healing power and is exceptionally nutritious. The medicinal plants also have strong healing powers when taken into or applied topically to the human body. Minerals here are equally potent. Using quartz and other minerals from these grid areas would enhance whatever ceremonies or healing and/or consciousness raising processes one might engage. I also feel that grid sites are particularly attractive to various types of nature spirits or Elementals, especially the zephrs (wind spirits), elves and gnomes (earth spirits), and the undines (water spirits). In addition I have often sensed felt and intuitively observed angelic presences throughout the southern Appalachians. The overwhelming presence, in terms of sheer numbers, of nature spirits in a given area helps to keep the region fertile and in good balance with the forces of nature. Their presence may very well account for the numerous Indian legends that tell of the Little People who were/are known to live in these mountains. In my personal experience as a writer, particularly in my book on Native American mythology, as well as in my interaction with native people of various tribes, I realize the Cherokees are unique in that they have far more myths that concern some form of nature spirits and/or Little People than any other I have encountered. One can only imagine what the population of such entities must have been before humans and civilization moved in! And although we may have lost our ability to "see" the Elementals and with it the opportunity to interact with them, there is no question in my mind that the early people who lived in these old mountains not only could see them, but that the elementals played an important role in their lives. I believe we can regain the sight necessary to make a conscious connection with the Little People and the nature spirits and that doing so can go far in helping us to extend our psychic sensitivity and assist in our reconnecting with the Earth Mother. Activities that came to light regarding the New Age community at Findhorn in northern Scotland and the more recent work of teachers like Michelle Small Wright at Prelandra in the eastern U.S., proves what can be accomplished and what may be gained from a carefully cultivated relationship between the elementals, the forces of Nature, and human beings.

The following is an identification of and a general overview of each of the grid areas.

SHINING ROCK WILDERNESS:

This electromagnetic grid was one of the first designated national wilderness areas in the eastern United States. The *Middle Prong Wilderness* is an integral part of its energy pattern. This is a popular hiking area that is criss-crossed with many trails. Within the grid there are two powerful *electrical vortexes;* two of the few really potent electrical peaks in the entire region. One is the 6,000 foot *Shining Rock Mountain,* an intense mountain vortex whose summit is composed entirely of quartz crystal! On the astral, this quartz mountain is absolutely clear and gleams with a powerful radiance of soft, pastel rainbow colors that spread in all directions. The crystal of which this mountain is composed, and all other quartz in the region, has been "programmed" by Mother Nature herself with the incredibly ancient memory of geological changes and mountain-building events that first formed these Old Ones. Shining Rock is also a reference name given to a rock that has strange markings on it. The Cherokees say that the interior of Shining Rock Mountain is a place where the Little People live and the home of Judaculla (Tsulkala), the slant-eyed giant who owns all the animals in the area. (Rossman; 1988, pg. 10) The other vortex is *Cold Mountain* whose peak soars to an elevation of 6,030 feet. I feel that Shining Rock Mountain is one of the few vortexes that has already awakened to its full power.

When I viewed Shining Rock Mountain clairvoyantly I "saw" that the peak has an indwelling spirit force unlike any I have ever seen. This great Mountain Deva appears to have a sheer, transparent form with great white wings and a pale complexion. Its crystal-like eyes radiate pure light like prisms. I felt a powerful and ancient energy being emitted by this Deva, and a sound that is similar to a shrill, high-pitched whistle.

I also sensed a "presence" at Cold Mountain. It was a Being who appeared wrapped in a silvery cocoon-like aura that glimmers in the light of the sun and moon. I also sensed the mountain sending out an audible vibration that sounded like the howling of wind and I felt very strongly that the wind spirits frequently center themselves around the area. Both Shining Rock Mountain and Cold Mountain are wonderful places for recharging yourself on every level: physically, emotionally, mentally, and spiritually. Crystal from Shining Rock and the area surrounding it) would serve as a wonderful energy-giving sacred object when worn on the person, or when carried in a medicine bag, or held in the hand during ceremony. Physically it would charge the body when one is experiencing low vitality. However, should you decide to take a small piece, remember to ask permission from the mountain first and leave an appropriate offering in its place.

The land in Shining Rock Wilderness is rugged and the views are spectacular. The forests of the area are easily accessible and seem to reach out and embrace you. Trail guidebooks and maps should be consulted before you set out for a hike. I sense that Cold Mountain's energy is currently elevating very rapidly and will be at its full power by the end of 1994.

ELLICOTT ROCK WILDERNESS:

This is a 3,030 acre *electromagnetic* grid is also rugged country located on the Chattooga River. Its energies and man-designated boundaries touch three states: North Carolina, Georgia, and South Carolina. Entrance into the wilderness is at Ammons Branch Campground and is called the Ellicott Rock Trail. *Ellicott Rock* itself, though it is not a vortex, is an intense source of natural electrical earth power and a place that is conducive to performing ceremony, particularly those that have to do with honoring and tapping into the power of Grandfather Sun and getting in touch with the Higher Forces, and for re-charging your energy on all levels. Keep in mind that the hike to the rock is a strenuous 7 mile round-trip excursion.

UPPER NANTAHALA WILDERNESS:

Upper Nantahala Wilderness is an *electromagnetic* grid that has only one electrical power spot within it: *Standing Indian Mountain*. Although it is a power spot, Standing Indian is not a vortex. According to Cherokee legend this mountain was once home to a huge mythic bird who was prone to stealing children! (Mooney; 1982) Allegedly the ferocious monster was destroyed by *lightning* sent by the Great Spirit in answer to prayers offered up by the people for protection. There is a legend which says that Standing Indian Mountain was created by the body of an Indian who was turned into stone for deserting his lookout post, leaving the people vulnerable to the terrifying bird. (Sakowski; 1990, pg. 50)

As a rule, places that are the origin of ancient legends are always special and sometimes sacred to the people of the area. Legends often tell a story of the *naturally inherent energy* of a place and can, as is the case with Standing Indian Rock, give that energy and the events surrounding it a sort of *identity*. The reader will take notice that *lightning* is the keyword in this particular legend and is therefore the primary energy associated with this place. Lightning is pure electricity. Due to the rather negative events involved with the story of this place it is likely that Standing Indian Rock and the area immediately surrounding it is a potent electrical spot and particular caution should be taken before spending an excessive amount of time there. I suggest that prayer, ceremony, and/or a special offering to honor the lightning spirits would be a good idea when you go into this grid. The Lightning Spirits are intensely powerful forces that constantly are in the process of recharging the earth's life energy. When we are in tune with and in harmony with their power they can provide us with valuable energy that we can channel to motivate and inspire us to completing difficult and challenging tasks in our daily lives. I also think of the Lightning Spirits as *messengers* of the gods and they are closely associated with The Thunders, the Winds, and other weather spirits.

SLICKROCK WILDERNESS:

Slickrock comprises a huge *electromagnetic* grid that covers some 14,000 acres. I do not feel there are any vortexes in the wilderness itself. But the nearby Santeelah Lake to the southeast is a large *magnetic* grid, making the lake area a wonderful site for meditation, dreams and dream recall, past life recall, and vision quests. Slickrock Wilderness is one of the few sites of virgin forests left in the eastern U.S. and contains over a hundred species of trees, some of which are grandfather trees that are over 300 years old and exceed a hundred feet in height.

For those who have a particular knowledge of or interest in the ancient tree cults such as that of the Celtic Druids, you will find this area a wonderful source of tree and plant power. Oak, one of the most prominent of all the trees held sacred by the Druids, Greeks, Romans, and Germanic tribes, is common in the area. (Matthews; 1991) The oak was long known among the ancient Celts as the "king of trees" because its wood is so tough. And oaks have been known to live to be as much as 2,000 years old! Most of us are familiar with the esoteric nature of the acorn, making the oak the sacred tree that embodies the deepest mysteries of life. Additional and more detailed information regarding the power inherent within trees and plants may be found in chapter seven of this book. I suggest that carrying an acorn from one of the oaks in the Slickrock Wilderness is a good way to tap into the power of the oak, as well as be in touch with the power of regeneration, fertility, and psychic power possessed by oak trees in general.

LINVILLE GORGE WILDERNESS:

The Linville Gorge Wilderness is an *electromagnetic* grid that is the location of two extremely powerful and rare *beacon vortexes: Table Rock (electrical) and Hawksbill Mountain (magnetic).* It is necessary for me to digress at this point in order to explain what a beacon vortex is, as they are unusual as vortexes go.

Lake Santeelah - Robbinsville, NC

Like all other vortexes, *beacons (vortexes)* possess one of the three charges of Life Energy; electric, magnetic, or electromagnetic. Beacons are always hills, large or small natural rock formations, natural mounds, mesas, or mountains. Occasionally beacons are man-created mounds of various sizes that have been erected for varying purposes. Examples of these include the famous Silbury Hill near Avebury in the southwestern English countryside and Newgrange Ireland. Other more elaborate examples include various stepped pyramid structures such as the elaborate Sun and Moon temples in the

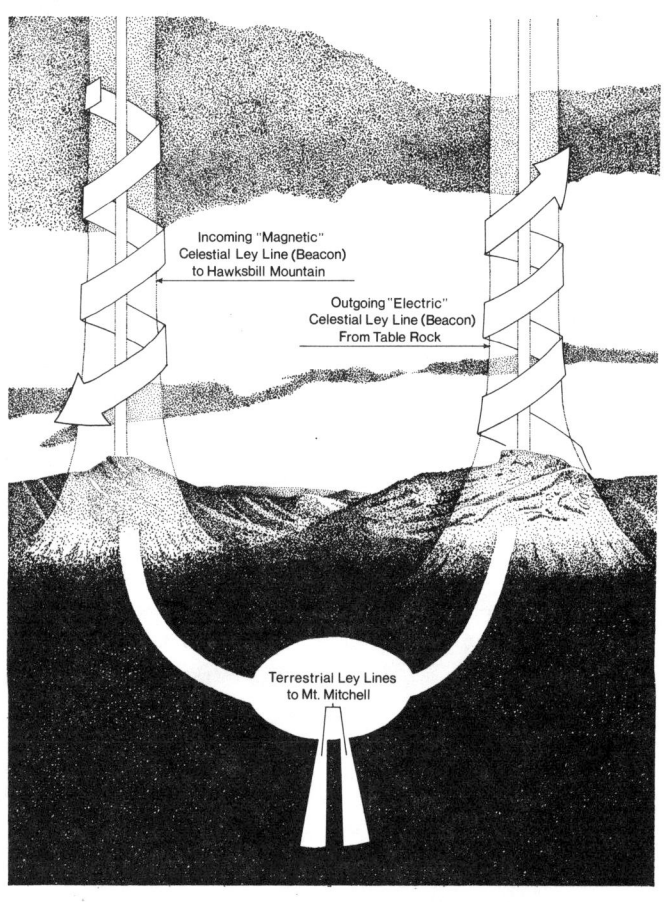

Yucatan, the monumental Zozer's pyramid at Sakkara in Egypt, and the intriguing ziggurats in the land that was once ancient Babylonia. Whether natural or man-made, beacons are always connected by one or more *celestial ley lines* that link them to the sun, moon, other planets in the Solar System, stars, or other galaxies.

Whereas the leys previously mentioned are purely terrestrial and run just above or just below the earth's surface, celestial leys are invisible lines or "threads" that are natural to the Earth but that extend out into extraterrestrial territory. There also exist celestial leys that originate from other heavenly bodies and connect to a beacon on the earth. Celestial leys, especially the latter type, are far less common than terrestrial ones and, as stated, serve to *link* the earth with celestial bodies within the solar system and beyond. Incoming systemic, galactic, and a variety of cosmic forces reach our planet via these celestial leys. And through them the earth's energy is transmitted into outer space. As a result of these leys the earth is linked to other bodies in the universe and is, therefore, not alone.

Some beacon vortexes are *electric* and *emit* pure earth energy to the extraterrestrial body or bodies to which they are linked. Others are *magnetic* and *draw energy* through them to our planet from the celestial body or bodies to which they are connected. This is a sort of inhalation-exhalation process that is an integral part of the living mechanism of the earth. To date I have not discovered any beacons that are electromagnetic. I think it is reasonable to believe that natural beacon vortexes were known by many if not all the ancient people, and that some cultures actually created their own (beacons) in the form of mounds and pyramids. I feel that both the natural and man-made ones were employed as special ceremonial sites specifically for the performance of star ceremonies or rituals that honored and/or involved communicating with and/or drawing upon the power of the sun, moon, single stars, constellations, other celestial bodies and powers, and sky deities. Natural beacons are found worldwide and include Bell Rock in Sedona, Arizona; Dreamer's Rock in Canada;

the Glastonbury Tor in England; and Stone Mountain outside of Atlanta, Georgia, to name but a few. Many of the natural sites such as Stone Mountain and the Glastonbury Tor have been altered by humans in some way for some reason which may or may not have had to do with the spiritual significance of the place or changed the energy in any way. Stone Mountain, for example, has been carved with gigantic images of Civil War generals which obviously has nothing to do with its spiritual power or its ever having been used for ceremonies by indigenous peoples. In my mind this kind of drastic alteration that is in no way related to the spiritual significance and/or sacredness of the mountain does indeed take away from the energy if not the value of the site. The same would hold true for Mt. Rushmore in South Dakota which, incidentally, was and is a sacred mountain to the Sioux. On the other hand the Glastonbury Tor was "terraced" ages ago by ancestral architects who most believe were the Druids, for what has been suspected to be for ceremonial purposes, as the seven terraces lead to the summit. Alterations of this kind and for such purposes would, in my opinion, not take away from the natural power or sacredness of the place. It might in fact enhance it.

The Table Rock/Hawksbill Mountain natural beacons are *extremely rare*, perhaps even unique, on the planet due to their being in such close physical proximity, as well as their being *"linked"* together in the task they perform for the earth. But before entering into any further explanation of these two peaks, let me say that I believe the ancient people, worldwide, who constructed various types and sizes of mounds created what I call beacons and that they did so in order to be closer to and therefore to "reach" the stars more efficiently! I propose the theory that the various mound-builders built ceremonial mounds, some of which were very large, for this precise purpose and that some of these mounds served a double role or purpose as they were also mass burial sites, family, or individual tombs, and council places.

Think about it. Mounds literally *elevated* star priests and shamans *closer to the heavens!* I might add that the Cahokia Mounds along the Mississippi and the astoundingly complex mound site at Poverty Point in Louisiana are, I believe, both examples of possible man-made beacons. The following is a related passage from my book *Terravision: A Traveler's Guide To The Living Planet Earth* (Ballantine Books) concerning a rare and ancient shamanistic practice that I call *starwalking*.

"The experience required for the living to enter into the supernatural, celestial worlds calls for unusually precise knowledge and skills. It could be said it is a 'calling', the business of specialists. Such specialists are shamans. Many of their visions, ceremonies, and other mystical practices are designed to carry them to the sky. Being connected to the Earth is surely considered desirable by all the native peoples. But, having access to the heavens is of equal value and importance. Visions obtained by the shamans in their contact with the Sky Gods is, to them, an echo of Cosmic Order. The shaman's interaction with the stars and other celestial bodies is a must. The shaman's interaction with the sky helps them....and us.... to understand the sky's role in human life. In short, to the shaman, intimacy with the stars and other celestial bodies is a must." [2]

So beacon vortexes, both natural and man-made, could have been (and many still may be) unique places where humans and the stars could *meet* in a powerful celestial dance of life and meaning. My perspective of the unique importance of sacred mounds and the purpose for which they were used is why my "discovery" of the Table Rock and Hawksbill mountains in the beautiful Linville Gorge sent chills up my spine and excited my imagination as to the possible purposes for which they have been used in the past by the indigenous people of the area.

*Table Rock* is an *electrical* beacon vortex. When I viewed it clairvoyantly I saw it surrounded by a clear blue haze or mist that emits a bright ray of darker blue light from its summit. Table Rock is connected to *all* the other planets in the solar system by individual celestial leys. Nowhere else have I encountered a beacon that is connected to all the other systemic planets. Because Table Rock is electric its leys serve the purpose of *transmitting* natural earth energy to each of the other planets in our solar family. This vortex is extremely powerful and should be approached with caution as it can "burn" or cause "tears" in the human astral body, resulting in mental distress, disorientation and mild sensory deprivation, and intense nervous tension that could last for several hours and cause you to put yourself at risk of physical injury during the time it is affecting you. Due to its celestial connections Table Rock's energy is conducive to deliberately induced astral travel experiences (which should only be undertaken by experienced persons) and for gaining access to the energies inherent in other planets. Table Rock, although I do not know of its past history in terms of any legends connected with it, is most likely a place that would be associated with frequent UFO activity as this phenomena seems common around many prominent beacon sites around the world. Examples are Cley Hill in England, Bell Rock in Sedona, and Ayers Rock in Australia.

*Hawksbill Mountain,* on the other hand, is an impressive *magnetic beacon* vortex whose physical shape resembles the bill of a giant bird of prey. Like those of Table Rock, Hawksbill's celestial leys are connected to each of the other planets in our solar system, and serve as leys through which those planetary energies *come to* the Earth. So this mountain is working in a magnetic way to bring in these energies to the Earth's body and atmosphere. I perceived the mountain as having an indigo-colored aura, giving it an unearthly air of mystery.

The first time I visited the Table Rock/Hawksbill "double beacon" vortexes I felt particularly drawn to Hawksbill. As I sat looking out over the magnificent Linville Gorge at the curious peak, my eyes drinking in the beauty and power of the place, my mind drifted, seemingly at the whim of the soft, gentle breeze, into an altered state. It seemed like the mountain suddenly transformed itself right before my eyes and I had a compelling vision of its indwelling Spirit. I watched transfixed as its summit became the head of a huge hawk. The vision of the giant bird slowly changed from having the appearance of a real hawk with reddish-bronze feathers and large black, piercing eyes, into being a great silver-colored Spirit Bird with dark eyes that radiated sharp and brightly flashing silver rays! The vision lasted for what seemed to be a full five minutes (though when one is in an altered state time is of no consequence) and it left me with a sense of having *bonded* in a special and powerful way with both the mountain and the Spirit that dwells within it. As my vision faded, and not entirely to my surprise, hawks appeared, one by one until there were seven, gliding and circling over Hawksbill's summit! It was at the same time both a wonderful and intense experience.

The energy that emanates from Table Rock and Hawksbill mountains, which appears as a translucent mist is emitted out of the apex of each of their summits. This activity constitutes the actual vortex power within which are found the celestial leys. (see illustration) I also noticed that from the base of the body of each peak there were two terrestrial leys that were no doubt present due to the very fact that these peaks are each earth vortexes in their own right. The terrestrial leys seemed to flow together, converging at a point between the two in the valley below. (see illustration) The presence and activity of the celestial leys accounts for the beacon vortexes that the two are, whereas the presence and activity of the terrestrial leys involves the peaks' relationship with the earth alone. For example; all beacons have one or more celestial leys, but they each have a terrestrial ley of a specific charge of Life Energy as well which connects them to other vortexes of the same charge worldwide. Collectively, the Table Rock/Hawskbill terrestrial leys and their energy flow forms what I have named the Linville (ley) Line which runs to and connects with Mt. Mitchell. (More will be given about Mt. Mitchell later in this writing)

These two mountains do indeed draw one to them in a powerful way. I see Table Rock and Hawksbill as forming a *cooperating pair* of natural vortexes that are forever locked in a partnership of sending and receiving planetary energies that both vitalize and release the earth's life force. I view this task as an integral part of the living mechanism of the earth's life process and does much to sustain her as a living entity. Again, this is the most unique double vortex site, beacons or otherwise, that I know about and it may very well be unique on the planet. It is a place where the Earth is breathing; where the two peaks and their interaction form, at least in part, the respiratory system of the Earth Mother.

This area would be a good place to go for various purposes that could include performing sacred ceremonies to honor the Earth, for experiencing the "breathing" and tap into a powerful fountain of the earth's living force, for prayer, for alignment of the mind and body with our planet's natural rhythm, and for healing. It is also a place where the ancient art of "starwalking" (drawing down star power) could be accomplished and where one can easily get in touch with the energies of all the brother and sister planets in the solar system.

The spectacular Linville Gorge is indeed a feast for the eyes. Called the "Grand Canyon of the East" by tourist brochures, this deep river valley is cut down its middle by the 14 mile-long Linville River. The entire gorge covers almost 11,000 acres; land that is abundant in plant and animal life, some of which are rare. The gorge is highly electromagnetic but its river is a magnetic grid that forms a geological energy configuration or pattern that is somewhat like a grid within a grid. This wild wilderness is without doubt one of the most intensely powerful grids in the entire region of the Smokies and the Blue Ridge.

BROWN MOUNTAIN:

East and a bit south of the Linville Gorge Wilderness off S.R.1328 there is a ridge known as *Brown Mountain*. I mention this place not only because of its being a small electromagnetic grid, one of the small grids within the larger one, but also because of its being the site of a famous "earth light" phenomena; the *Brown Mountain lights.* The lights have been reported for many years and have baffled scientists and laypersons alike with their mysterious appearances. Over the years I have heard many stories about them along with various explanations of their origin which range from their being the headlights of locomotives rumbling through the valley below, to ghosts, and even flying saucers! Other theories have included foxfire, natural gas emanations, and St. Elmo's fire. Attesting to the longevity of the lights, there is a Cherokee legend that says they have existed as far back as the 1200s. The Indians claim that the lights are the spirits of the distraught widows of Cherokee and Catawba warriors who still search for their dead husbands. Another popular story tells of the lights being the ghost of an old slave who vanished while on a hunting trip. Still another tells of the enigmatic lights being somehow related to the strange disappearance of a young mother and her child. (Sakowski; 1990, pgs. 243-46)

In Issue 31 of Katuah Journal (Summer, 1991, pg.2), an informative article by Clyde Hollifield sheds some light on the mysterious lights of Brown Mountain. Hollifield says the lights, called "jack-o-lanterns" by the locals, usually appear in late evening or early morning hours and have the color of mercury vapor. "Sometimes they move around- sometimes they pop off like light bulbs all over the mountain."[3] It seems there are also times when the lights appear to move around atop the ridge or go in and out from behind the hill! They have even been known to bump together and pull apart again. There may also be a hidden clue as to what they are in the fact that the lights appear most frequently after the passing of a thunderstorm. Hollifield discounts the popular theory of the lights being gas "as they do not diffuse with the wind". (Katuah Journal, Issue 31, Summer 1991) The famous lights, like luminous balls, have also been seen in the Linville Gorge itself and all around the Hawksbill area. The same type of phenomena has been witnessed on Grandfather Mountain and at Mt. Mitchell. According to Hollifield they seem most likely to appear at these two locations at the highest elevations above 3500 feet and during cold weather. Similar light phenomena has also been reported in the Andes mountains in Peru, the Long Kennet Barrow in Wiltshire, England, in the Himalayas, and in western Texas. To me the entire phenomena of earth lights is both intriguing and compelling. While I cannot prove it I do believe that the lights are spirit forces; perhaps the souls of some nature spirits manifest as "lights". Or perhaps they are natural earth energy that is simply being used by intelligent, living spirit forces for some purpose. It is difficult to say for sure. What is certain is that reports of similar *earth lights* have been reported over time throughout the world. British geomancer/investigator and author Paul Devereux has investigated the subject of earth lights in depth and presented detailed accounts of his research and experience in his book by the same name.

Brown Mountain is not a vortex nor is it magnetic in its charge. Its lights however are evidence of a mysterious phenomena that one might expect to be present due to Brown Mountain's association with the Table Rock/Hawksbill beacon vortexes. After all, the term UFO *does* suggest *unidentified flying objects* and the lights at Brown Mountain are airborne and certainly unidentified! I also think that at places where unusual phenomena can and does occur are places where the *veil* between the physical and non-physical dimensions is unusually thin, making this type of area a sort of "gateway" into the world of spirits. In these types of places spirits may be more easily contacted and spirit communication is easier to achieve.

Two other places of interest in the Linville Gorge Wilderness are *Linville Falls,* an electromagnetic spot that emits a powerful healing energy, and the *Linville Caverns.* The caverns, the only ones discovered thus far in North Carolina, are inside *Humpback Mountain* which is a magnetic peak. Entrance into the caverns is four miles south of the Blue Ridge Parkway, just 15 miles south of the community of Linville and Grandfather Mountain on U.S.221. The lovely caverns were found after the mysterious disappearance of fish swimming out of the mountain, leading curious explorers to follow an underground stream through passageways whose ceilings have been described in tourist brochures as "the arch of some grand old

Linville Falls - Linville, NC

cathedral." Keep in mind that caves and caverns are *"entranceways"* into the body of the Earth Mother and are generally sites that are intensely magnetic. This makes them excellent places for meditation, cleansing ceremonies, and vision quests.

### THE MT. MITCHELL (BLACK DOME) GRID:

The area extending out from the base of Mt. Mitchell in an approximate one-mile radius comprises what I label the *Mt. Mitchell Grid* or *Black Dome Grid.* The 6,684 foot Mt. Mitchell located in the Black Mountains east of Asheville is the highest peak in the Appalachians, as well as the highest peak east of the Mississippi. The

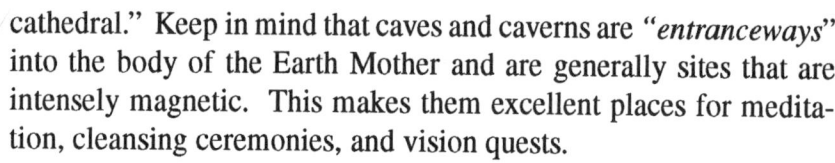

Mt. Mitchell, NC

mountain lies at the center of the Mt. Mitchell *electromagnetic* grid that is filled with large stands of spruce and fir. The beautiful mountain is preserved by a 1,400 acre state park, the first to be so designated in North Carolina.

Mt. Mitchell was originally called *Black Dome* and I for one prefer that name. Black Dome is an intense *electromagnetic vortex*, one of the few mountain vortexes in the world that holds such a charge. The mountain's task is to perform as a *generator* of pure electromagnetism that does a great deal to sustain the charge or vitality of the entire area; an energy that provides healing and balance. A 5.2 mile hiking trail leads to its top and the summit is a great place to go for awakening the soul consciousness and to pay ceremonial tribute to the Spirit of this powerful peak.

The Great Deva who dwells within and embodies the power of Black Dome is a magnificent winged one whose wings and body shine like pure gold. This intensely powerful one emits shimmering golden rays in all directions and gives off a sound I found to be similar to that of the rapidly-flapping wings of a giant bird. Going to the top of such mountains anywhere can be a high-powered and meaningful symbolic pilgrimage of spiritual ambition and self-discovery. Pilgrims wishing to journey to the summit of Black Dome are advised to be well-informed of current weather conditions and forecasts, as there can be frosts at the higher elevations even in the summer months and nights are always cool.

In addition to its being an electromagnetic vortex Black Dome is what I call a *ley terminal;* a site, oftentimes a mountain, where a large number of global and/or local ley lines converge. The joining of energy always results in the convergence point becoming an intense vortex. In the case of Black Dome, even though electrical and magnetic leys may run close to or through the mountain's area, the *converging leys* that terminate there are electromagnetic because, again, the mountain is electromagnetic in its natural charge. The presence of the ley terminal and the mountain vortex, together, in conjunction with the pure quality of electromagnetism coming into the area makes the electromagnetism at the point of the actual ley terminal incredibly intense. Furthermore, such a terminal is the geographical location and primary source of natural electromagnetic power for a vast region, as is the case with Black Dome which supplies electromagnetic power for the entire eastern United States!

All of the electromagnetic ley lines that originate in other grids in the Smokies and the Blue Ridge mountains terminate at Mt. Mitchell, along with all the other leys that have the same charge but originate in other eastern parts of North America. In addition to the ancient mountain spirit I felt at Black Dome I also sensed that the entire peak is enshrouded by an etheric *dome* which serves to protect the mountain and to contain the energy of its omnipotent summit from becoming depleted. As a result this wonderful dome is an ever-generating and distributing dynamo of Earth's pure healing force. This mountain, like Mt. Shasta in California and Denali (Mt. McKinley) in Alaska (both of which are electrical rather than electromagnetic), provides a self-healing, self-sustaining source of power for the planet and in this way is part of the earth's immune system. Water from the falls in the area, namely *Black Dome Falls* and *Mitchell Falls*, are particularly potent for healing the human body. But proper precautions must be taken before ingesting or getting into the water at any site, as pollution and other harmful elements may be present.

Interestingly, there is a relatively small region around the Black Dome area known as *Point Misery*. I sense this to be a negative part of the grid. I felt its energy to be similar to a pyramid-shaped mountain I experienced some years ago when I visited Mt. Shasta in California. While there I perceived a nearby peak as a place where some of the earth's toxins (from areas throughout the Pacific Northwest) were being drawn in and processed. I view the Point Misery area to serve a same or similar purpose. Negative energy drawn in by the Black Dome ley terminal from other parts of the planet are stored here until the Earth Mother can *recycle* it and use it once again as purified life force. I suspect that only ley terminals such as Mt. Shasta, Denali, and Mt. Mitchell have such "storage" areas and that these are necessary due to the excessive amount of energy coming into these sites. Such places can be somewhat negative and are not, as a rule, sites that are not conducive to ceremony or other spiritual activities.

GREAT SMOKY MOUNTAINS GRID:

The Great Smoky Mountains National Park area is in itself a natural grid, but I must technically refer to it as a man-made grid due to the *actual boundaries* of the area having been defined by humans. So for the purpose of clarity, I will rely on the man-imposed boundaries of the Park to identify this largest of the grids in the region in question. Cut almost in half by the state lines of Tennessee and North Carolina, this huge grid is *electromagnetic.* Within it are numerous vortexes, sacred sites, and power spots. Several leys also run through it.

One particularly powerful vortex in the Park is the well-known mountain that was sacred to the early Cherokees: *Clingman's Dome.* (Mooney; 1982) (Other special sites in the Park are mentioned throughout this writing) I think of the Park as being a great "teacher"........Nature's classroom; an actual entity whose task it is, by being itself for all human eyes to behold, to teach us the true nature of beauty and what lies behind that beauty; what state the land, worldwide, must be kept in for the earth to be a healthy, vital entity. The land is so delicate.....all these grids in the Smokies and Blue Ridge. We stand by daily and watch the ills of our modern industrial society creep silently into these magnificent woodlands and upset and threaten the fragile balance of nature. But at least an effort is being made within the boundaries of the Park to keep the land and all that lives upon it healthy for future generations. In this way the land is our teacher. May our prayer be that the land will survive long enough to teach us well; well enough to cause us to change our values and our environmental consciousness, collectively as human beings, before it is too late.

THE MAGNETIC MAN-MADE GRIDS:

In order to explain the nature of the man-made magnetic grids adequately (and there are also some natural ones that will be discussed later in this writing) that are located in the Great Smoky and Blue Ridge mountains I will use *Fontana Lake* as my example. This immense grid covers 10,640 acres and stretches 29 miles in length; making it one of the most potent of the artificial magnetic grids in North America, comparable in power to the Great Salt Lake in Utah and the Great Lakes themselves, which are among the largest magnetic grids in the world. However, because Fontana Lake is not a natural vortex, its energy is rather fragile and can be depleted very easily with any imbalance of rainfall or other water source problems.

The beautiful Fontana Lake was created by the construction of the 480 foot high Fontana Dam. (Sakowski; 1990, pg. 10) When at full power such vortexes can be quite potent. Good or bad, sites like Fontana Lake stand as evidence of and as a result of the effect humans can and do have upon the environment which, in the case of Fontana, appears to be positive. But this is by no means the rule. Other aquatic grids in the Smokies and Blue Ridge include Hiwassee and Chatuge Lakes (both man-made); Nantahala Lake; Santeelah Lake; Glenville Lake (man-made); and Lake James, located south of the Linville Gorge Wilderness.

Because there are seven natural grids in the Great Smoky and Blue Ridge mountains, there are also seven major ley lines that originate from these areas and terminate at the Black Dome/Mt. Mitchell vortex/ley terminal. While these leys are the ones that originate here and basically serve to transport the energy of the region into a point of conjunction, there are many other natural ley lines that run through the area of western North Carolina and eastern Tennessee that are part of the *global* ley system. Collectively, global leys form what might be called the circulatory system of our planet. A more complete description of the massive and complex planetary ley system may be found in my earlier book *The Earth Changes Survival Handbook* (Sun Publishing).

The following is a brief discussion of each of the ley lines that originate within each of the seven major grids and terminate at Black Dome. I have assigned names to each of the leys for purpose of identification. All of the leys are electromagnetic in their charge.

## THE GREAT SMOKY AND BLUE RIDGE MOUNTAIN LEY LINES:

### THE BLACK MOUNTAIN LEY:

The *Black Mountain Ley* constitutes the first of the major ley lines in the Smokies and Blue Ridge area. This line originates in the area of Table Rock State Park and runs through Cedar Mountain, Jeter Mountain, passing just west of the city of Hendersonville; on through the town of Swannanoa; through the town of Black Mountain and terminates at the Black Dome/ Mt. Mitchell vortex.

### THE LINVILLE LINE:

The *Linville Line* originates between Hawksbill Mountain and Table Rock in the Linville Gorge Wilderness. From there it runs west and slightly south through the Honeycutt Mountain range and through the Carolina Hemlocks Recreational Area, into Black Dome/ Mt. Mitchell.

### THE TRANSYLVANIA LEY:

The Transylvania Ley originates from the approximate center of the Ellicott Rock Wilderness area on the Jackson and Oconee county line. It runs through the Sapphire Valley; through the northwestern corner of Lake Toxaway; directly through John Rock and Looking

Glass Falls; through Black Mountain (not the town); across the Transylvania and Henderson county line; slightly north of Avery Creek; intersecting the Blue Ridge Parkway, slicing through the Great Craggy Mountains. From there the ley runs into the Black Mountains and directly into the Black Dome/Mt. Mitchell vortex.

THE NANTAHALA LEY:

The Nantahala Line originates in the Upper Nantahala Wilderness. From there it runs through Standing Indian Rock; across the Nantahala Mountains cutting across the Little Tennessee and Cullasaja rivers, slicing right through Ammons Knob that lies between them. From the Cullasaja the line runs through Wolf Knob; across the Cullowee Mountains just south of Tuskaseegee. The ley then cuts through the northwestern tip of the Middle Prong Wilderness, just south of the Sunburst Campgrounds and on through the northern part of the Shining Rock Wilderness near Cold Mountain; through the town of South Hominy; just south of Enka and Candler and on through the Great Craggy Mountains before terminating in the Black Dome/Mt. Mitchell vortex.

THE CHEROKEE LEY:

The Cherokee Ley has its origin in the area of the Joyce Kilmer Memorial Forest, which is another sort of grid within a grid within the larger Slickrock Wilderness grate. From there it runs across Santeelah Lake; just north of Tuskeegee; across Fontana Lake (actually it crosses the lake at two different point due to the shape of the lake); through Noland Divide and Thomas Ridge and on through the Cherokee Indian Reservation where it passes right through the Oconoluftee Visitor Center; through the southern part of the Cataloochee Divide; through the town of Cave Creek; across the Pigeon River crossing the Haywood and Buncombe county lines; through Leicester, Reems Falls, Weaverville, and Beech; on through the Craggy Gardens Scenic Area into the Black Mountains and directly into the base of the Black Dome/Mt. Mitchell vortex.

## THE BALSAM MOUNTAIN LINE:

The Balsam Line has its origin in the Slickrock Wilderness grid near the Stratton Bald area. From there it runs across the Cheoah River and across the Yellow Creek Mountains, directly through the Cable Cove Campgrounds. It then slices through Fontana Lake; on through the Welch and Forney ridges; across the Noland Divide and Thomas Ridge. It then goes through the Cherokee Reservation; through Balsam Mountain, the town of Cove Creek, and across the Pigeon River, running parallel with the Cherokee (ley) Line through Weaverville; through Little Snowball Mountain; through the Black Mountains into the Black Dome/Mt. Mitchell vortex.

## SMOKY MOUNTAIN LEY:

The Smoky Mountain Ley begins at Clingman's Dome within the boundaries of the Great Smoky Mountain National Park. From there the line runs across the Noland Divide Trail and Deep Creek across Thomas Ridge and the Oconoluftee River. The ley runs close by the Heintooga Overlook just north of Cove Creek, just north of the town of Leicester and on through Weaverville and on into the Mt. Mitchell vortex.

Keep in mind that the tracking of the leys must be termed as approximate although I have sought to trace them as close to their actual energy track as I could. One has to either *feel* the presence of ley energy or dowse their track with simple rods, a pendulum, or other implements designed for that purpose. Keep in mind that leys are *transporters* of pure living earth energy. When one is on or near the leys one can tap into their power and is affected by it, dependent of course upon the nature of their charge: electric, magnetic, or electromagnetic. Living near or on a leys would, for example, greatly affect the potency of your land as well as the quality of your domestic and personal life. This statement is in keeping with the fundamental principles of Feng Shui, the ancient Chinese art of geomancy. Because the energy in this particular region is electromagnetic, it is extremely potent in healing/balancing power. Generally the land is quite fertile, especially if there is a stream, creek, river, deep natural spring or well, or some other good water source nearby. Crops and herbs grown here are particularly healthy. Such land would also be good location for retreat and healing centers and for teaching and light centers. Places all along the leys are also especially conducive to enhancing prayers and ceremonies, as well as the general quality of life. As you discover and follow the leys throughout eastern Tennessee and western North Carolina don't forget that this part of the earth is waxing to full power. You can be a part of this process, and you and the quality of your life will certainly be affected by it. You can participate in the awakening and the surge of power involved with it and you can learn from it. You can feel it happening. You can re-connect to the entire planet through being aware of and consciously tapping into the energies here. Once accomplished, you will have taken one more step towards becoming a whole, fulfilled human being.

[1] Katuah Journal; Issue 31, Summer 1991; pg. 2.
[2] <u>Terravision: A Traveler's Guide To The Living Planet Earth</u>; Bryant, Page; Ballantine Books; New York, New York: 1991.
[3] Katuah Journal; Issue 31, Summer 1991.

# THE SPIRITUAL REAWAKENING OF THE GREAT SMOKY MOUNTAINS

## THE SOUL OF THE GREAT SMOKY/BLUE RIDGE MOUNTAINS

### CHAPTER 6

"As with other tribes and countries, almost every prominent rock and mountain, every deep bend in the river, in the old Cherokee country has its accompanying legend. It may be a little story that can be told in a paragraph, to account for some natural feature, or it may be one chapter of a myth that has its sequel in a mountain a hundred miles away."

James Mooney
Myths Of The Cherokee

In the eastern part of Turtle Island....."there is an apex of intense energy: the Blue Ridge and surrounding mountains, with the Great Smoky Mountains as the energy center."[1] This region of Grandfather Mountains is a place that generates some of the most potent living energy on Earth; energy that is the life and breath of our planet; a power by which the Earth Mother heals and replenishes her body. This spectacular land is known as the Great Smoky and Blue Ridge Mountains, ancient peaks that comprise the southern Appalachians. The Great Smoky Mountains National Park and the vast area surrounding it is a sacred landscape indeed and contains what most geologists agree are the oldest mountains on our planet. This chapter is designed to point out the vortexes, power spots, and sacred sites within the Great Smoky and Blue Ridge mountains and other areas throughout western North Carolina and eastern Tennessee. With each location I identify I will qualify the type of Life Energy present there and any legendary or spiritually-oriented information of which I am currently aware. The sources of my information are numerous and have been noted accordingly. Most of the sites are well known. And I have interpreted the esoteric nature of the sites according to my own unique system of energy identification and geomancy explained in chapter five of this writing. I cannot and do not make the claim that my knowledge includes the total number of power spots and sacred sites in the area, but I have made every effort to locate and identify all of those I have learned about through outside sources or came across through my own intuition and my years of experience with and teachings about earth energies. It is my intention and desire to provide a guidebook that will assist the earth-minded and ecologically-sensitive spiritual seeker to come into a closer and hopefully better relationship with Mother Earth.

Whenever going to a sacred site, power spot, grid, or sacred mountain it is appropriate to carry an offering as a giveaway to the Earth Mother as well as to the spirits who live there, the omnipotent Mountain Devas, or the angelic presences who guard such places. The giving of an offering is also an act of giving of yourself.....from your heart. It is also good to keep in mind that many of the places named in the book and that you will visit are public areas and can at times be very crowded. The experiences of others who might be present should never interrupted or otherwise disturbed or tainted by your attracting undue attention to yourself by your doing ceremony or other activities that might run the risk of taking away from another's experience of the moment and the place. In regards to your offering; if it is a non-physical one such as a chant, a song, a ceremony, a dance, or audible prayer, it should be given at an appropriate time in silence and privacy if others are present; aloud if you are alone. On the other hand, if your offering is a physical object it is good to choose it with careful thought. It may be flowers, a crystal or some other mineral, one of your own hairs, a sacred herb, or even a coin, to offer but a few suggestions. Keep in mind that any object taken to and placed in a given place *will*, to a small or large degree, change the energy of the site. Therefore the object should be small and unobtrusive and should in no way mar the environment. All the more reason why careful thought should go into your choice.

As stated earlier, as we make our journey around the Blue Ridge and Great Smoky Mountain region I have made an effort to point out as many of the individual vortexes, sacred sites, and power spots of which I am aware. Readers are encouraged to inform me of any additional sites of which you are personally aware and perhaps share your personal experiences of these places or any of those mentioned in this book if you care to. This would make for a wonderful second edition of this writing which is already planned. I have also tried to be as specific as possible with the locations of the places I have listed and/or discussed. The reader will see that the directions to some sites are more exact than others, as some are more well-known and/or more easily accessible. These directions reflect my personal familiarity with the region gained over my three and a half years of residency. Readers more familiar with the area are invited to suggest more exact directions for the future edition. Any such assistance would be appreciated. All the locations listed are easily found on any detailed map of western North Carolina and eastern Tennessee.

POWER SPOTS/VORTEXES/SACRED SITES:

GREGORY BALD:

Let us begin our journey of planetary discovery at *Gregory Bald* which is located directly on the N.C./Tennessee state line. This is an *electrical power spot* but not a vortex. Gregory Bald was recognized by the early Cherokees who called it "Rabbit Place" because they believed it to have once been the home of Great Rabbit, the huge chief of the rabbits who had a council house beneath this mountain. (Mooney; 1982) This is also one of the four sites where the bears once had a lodge (and perhaps they still do) and where they held a sacred dance before going into their winter hibernation. (Mooney; 1982) I feel that Gregory Bald should be considered a sacred site as well as a power spot because I feel that it is quite possibly the location of an animal lodge. Let me explain.

The existence of the *animal lodges* is common among various Native American tribes. These sites were believed to be invisible places (to humans at least) that were oftentimes depicted as being actual dwellings or structures. These were lodges where animal chiefs and/or councils gathered for sacred ceremonies and decision-making activities. An example of just such a site is *Pa-ha-tu*, which means "Hill In Water Settlement".[2] Pa-ha-tu is located on the inside of a specific bluff, underwater, along the Platte River in Nebraska; a site once held sacred by the now-extinct Skidi Pawnee Indians, the star cult of the Great Plains. My husband and I were taken to Pahuk (accepted spelling) by a friend who is one of Sun Bear's apprentices in Omaha, Tom Workman, to do ceremony and smoke pipe. Inside the Lodge there dwelled one of each kind of animals, including birds and reptiles, that lived in that area of the earth. They lived there along with one male human being. The Skidi believed that it was the animals who first received the traditional spiritual, religious wisdom teachings and that humans must go to the animals in order to learn this knowledge. Interestingly, the only way that a human could gain entrance into the Animal Lodge was through a dream and to do so was a great honor. Healers gained their power there. It was also said that the wind is very strong at Pa-ha-tu and that the doorway of the Lodge was once marked by a large cedar tree that was always filled with all kinds of birds. The Lodge was guarded by a big fish who spat fire from his mouth. I would imagine that as a guard he was quite effective!

Another example of an animal lodge site is the famous natural rock formation known today as Devil's Tower in Wyoming. Called Mata Tipila, Bear Lodge, by the Sioux, this 1,267 foot natural rocktower is an imposing site indeed. Sacred to the Sioux and the site of the annual Sun Dance, Mata Tipila has a legend connected with it that tells of a warrior who went into the wilderness so he might be in solitude. On one occasion the warrior took his buffalo skull and went to the base of Mata Tipila where, after two days of praying he suddenly found himself on top of the steep rock tower and he did not know how to get down. After falling into a deep sleep, suggesting again that entrance into such places was accomplished during sleep or some other altered state, he once again found himself at the tower's base and standing at the door of the bear's lodge. He then knew that the strange crevices and marks on the sides of the stone column had been made by the bear's claws. Incidentally, some say that the buffalo skull taken atop the tower by the warrior may still be seen there! (*Native American Mythology;* Bryant, P., pg.97) I think there is good reason to suspect that Gregory Bald, like Pa-ha-tu and Mata Tipila, is the location of an animal lodge and may not be the only place of this kind in the Smokies or the Blue Ridge mountains. There are numerous sites mentioned in various writings I used for my research whose only claim to fame, so to speak, is their legendary association with various animals and/or reputed to be animal dwellings. These places are usually very powerful and are excellent places to go for communication and connection with one's totem and with the animal kingdom in general. Always remember, please, to take an appropriate offering to the animals when visiting these places. An animal, bird, or reptile fetish is a wonderful offering, depending upon the kind of creature associated with the place. With Gregory Bald, a rabbit or bear fetish would be fine, as would a small piece of rabbit fur or bear hide. Ultimately, however, the choice of an offering is up to the individual.

ROCK CAIRNS:
    From Gregory Bald we move along the south banks of Slickrock Creek on the Cheowa River in Graham County. Here lies a series of rock cairns that line both sides of the trail down the south side of the

river. The cairns extend for several miles. Although the suggestion has been proffered that the cairns may have once marked the site of an ancient battle, (Mooney; 1982) I disagree. I feel the cairns form what was once a ceremonial "avenue". If I am correct this would make it a truly sacred place. I understand that it was once a custom that when passing through the cairns, once held sacred by the Cherokees, one would always throw a stone on the pile, believing that bad fortune will befall those who do not. This, to me, is evidence that the early Cherokees, and perhaps the whites too, either knew or sensed that this was a special site, even though its original purpose may have long been lost. There are other rock cairns on the west side of Slickrock Creek about a mile from the Little Tennessee River, and others are found south of Robbinsville where the trail crosses the ridge at Valleytown in Cherokee County.

AGISIYI:

A curious place, Agisiyi, (I have also seen it given in Mooney's writing as Gisehun yi) "where the females live", is located on the Tuckasegee River above Bryson City. (Rossman; 1988, pg.11) This is where a strange family of supernatural white people were once seen washing their clothes in the river! The spirit people, if this is indeed what they were, were believed to be members of the family of the Great Female, a spirit invoked by Cherokee shamans. This is a strong magnetic site due primarily to its proximity to a strong and constant water source. You will remember that since magnetic sites are often places where the veils between dimensions is thin, I suspect the unusual sighting of the supernaturals may have been the result of a dream or vision experienced by the people and they were most likely medicine people though this is only a thought on my part. The visions could have revealed the presence of spirit people or, perhaps they were "memory visions" of the ancient people who once inhabited the area before the arrival of the Cherokees. If the latter is the case, Jung might say the inhabitants of the vision are but a part of the collective unconscious of the area where they were seen and of the people themselves. In other words the visionaries saw their own ancestral spirits. Readers are encouraged to go to this vicinity and make their own psychic attunement to the spirit forces there. Also remember that magnetic places usually provide good energy for dreams, meditation, prayers, vision quests, healing and cleansing ceremonies.

RATTLESNAKE MOUNTAIN:

Located 2 miles northeast of the town of Cherokee in Swain County, *Rattlesnake Mountain* is an *electrical power spot*. An intriguing legend is associated with this peak; a tale that concerns a sacred crystal once seen flying through the air in the form of a ball of light that landed on the mountain! (Mooney; 1982) I wonder if there have been any recent witnesses to any unusual light phenomena on or near this peak, because I suspect that the sacred crystal or ball of fire seen in the early times may have been a meteor. My primary reason for thinking this is the fact that the legend tells of the object flying through (falling from?) the air and that it was described as "fiery"; an apt description of a meteor if I ever heard one! It is also interesting that Rattlesnake Mountain is not the only site in the Blue Ridge and Great Smoky Mountains with which light phenomena of a similar and mysterious sort have been reported. In fact such reports are fairly common throughout the world, particularly near ancient sacred and vortex sites. Another of these in our local region regards two small bald spots on a mountainside at the head of *Little Snowbird Creek* located southwest of Robbinsville in Graham County. Here it is said that a giant mysterious being, whose head blazed like the sun, was seen to *fly through the air and land at this spot!* After standing for a while, peering out over the land the being flew away. When the people went to the place where the landing site they found that all the trees and plants had been burned away! (Mooney; 1982) Again, it sounds like a meteorite fall site to me. The Cherokees felt that the giant may have been the Sun god. Again it is my feeling that this could have been the be site of a meteorite fall, although I am not saying that all sites where light phenomena occurs are. I definitely feel that places where a meteorite fall has occurred are powerful sites where one can make a soul "connection" with the Great Star Nation. It is also interesting to note that meteorites were considered highly sacred to the Skidi Pawnee Indians who believed them to have healing powers and the power to protect warriors in battle. Meteorites have also played important roles in the spirituality of other ancient cultures; a prime example being the Kaaba stone at Mecca which is a large meteorite.

## FODDERSTACK MOUNTAIN:

Located a little over a mile southeast of the town of Highlands in Macon County, *Fodderstack Mountain* is an *electromagnetic power spot*. This was one of four mountains that the bears once had a council house for holding ceremonies. (Rossman; 1988, pg.18) Another, you will recall, is Clingman's Dome. Again, such places are excellent sites to go to for communicating with the animal kingdom and ones personal totem. Don't forget to take an offering.

## DEVIL'S COURTHOUSE:

Located on Forest Road 240 off N.C. 215 (base of the mountain) there is an *electrical power spot* called *Devil's Courthouse* (not to be confused with a place by the same name in Hickory Nut Gap). The Cherokees believed this to be a place frequented by the giant, Judaculla, who held judgement sessions there. Other legends tell of the Devil himself being associated with this site. Devil's Courthouse's peak is clearly visible on a pull-out on the Blue Ridge Parkway. I feel that when negative stories have been associated with a given site over a long period of time, this results in "bad vibes" or thoughtforms manifesting there. This kind of thoughtform can, in turn, have a subliminal effect on people who go there and who are open, consciously or unconsciously, to the energies that are present. I felt extremely powerful energy at this site, but I cannot say that it seemed negative, just very powerful and empowering. Nearby its base area, on U.S. 64, are the beautiful *Toxaway Falls,* an *electromagnetic vortex (man-made)* and *Lake Toxaway,* a 640 acre man-created *magnetic grid.*

CLINGMAN'S DOME:

Inside the boundaries of the Great Smoky Mountains National Park, very near the Tennessee border, there is the powerful *electrical vortex* known as *Clingman's Dome.* During my first visit to this area, I experienced the presence of an intense Mountain Deva who resides within and embodies the potency of this ancient peak. I perceived the Great Deva as a violet-colored Light Being with huge white wings and piercing violet eyes. As we drove the road leading up to the Clingman's Dome overlook area, I "saw" the immense wings stretching east to west on either side of the Great Being and perceived them to be agents for sending out the power of the mountain and for protecting the area around it. This Ancient One is the *guardian* of the entire grid that is the Great Smoky Mountains National Park.

Clingman's Dome is the type of vortex that I call a *synthesizer.* These vortexes, and there are many of them worldwide, serve the role of synthesizing or blending and harmonizing the natural terrestrial and atmospheric energies over a vast region. In this way, such vortexes, which are often considered as sacred mountains by the area's indigenous peoples, serve the role of being the "healer" for a given region that may cover many square miles. These "healers" keep the necessary ecological balance. In light of the current environmental problems affecting both land and sky, such synthesizers are having a difficult time of it and many are all but shut down.

Clingman's Dome is the highest peak in the Park and the second highest in the eastern U.S. There are many legends associated with this famous summit, many of which have to do with the animal kingdom. (Mooney; 1982) It is truly a sacred mountain in every sense and should be preserved at all costs. Based on these strong feelings, I have tremendous concern for the ecological condition of not only Clingman's Dome, but the entire area of the southern Appalachians. There are so many dead trees that can be seen along the road leading up to the Dome's summit. The life force and general vitality of the area seemed much weaker and lower than I had expected it to be. However, with the reawakening of the Smokies, I have great hopes that this vortex, along with others, over time, will regain its health and full power. Clingman's Dome is a good area to go to do needed earth- healing ceremony and to make prayers for our planet. Helping the Earth Mother through Clingman's Dome and other damaged sites will result in the planet returning energy to you that will help you to bring balance to a particular problem that you may be having and, telepathically, help you to quiet yourself so that you can hear your own inner voice. When we are quiet, we stand a much better chance of "synthesizing" what we know and how to use our knowledge.

CADES COVE:

I feel especially strong about the energies in *Cades Cove* and the area immediately around it in the Great Smoky Mountains National Park. The rich bottomland of the coves and valleys of Cades Cove comprises a smaller *electromagnetic grid* within the much larger Great Smoky Mountain National Park grid. The cove is a prolific habitat for wildflowers and a wide variety of other plant life. Moisture is abundant, which helps to hold the "memory" of human lives and times long past, as all highly magnetic places do. This is an especially relaxing area to go to for meditation and for just being with the Earth Mother.

Interestingly, there is a faultline, the Oconoluftee Fault, that runs through Cades Cove. (Hubbs, Maynard, and Morris; 1992, pg.39) There are also numerous waterfalls and cascades located throughout the Cades Cove area. The one that I feel is a full, intense *electromag-*

*netic vortex* is Abrams Falls. Details about the falls and directions to it are defined in a later chapter of this book.

THUNDERHEAD MOUNTAIN:
Located inside the Great Smoky Mountains National Park, *Thunderhead Mountain* is a potent *electromagnetic vortex*. Perhaps due to its name, I associate it with the Thunder Beings and it is, in any case, a wonderful spot to attune to these powerful elemental spirit forces. Other places where I feel there could be close contact and communication with nature spirits or elements and the forces of thunder and lightning, inside the Park, are Chimney Tops, Cold Springs Knob, Mt. Sequoyah, the Cataloochee Campground area, Smokemont, Mount Sterling, and Spruce Mountain. Outside the Park, I direct the

Looking Glass Falls near Brevard, NC

reader to Ceasar's Head (just over the border into South Carolina on Hwy. 276), the Cullasaja River Gorge, Roaring Fork in the Gatlinburg area in Tennessee, and Looking Glass Falls. I feel that getting in conscious contact with the Elementals can indeed improve upon the quality of ones relationship with the Earth Mother and Nature in general. Other such sites within the Park itself will appear throughout this chapter.

RUMBLING BALD MOUNTAIN:

Once we leave the Park area, the landscape is filled with power sites of varying kinds. In the lovely region of *Lake Lure* in Rutherford County, near the South Carolina border, lies *Rumbling Bald Mountain*. I believe this peak to be a rare *magnetic vortex* that is in the process of *imploding*....in other words, being gradually (geologically) "swallowed" into the body of the Earth. And, I do have some geological foundation upon which to base my intuitive feelings about this curious mountain. Rumbling Bald Mountain has an unusual reputation that dates, by human records, back to the mid-1970s. But I suspect that the sometimes frightening and powerful geological events going on here have been going on over many thousands of years. Series of "rumblings", hence the name, or "shocks" have been known to dislodge huge boulders and to open fissures inside the body of the peak. Scientific investigations in 1940 revealed that the noise was the result of the large boulders breaking loose from the ceiling of subterranean crevices, sending them crashing to the cave floors inside the mountain! (Sakowski; 1990, pg.157-8). It has been my experience that when there is something physical/geological happening at a given site, there is bound to be a "reflection" of those events occurring on the astral plane or *energy level*, the invisible level, whether it is a person, object, or place. An example may be seen with humans who, due to some inner *emotional* turmoil, have *physical* health problems. Also, places where physical events, such as a battle, has occurred, its "mark" is left on the area. Because of the geological activities at Rumbling Bald Mountain, I do not feel that this would be a good place to go for ceremony. However, it would be a wonderful place to tune into the changes that the Earth Mother is currently undergoing.

JOANNA BALD:

*Joanna Bald,* located on S.R.423 in the Snowbird Mountains in Cherokee County, is the site the Cherokees called *Lizard Place.* I consider this to be an *electrical power spot.* This is but one of the many places located throughout Cherokee County that have a mythological creature associated with them. It is my feeling that such places are not always sacred sites or vortexes, although they can be, but they *are* places where the natural earth power is quite intense. Also, because these places have Cherokee myths associated with them, and because these myths are a part of the whole body of Cherokee mythic and spiritual tradition, I feel that by going to such sites one can "tune in", if you will, to that collective body of traditional teachings and wisdom. It is like touching into the "oversoul" of the power of the sacred teachings. I can only suggest that the reader work with this theory at a couple of these locations and see what comes of it for you as an individual. The location of many of these places may be found in Douglas Rossman's book *Where Legends Live* (Cherokee Publications).

SACRED MOUNDS:

Let me digress for a moment to take up a subject that is vitally relevant to any discussion of sacred sites and natural earth energy. Not only do power spots and sacred sites found in various types of terrain sometimes have legendary and/or spiritual meaning, they often have historical significance as well. Mounds often fall into this category. Usually built as a part of ancient village sites, mounds have important archeological and historical value. Furthermore, all mound sites should be considered *sacred,* as they were almost always places where ceremonies were held. This was certainly true with the Cherokees. There seems to be some confusion as to exactly who built some of the mounds in the Great Smoky Mountains. Some say that they were not erected by the early Cherokees. But there is clear evidence that at least some of them were, as it is known that these people had certain ceremonies and procedures and purposes for which the mounds were used. Just how the Cherokees went about erecting their mounds and for what purpose is of interest here.

First, several stones were gathered and placed in a circle. In the center of the circle a sacred fire was kindled. Next, the bodies of seven (the sacred number) recently deceased chieftains were placed beneath the mounds of earth, along with other sacred objects such as eagle feathers and seven special beads, each of which were colored with one of the sacred colors. A hollow cedar log was then placed in an opening left in the mound. The log fit around the sacred fire so that it would not go out. The dirt was piled up around the log and the entire mound was finished off to a smooth texture. Then a "townhouse" (ceremonial lodge) was built on top of the mound. One man, called the *firekeeper*, remained, at all times, in the townhouse to tend the fire. The fire always smoldered below, and some say it still does. (Mooney; 1982)

Just such a place is the *Peachtree Mound* and village site in Cherokee County. Interestingly, this special place is located at a *conjunction* of Peachtree Creek and the Hiwassee River. Where rivers, streams, and creeks join have always been places many Native Americans considered sacred. The village at this site is believed to date back to the period between 8000-1000 B.C., and may have been home to the Gusili, an ancient tribe of Cherokees. (Sakowski; 1990, pg.32-33) The mound is thought to have been a ceremonial structure. It is made of stone and wood and is capped by a small round-topped mound, which itself was the site of at least three ceremonial buildings.

Another intriguing mound still stands in the town of Franklin. Called *Nikwasi*, the mound sits on the site of what was once an ancient Cherokee village and ceremonial center. The village was a place that possessed the "everlasting fire" which had tremendous significance in ancient rituals. The early Cherokees associated Nikwasi with the Nunnehi, the "Immortals", another type of benevolent spirit entities who are similar to, but apparently different from, the Little People mentioned earlier in this writing. The Immortals live(d) in the high peaks, specifically in the balds where no trees grow. (Sakowski; 1990, pg.52-53) Aside from the Nikawsi mound, the Immortals are also associated with a place called *Pilot Knob* in the old town of Kanuga on the Pigeon River, and at *Blood Mountain* in Georgia, and a placed called *Set tsi* near Lone Peak at the head of the Cheowa River on the line between Graham and Macon counties in western North Carolina. It was the Immortals who kept the sacred fire burning at Nikwasi and perhaps other mounds. It seems that the Nunnehi wished to protect the Cherokee people and their traditional ways. Legends tell that, after fasting for seven days, the people were lifted up to Lone Peak by the Immortals. Long since turned to stone, it is said that the village of the Immortals can still be seen atop Lone Peak. (Mooney; 1982) I would certainly consider Lone Peak to be a sacred site as well as an electrical vortex.

It is also worth noting that sacred fires are fairly common in many of the legends associated with sacred places throughout the world. The burning of the Yule Log, the balefires of May Day of the ancient Celts, and the fires of the sacred Sweat Lodge of the American Indians, and the fires related to the Cherokee mounds are prime examples.

Another mound site is *Kitu'hwa,* whose ruins are located some 3 miles northeast of Bryson City in Swain County that, like Nikwasi, was said to have the sacred Everlasting Fire. Mooney called it one of the seven "mother" towns. Some writers say this mound was once the major ceremonial center of the Eastern Cherokees; the place that I feel is the *"heart center"* of the entire Blue Ridge and Great Smoky Mountains region. I think that each of the mound and village sites of which I have become aware are *electromagnetic* areas and, therefore, should be considered to hold that same charge. Douglas Rossman, in his book *Where Legends Live* (Cherokee Publications) makes a foreboding comment: "Unlike the Nikwasi Mound in Franklin, North Carolina, the Kitu-hwa Mound is not protected. If it continues to be subject to cultivation (it is in a field/comment mine), it will not be long before all that remains of what was once the principal ceremonial center of the Eastern Cherokee will be lost forever."[3] This brings to mind the peril that so many sacred sites, worldwide, suffer at the hands of humans, who are motivated by progress and the relentless development of the land. I am reminded of the moral of the story of the Fisher King in the legends of King Arthur. The King, the symbol of and sovereign of the land, was lame and sick and his land was laid to waste and bare. In these modern times we have lost our connection to the land, and in doing so, we have forgotten, all too often, that the state of the land is a direct reflection of the state and condition of the people and vice versa. If Kitu'hwa is lost, forever, is this prophetic for our future....those of us who live in these old mountains? It is something to think about.

NANTAHALA GORGE:

The scenic *Nantahala Gorge* was held in high esteem by the Cherokees who called it *The Land of the Middle Sun*. It is a small *electromagnetic grid* and a *power spot* that, according to legend, was home to Uktena, the dreaded monster snake. (Mooney; 1982) Others say that it was home to Spearfinger, one of the most feared female mythical monsters in Cherokee lore. Spearfinger, a "shapeshifter", could take on any form and appear as anyone she chose and seemed to have the nasty habit of stealing the liver from unsuspecting victims. (Rossman; 1988, pg.9). Although the gorge is electromagnetic, its degree of *magnetism* is very strong. This is a wonderful place to go to be with the Earth Mother, to attune to the water spirits, for cleansing ceremonies, and for quiet time, prayer, and meditation.

WAYAH GAP:
*Wayah Gap* in the Nantahala Mountains in Macon County, is called the "Shouting Place". (Sakowski; 1990, pg.67) The early Cherokees believed this place to be the home of Ulagu, the Great Yellow Jacket; a mythic creature who also had the bad habit of stealing children! The gap is a beautiful, mature hardwood forest that is highly *electromagnetic* in its charge. Trails through it begin at Wallace Gap, located 15 miles southwest of Franklin on U.S.64.

WHITESIDE MOUNTAIN:
*Whiteside Mountain* on the Blue Ridge was once called Tree Rock. (Mooney; 1982) This is an unusual peak that boasts the largest amount of exposed rock east of the Rockies! (Sakowski; 1990, pg.87) The majestic dome is marked with deep horizontal white rock rifts across its face. Its summit reaches 4,930 feet and is relatively easily accessible. The western side of the summit is said to have been destroyed by the Thunders. (Mooney; 1982) Whiteside is located on S.R. 1107 (Whiteside Cove Road). There is a lake at its base that shows the visitor a watery reflection of the beautiful mountain. I feel that this is a sacred lake whose waters may possess strong healing qualities.

The Cherokees say that Whiteside is home to the ogress they called Spearfinger remember the crafty shapeshifter? It was she who was the architect of a great rock bridge that extended from Whiteside Mountain to the Hiwassee River near Hayesville on the Georgia border. (Sakowski; 1990, pg.88-89) A cave near Whiteside is believed by many to be the home of the Devil himself! As I see it, Whiteside Mountain is a huge and very powerful *electrical vortex* that, were it a little larger, would constitute a grid. When the Whiteside Mountain area comes up to its full power in 1994 or 1995, I feel it will become a popular vision quest and ceremonial site. When I first viewed Whiteside, I had a strong sense that there was once a secret medicine society who used the caves in the area for sacred initiations.

## JUDACULLA ROCK:

Judaculla Rock near Sylva, NC

The first power spot I visited after moving to the Smokies was *Judaculla Rock*. Prolifically etched by ancient human hands, this enigmatic rock is located less than a mile off N.C.107, where it intersects with S.R.1737 (Caney Fork Road). Follow 1737 along a well-marked 3 miles and it will direct you to the site. I consider Judaculla Rock to be a sacred site as well as an intense power spot that is highly *magnetic*. The Rock itself is an impressive chunk of soapstone that has been inscribed with strange symbols which, to date, have not been deciphered. Nor is it known who carved the stone or why. The Cherokees, who have never claimed to be the stone's carvers, have long associated it with the outrageous slant-eyed giant, Judaculla, whose footprints were alledgely responsible for the rock's mysterious marks. I, for one, do not place much stock in this legend as having any roots in truth, as legends often do. I do not disbelieve that the giant may very well have existed at one time, but the etchings predate Cherokee mythical history.

To me, Judaculla's etchings have a truly "intelligent" appearance. In other words, when I saw the rock and its crude markings, I distinctly felt that they had been put there by someone for a *specific* reason and were meant to depict a specific place, or relate some specific *message*. Theories offered over the years have suggested a simple boundary marker. However, while I concur that it may have indeed once served as some sort of a "marker", I feel, intuitively, that it had far more significance that may not have been terrestrial in its nature.

As I stood before the great stone, at least what of it is above ground, I had distinct feelings that it was a *star map*; a map of some region of the heavens, perhaps drawn in honor of and/or to indicate the actual or legendary *origin* of the ancient people who once lived in the area. Belief in their having extraterrestrial origins is not uncommon to many Native peoples, including the American Indians. The reader will recall that the Cherokees say they came to Earth from the Pleiades. The energy of the area surrounding Judaculla is generally *electromagnetic*, but I felt strong *magnetic* forces coming from the rock itself and the immediate area for about ten feet around it. I also felt that at one time there had been mounds in the area, although I saw no remaining visible evidence of them.

## HICKORY NUT GAP:

*Hickory Nut Gap* is a lovely area that comprises a small *electromagnetic grid*. The Cherokees have a legend of a warrior who was sent to fetch tobacco from the east, as the people in the Gorge had run out of the prized plant. In order to fulfill his task, the warrior had to get past the malefic Little People who were known to viciously attack anyone who tried to do so. When the warrior failed to return, a shaman tried by first changing himself into a mole so he could get past them by going underground, and then into a hummingbird so he could fly over them. Both failed. It was not until he changed himself into a whirlwind that the shaman was successful at frightening the Little People away! (Sakowski; 1990, pg.153-154)

Tobacco, a sacred plant to many Indian peoples, still grows abundantly in Hickory Nut Gap; a good place to go and gather some for ceremonial purposes. Also, due to tobacco's ability to absorb negativity from its immediate environment, it is good to keep some of its leaves in an open container in your home. According to the Cherokees, tobacco is a very ancient plant. (Mooney; 1982) They call it the Old One, saying that it was second only to the sacred and powerful ginseng. To them, tobacco was a feminine plant that can rid the body of negative energies and problems that cause sickness. Tobacco was smoked prior to sacred rituals as well as on certain on social occasions. (Katuah Journal; Issue 12, Summer 1986). More detailed information about tobacco appears in a later chapter of this writing.

## CHIMNEY ROCK/ROUND TOP:

Hickory Nut Gap is the location of several power spots and

vortexes. One is *Chimney Rock,* which drew me to it like a magnet. Called *Sohiyi* by the early Cherokees, Chimney Rock; a curious circular granite knob that has been worn to a smooth texture by rains and time, attracts thousands of tourists each year. The rock itself and the stream of water that falls into some unknown, undiscovered pool

Chimney Rock Park - Chimney Rock, NC

below, gives this power spot/vortex a strong *magnetic* charge and feeling, although it is clearly in an *electromagnetic* environment. While Chimney Rock is easily accessible during tourist season, it is usually crowded. I would suggest that any meditation or ceremony done there would best be done in the wooded area around the base of the mountain upon which the rock is located. This is a good place for meditation and for connecting with the forces of Nature.

In addition to the tremendous appeal of the terrain, curious tales have been associated with Chimney Rock. One 1896 account tells of the sighting of a "very numerous crowd of beings" atop the rock, dressed in brilliant white garments, who levitated, in unison, before the very eyes of witnesses! (Sakowski; 1990, pg.155) And that's not all. In 1811, an even more curious sighting of two groups of *winged horses,* complete with *riders,* who appeared to be preparing to do battle with one another, was also "seen" by startled witnesses. Sure enough, a skirmish did ensue with the astonished human observers claiming not only to see it, but to have heard the clashing of the swords carried by the mysterious warriors! (Sakowski; 1990, pg.156) Needless to say, both of these events and the subsequent reports must have created quite a stir among the witnesses and those they told about their experience. When I first read these accounts I was baffled. But after thinking about it for some time, I have come to think that it is possible that the "spirits" could have been ghosts of the ancient people who once inhabited the area, possibly those of the Atlantean migrants mentioned earlier in this book. But, another thought that has come to me is that they might have been angels, as angelic presences are often associated with sacred sites worldwide. *Round Top,* the mountain opposite of Chimney Rock, is also a *vortex* that has a much more *electrical* charge than its neighbor.

## MOUNT PISGAH:

*Mount Pisgah* is a powerful *electromagnetic vortex* located off the Blue Ridge Parkway in the Pisgah National Forest. The 5,721 foot peak and the surrounding area is a good area to do ceremony. While there, I sensed the presence of a magnificent Mountain Deva who dwells within the peak and serves as a sort of "Guardian" over the entire place. I distinctly detected that this beautiful and powerful being emits an energy that is especially beneficial to all members of the plant kingdom in the entire Blue Ridge and Great Smoky Mountains region. Herbs and plants from the mountain's immediate area are particularly potent and useful for sacred ceremonies, especially for healing rites.

PINK BEDS:
Located just off U.S.276 near the Slide Rock area lie the *Pink Beds*, an unusual forested bog site that is a strong *magnetic power spot*. This is an excellent and easily accessible place to go to meditate and pray, as well as for performing any kind of cleansing or earth healing rituals. *Slide Rock* is a beautiful and exciting place (but not a vortex or power spot); one that is highly magnetic in its charge.

PILOT MOUNTAIN:
*Pilot Mountain*, located in Transylvania County, was said to be the home of the Thunder, Kanati, and his family. (Mooney; 1982) I have heard stories about this once having been the site of a great cave from which all the game animals and birds originated but that was torn away by the Great Spirit and replaced by a steep cliff, punishing the Cherokees who would now have to always search for their food. While doing research for this book, however, I found it interesting, and somewhat confusing, that this same legend is also associated with Black Mountain and Mt. Mitchell. In any case, Pilot Mountain is a very *electrical power spot* that is also reputed to be the site of a Nuhnehi council house. Pilot Mountain may be reached by traveling U.S. 276 for about 5 miles from U.S. 64 at Brevard, to the Pisgah Forest National Fish Hatchery road and on to Gloucester Gap. A trail leads to the slope of the mountain. (Rossman; 1988, pg.30)

For many years, through my close association with Sun Bear, the well-known Chippewa medicine man whose "medicine" was the Thunder Beings, I gained a healthy respect for the power of these powerful Nature Spirits. And, having gained some knowledge and alliance of and with their force, I am particularly drawn to Pilot Mountain, a place that I often go to connect myself with and communicate with them. I find the Thunder Beings especially helpful in their willingness to, telepathically, allow me to know about forthcoming weather conditions, earth changes in a given area, and in empowering my connection with the Sky Country and the Sky Gods. Taking an offering to the Thunder Beings is always appropriate when visiting places such as Pilot Mountain that have legendary associations with them.

FLAT ROCK:

An intriguing and powerful sacred site located some 3 miles south of Hendersonville, *Flat Rock* is an *electromagnetic vortex* that was once an important ceremonial site to the Cherokees. (Sakowski; 1990; pg.120) Because Flat Rock was the site of hunting rituals, I consider it to be related closely to the animal kingdom and would, therefore, be a good place to get in touch with one's totem and the animals in general. For those of my readers who may be hunters, I suggest that a trip to Flat Rock prior to your hunting trip might be a good thing. Also, when visiting this site, I feel it would be good to give thanks, through prayer, for the animals that give of their bodies so that our bodies might be nourished.

PAINT ROCK:

*Paint Rock*, located on S.R. 1304 (Paint Rock Road) in Madison County, is an ancient sacred site and power spot that I feel is *electrical* in its charge. Although scant evidence remains visible, Paint Rock is painted in red images and symbols that include animals, birds, fish, and humans. Who painted them or why is not known.

Such sites are like "storyboards" that tell of the lives and of what was important in the lives of the ancestral people who drew them. I also find that such sites are good places to attune, intuitively, to those humans long gone. Their voices can still be heard and this is a way, the only way left to us, to learn about and from them.

ROAN MOUNTAIN:

*Roan Mountain* is one of the most potent magnetic vortexes that exists in the enchanted region that is the Smokies and the Blue Ridge. The magnetic power that the mountain emits is so intense that it may very well be responsible for the fact that no trees grow on its 6,285 foot summit, although they grow prolifically on all the other peaks in the area. (Sakowski; 1990; pg.207)

This powerful mountain, located in Carter County, Tennessee, and Avery and Mitchell counties in North Carolina, is near Bakersville, N.C. and Roan Mountain, Tennessee. It is one of the world's oldest peaks and, like other Southern Appalachian summits, has supported life for over 250,000 years. The winds at Roan Mountain average 24 m.p.h. year round. The potent magnetism of the mountain is evidenced by its having originated the first flowering plants above the conifers 95 million years ago! Roan preserves and maintains the most varied plants on the planet and attracts botanist from all over the world. Aside from being the site of a few battles, Roan was also a place where Indians gathered for celebrations. Legend tells that it was a result of a bloody confrontation between the Cherokee and the Catawba tribes that spilled drops of blood that later blossomed as the rhododendron flowers for which the mountain is famous. (Sakowski; 1990, pg. 208) These lovely flowering plants are now called Catawba Rhododendrons. Roan Mountain's magnetism still "gathers" (attracts), as all magnetic places do, people to it. Hundreds come annually to view the beautiful gardens maintained on the peak and to gather to celebrate the Full Moon at the time of the Summer Solstice.

Roan Mountain is the home of a powerful and beautiful Mountain Deva whose body, as it appeared to me, seemed to be composed of brilliant blue, violet, and lavender flames. Its eyes were like golden crystals, very piercing, that shoot intense rays of energy from them in a penetrating stare that was both loving and foreboding. Also, aside from its terrestrial ley connections to other magnetic vortexes worldwide, Roan Mountain has a celestial ley that extends out from its summit in a wavy-ray-like energy pattern and connects directly to the Moon. This ley receives lunar energy and the mountain, in turn, radiates lunar power to a wide area that encompasses a radius of over a hundred miles! This means that Roan Mountain is also a powerful beacon vortex. The peak is a perfect place to do ceremonies in honor of the Moon and to draw upon her great feminine power. It is also conducive to meditation, prayer, and any kind of cleansing and healing ceremonies. It is also a wonderful place for women (and men) to go for the purpose of getting in closer, conscious touch with their individual and collective feminine power.

GRANDFATHER MOUNTAIN:

Another powerful mountain vortex, also *magnetic*, is the wonderfully exquisite *Grandfather Mountain*, the highest peak in the Blue Ridge. To reach the mountain from the Blue Ridge Parkway, take the U.S.221/Linville exit at milepost #305. The mountain can also be reached by traveling south of Boone on N.C.105, or by going northeast of the town of Linville on U.S.221.

Named appropriately, Grandfather Mountain is said by geologists to be over 140 million years old, making it one of the oldest mountains on Earth! The mountain got its name because of its profile, which looks like the face of an old man looking skyward. I have heard since I was a child that the mountain is home to Grandfather Elf Spirit. When I visited there recently, I perceived and communicated with an ancient Mountain Spirit (who may have been the Elf

Spirit) whose body manifested to me as a brilliant silver-colored energy pattern. The magnificent Being gave off a continuous humming or buzzing sound, no doubt due to the pure charge of magnetism being generated and emitted by the mountain. This Being is what my Spirit Teacher, Albion, calls *The Watcher*; one whose task it has been to over-

Pilot Knob at Grandfather Mtn. near Brevard, NC

see the comings and goings of all in the area over eons of time past, and continuing, always, into the future. Nothing comes or leaves, no event occurs, without the eyes of the Great One of Grandfather Mountain upon it. This is a wonderful place to carry offerings and to do ceremony in honor of the Earth Mother and to honor and get in touch with all the mountains on our planet. It is important to note that the Native Americans, along with all other indigenous peoples of the mountainous regions of the world, realized the power of the greatest peaks. The people often made pilgrimages to the summits of specially chosen peaks in order to communicate with the indwelling mountain spirit and/or the Creator. Grandfather Mountain is a great mountain to go to for such a purpose. Before going, however, I suggest that a short period of fasting and prayer will help to prepare you for your sacred journey.

Grandfather Mountain has a particularly potent power of influence upon and relationship to the plant kingdom. Tourist literature tells us that, in fact, the Southern Appalachians, Grandfather Mountain in particular, may be the origin point of the plants in this hemisphere! This is an incredible piece of knowledge that lets us know that Grandfather Mountain is certainly a place where we can get in close touch with the plant kingdom; a place to go honor and celebrate the plants and the gifts that they give to us. It is a place that is a true pilgrimage site for all plant lovers and especially for those who work with plants that feed, clothe, heal, and assist us in our sacred rituals and tasks. It is also an indication to me that Grandfather Mountain, which is located in a highly electromagnetic environment, emits an extremely powerful magnetic force. It is perhaps the most potent of all magnetic mountains in the world. Anyone visiting The Grandfather should remember to take an offering to the mountain and to the plant kingdom.

As an afterthought regarding the plant kingdom, the early Cherokees believed that when we come across two trees that have grown together, the loop made by the tree bodies marks an"entranceway" into the Under or Otherworld. (Mooney; 1982) Also, aside from the power inherent within ginseng, tobacco, and other plants in the area, I have learned that bark from a tree that has been struck by lightning is a potent magical object which can help us get in touch with the Lightning and Thunder Spirits. A small piece of the wood can be carried in a medicine pouch and used for personal empowerment; a true gift from Nature. Just keep in mind that it is a sacred object and must be treated that way. Such natural medicine helpers must never be exploited or misused in any way for any purpose.

Grandfather Mountain is the true "grandfather" of all the Earth's mountains; the greatest, most powerful of all the elders. We should go to its summit with only love and peace in our hearts.

SITTING BEAR ROCK:

*Sitting Bear Rock*, so named because of its similarity to a bear in appearance, is an interesting *electromagnetic power spot* located off S.R.1264 near the Table Rock Picnic Area in the Linville Gorge Wilderness. This electromagnetic area is a good place to go to make offerings to the animal kingdom and/or to be in psychic contact with your totem spirit.

JUNALUSKA'S GRAVE/LAKE JUNALUSKA:

As stated in an earlier chapter, not all sacred sites or power spots are natural. A man-made sacred site is the grave of the famous chief of the Cherokees, Junaluska. He is buried alongside his wife, Nicie. (Sakowski; 1990, pg.20) A memorial marks the gravesite which is located in the town of Robbinsville in Graham County. This is a good place to go to honor Junaluska and to make prayers for all Native American peoples, particularly the elders and leaders, living and dead. Also, a man-made *magnetic vortex* is Lake Junaluska in Haywood County. This site is a vortex due to the spiritual activities that have taken place here over the years. It is a retreat center for theUnited Methodist Churches in the eastern U.S.

## BLOWING ROCK:

*Blowing Rock* is a huge cliff, 4,000 feet above sea level, that overhangs the Johns River Gorge 3,000 feet below. The rock itself is an intense *electrical vortex* set in a highly *electromagnetic* environment.

There is a legend about the rock that tells of a Chickasaw chief who was afraid that his beautiful daughter would marry a white man. So he traveled to the Blowing Rock and left her in the care of a surrogate Indian mother. One day, the maiden saw a Cherokee brave wandering in the wilderness below, so she playfully shot an arrow in his direction to get his attention. The tactic worked and the young girl and the brave soon became lovers, spending time walking through the forests and along the streams.

Blowing Rock - Blowing Rock, NC

And then a strange, ominous phenomeon ccurred. The sky turned red, signaling that the young brave must return to his people in the plains. Although the maiden pleaded with her lover to stay, it was to no avail. Torn by the inner conflict that he felt between what his head and his heart told him to do, the brave leaped from the blowing rock to his death in the wilderness far below.

The grief-stricken girl prayed daily to the Great Spirit, for the return of her beloved brave. One day, curiously, the sky turned red again and a gust of wind blew her lover back onto the Rock and into her waiting arms! It is said that since that day the wind has blown up onto the Rock from the valley below. And the incredible winds still can be felt; currents of air that flow upward from the Blowing Rock and that forms a flume through which the northeast wind sweeps with such a force that it returns light objects cast over the void. (The preceding information was taken from a tourist brochure)

Albion commented on the wind flume at the Blowing Rock vortex, saying that it is a good place to go to get in closer touch with and take offerings to the wind spirits. I am also reminded of the words of the famous Oglala Sioux holy man, Black Elk, who once said that the Voice of the Great Spirit speaks to us in the wind. Like the Thunder and Lightning Spirits, the Wind Spirit is a powerful Being whose force can be both constructive and destructive. During recent earth changes, the wind has "spoken" to us very loudly, what with the frequent hurricane and tornado activity that has occurred in the U.S. I feel that our coming to understand the "language" of the Weather Spirits is of tremendous value and a necessary part of our coming to re-connect ourselves with the forces of Nature so that we might walk in greater balance with the Earth Mother. I feel that Blowing Rock, therefore, is a wonderful spot to go to for the purpose of *listening* to the Great Spirit, and to ask for and receive guidance in our lives. The Blowing Rock is located in the town of Blowing Rock on Highway 321. There is an entrance fee to get to the Rock. The visitor's center is open from March through November, weather permitting.

CEASAR'S HEAD:

*Ceasar's Head,* located on U.S.276 southeast of Brevard is an *electric power spot* but not a full-blown vortex. This would be a good place to go for ceremony and for getting in closer touch with the Earth Mother.

MYSTERY HILL:

*Mystery Hill* brings to mind some information I channeled years ago during the writing of *The Earth Changes Survival Handbook* (Sun Publishing). Albion was giving information about the various types of vortexes, one of which he referred to as a *time warp*. He defined these as places, worldwide, which display a curious phenomena that contradicts what we normally consider natural law. The energy of these places is not necessarily negative, but it certainly confounds the mind. Just such a place is *Mystery Hill.* (I have heard that similar places exist in Oregon, South Carolina, and in other states but I have never been to any of them.)

Located on Highway 321 in the town of Blowing Rock, Mystery Hill is a place where water runs uphill, where people, when walking into the so-called Mystery House, cannot stand up straight, and where other strange things occur. Mystery Hill is now an entertainment complex that caters to tourists. It is open year round, seven days a week and there is an admission fee. I think that, if for no other reason, it is interesting to experience such a place so as to get a feeling for these planetary anomalies. Albion considers such sites to be places where a natural vortex has lost its power and has completely "inverted". He considers such inversions to be natural, albeit rare, occurrences.

MT. MITCHELL/BLACK DOME:
Please see Chapter 5.

## LOOKING GLASS ROCK:

*Looking Glass Rock* was the first natural vortex I spotted upon moving to western North Carolina. Easily viewed from the Blue Ridge Parkway, the mountain caught my eye when I saw, psychically, and felt the intensely powerful magnetic energy being emitted from it. I was startled to find a mountain that was magnetic, experiencing for the first time the fact that such mountains do indeed exist. I also perceived the presence of a wonderful Mountain Deva that seemed to hover over the summit of Looking Glass, its wide wingspan stretching out as if to wrap the mountain in a protective shell. I also perceived that this is an ancient rock that, although I do not know for sure, must have been sacred to the ancestral people of this area. Those wishing to go to Looking Glass, which I feel is a good place for getting in touch with the spirits of the mineral kingdom and for doing earth healing and personal healing ceremonies, a short trip down (Forest).R.475, turning right at the Pisgah Forest Fish Hatchery, will take you to a trail to Looking Glass Rock. (Sakowski; 1990, pg.114) It is just over a 3 mile hike to the top of the 3,969 foot summit of Looking Glass. Author Carolyn Sakowski, whose wonderful travel book *Touring The Western North Carolina Backroads* has been such a tremendous help in my research, tells how, during rainy spring and winters, the water freezes on the face of Looking Glass, resulting in its acting as a giant mirror that reflects the sheer cliffs and other features of the surrounding area. This must be a beautiful sight indeed. The Cherokees called it the Devil's Looking Glass because of its being so close to the Devil's Courthouse, a site mentioned earlier in this chapter. I also feel that Looking Glass Rock is the place where the Archangel of the Mountains resides; the Divine Presence, if you will. I have perceived this Shining One as a typical archangelic angelic Being, with great "wings" that extend out to embrace and protect the entire Blue Ridge/Smoky Mountain region. This is the One who "represents" the Creator in these old mountains. To this Being we can make prayers for peace and harmony in our lives and for our planet. I feel there is no other place in this area we can go to be in closer contact with the Great Spirit; Looking Glass is an earth "temple" in the truest sense of the word.

## COWEE VALLEY:

Located about 6 miles from Franklin on S.R.1341, the *Cowee Valley* is a small *magnetic grid* that has been called The Valley of the Rubies because of the discovery of this mineral in the creek bed. (Sakowski; 1990, pg. 61). This would be a good place to go to honor and get in closer touch with the mineral kingdom. Don't forget to take an offering.

## CAVES:

Caves are openings in the body of the Earth Mother and are, as a rule, extremely *magnetic* in their nature and charge. Living on the earth's surface does not always give us an awareness, in the truest sense, of our planet. But when we go into a cave, we become instantly aware of our environment; like being embraced and, at the same time, perhaps a bit intimidated by the depth and darkness that such places possess. When we stop and really think about it, when we go into a cave, we literally enter *into the body* of the Earth Mother. In ancient times, caves were often the sites of initiation rituals and other sacred ceremonies. I am reminded of the what archeoastronomers have named *Planetaria*.....the huge caves in Navajo country in northeastern Arizona, whose 300 foot ceilings are adorned with countless stars, painted by unknown hands of long ago. There are also the famous caves in France, they too painted by Ice Age ancestors with scenes of their daily life.

The Great Smoky and Blue Ridge Mountains are filled with caves and caverns. Caves, in particular, are nice places we can go for prayer, meditation, ceremony, and for refreshing, healing quiet time; time to be with the Earth. We must keep in mind, however, that caves can be dangerous places and proper caution and, oftentimes, permission (should the site be on private or federal property) must be the rule when entering these places. It is my understanding that you must get a permit before going into a cave in the Great Smoky Mountains National Park. The Superintendent's office for the Park may be contacted regarding cave rules, regulations, and permits. Caves can also be home for animals that may not welcome humans. It is a good idea not to go alone or, at least, inform someone else of your venture into caves or caverns, especially those located in the depths of the wilderness. The following is a list of some of the caves that I have become aware of, primarily through my study of maps and books on the area. I know that there are many other cave and cavern sites and any reader having such information is encouraged to contact me so that I might include them in the second edition of this work. Relying on my intuition (I have not gone into these places), I offer these as particularly strong magnetic power spots. I am not aware whether or not any of these were sacred to the early Cherokees.

GREGORY'S CAVE: This is a limestone cave located in Cades Cove.

BULL CAVE: This cave is also near Cades Cove.

BLOWING CAVE and RAINBOW CAVE: Both these caves are located near Whiteoak Sink.

BAT CAVE: This cave is located in Hickory Nut Gap near Lake Lure and Chimney Rock. It is open to visitors.

ENCOUNTER WITH THE FOREST PEOPLE:

One of the areas, itself a *magnetic grid,* I had not visited until late in my writing this book was *Roaring Fork,* located in the area of Gatlinburg, Tennessee. Having done much of my early work on this project through map dowsing, I had come across some spots that particularly attracted me and Roaring Fork was one of these. But there were so many places to go so that I might have my own personal experiences with the sites I was to write about, it was not until mid-June of 1993 that I, in the company of my brother, made the journey to Roaring Fork. Boy! Talk about unconsciously saving the best for last! I could hardly believe my eyes! I found myself embraced by my favorite type of landscape; virgin, damp, green forest...a playful, babbling creek....emerald moss that carpets fallen logs, rocks, and boulders....ferns....it was lovely. The beauty....the "feel" of it.....the quiet sanctity of the place almost instantly took me into an altered state of consciousness. Little awareness of the mountains was present here except for the obvious and few rather steep up and down grades and a couple of viewing sites that look out over magnificient panoramas of the Smokies. Otherwise, one is enveloped in moist, green forestland that is unmatched in beauty anywhere in the Great Smoky Mountains. My mind drifted back to a time some two years earlier when my husband and I, while working in the Seattle area, had been taken to a rain forest near Mt. Ranier. The vibrations seemed quite similar, though Roaring Fork is much more magnetic; a magnetism that penetrates into and nourishes the inner etheric and astral bodies, as well as caressing the physical one. As I said, I have always been partial to shady, misty forests, and in Roaring Fork I surely got my fill.

    Located off Highway 321, there are two ways of reaching Roaring Fork from the eastern parts of western North Carolina. The first is by following U.S.40, west, to the Gatlinburg/Foothills Parkway exit. Ride the scenic road into Gatlinburg, staying in the left lane when you get into town. At stoplight #8, make a left turn. (All the stoplights on the main street in Gatlinburg are numbered/look for the sign above each light) Shortly, you will see signs for the Roaring Fork Auto Trail. Another way is to drive across the Great Smoky Mountains National Park from the town of Cherokee into Gatlinburg. You will make a right turn at stoplight #8 and follow the signs to Roaring Fork. Readers should be aware that there are no picnic or camping facilities in the area proper, but you are welcome to picnic from your car at one of the numerous pull-off areas provided all along the drive or at a picnic park located just before entering the auto loop drive. Check with the Gatlinburg Chamber of Commerce regarding campgrounds. There are many well-marked hiking trails throughout the area; two of which lead to waterfalls (Rainbow and Grotto Falls) each of which constitute highly *electromagnetic power spots*.

It was immediately apparent to me that Roaring Fork, whose boundaries are man-set, is one of the most magnetic places I have ever been, though some of the islands and select places in the Lake District and other areas throughout the British Isles (England in particular), the rainforests of the Pacific northwest, and some coastline spots come close. Never in my life have I entered into such a paradise, one of which I am sure rivals any rainforest anywhere. Lush and green, the earthly fragrance created by the natural symphony of trees.....rhododendren thickets, hemlocks, pine, mountain laurel....and the massive old grandfather trees....the mosses, ferns, and other members of the Green Nation......the sound of the creek......the waterfalls and cascades.....makes this area one that is sure to delight the senses of anyone who loves Mother Earth. Cool, due to evaporation during the summer, the region draws you like a magnet, as I discovered....making three trips there within a ten-day period!

My first journey was purely a sight-seeing one. It was during the second trip that I really "opened" to the true energy of the place, resulting in one of the most rewarding psychic experiences I have ever had; an experience that opened my consciousness to another kingdom and its life forms. Let me explain.

My husband and I, along with two friends visiting from Florida, went to Roaring Fork on an overcast, misty afternoon. Just before our arrival, the area had been gifted with a typical summmer downpour which had left the forest smelling sweet, with gentle mists floating among the trees. It was as if we had entered the land of the fairies. Ahhhhhh....little did I know. As we wound our way through the steamy woodland, we stopped often to take in sites that were of particular interest; a stately grandfather hardwood.....a huge moss-covered trunk of a fallen tree that created a make-believe bridge leading deeper into the forest....gnarled vines that hang like great ropes strong from tree to tree.....and the babbling creeks that weave in and out of view. After a while we pulled over to park in a place just before the pull-off for the site where the Roaring Fork and Cliff Branch Creeks converge, forming the incredibly lovely Place of Ten Thousand Drips. Green ferns, moss, and hemlocks make this an especially lush and beautiful spot where the water tumbles 80 feet in 10-20 foot streamlets over Thunderhead sandstone. But where we were at the moment was no less enchanting. As I sat drinking in the sounds and fragrances, I looked up to see my husband, Scott, standing, precariously, on a large rock in the middle of the creek; his arms stretched out to help him maintain his balance! The thought of him falling into the cold water instantly flashed into my mind. Suddenly, that thought was replaced by a soft, masculine-like voice that assured me that Scott would not fall, and even if he did he would not be hurt, for this was a special, sacred place......"a place of *baptism*", the voice said......"a site holy to the Forest People". The next moment, my thoughts were replaced by a vision and within it a "knowing". I knew that I was in a place where there is an "opening".....no....many openings...into another dimension of Time/Space.....a place not unlike the Otherworld of the ancient Celts. My eyes, both my physical and psychic ones, looked around me and I saw the area where I was in a different light, literally. The flat rock where Scott was standing was surrounded by a natural rock wall and, adjacent to it, was a shallow pool. I realized this was the "baptismal pool" that the "voice" had indicated. My psychic sight showed me that where the water emptied from the pool, forming a little waterfall only inches high, was what carried all negative energies downstream. Beside where I sat there was a tree that had split in its growth to form two trunks...."a fairy tree" (according to the Cherokees).....this must be the "Guardian", I thought, of this special place. It also seemed as if the rocks and small boulders that surrounded and created the pool formed a sort of fairy ring...an aquatic fairy ring! Such stone rings(like those found on dry land throughout the countryside of the British Isles and other places throughout Europe) have long been considered by the ancient Britons and others to be sites where the fairies danced and did ceremony, as well as being "entrances" into their world, the World of Anwynn, as it was called. I was both startled and mesmerized by what I was able to consciously allow myself to perceive and "see".

Still my vision unfolded. The area was so magnetic, I was able to consciously allow what I was experiencing to continue without my intellect interferring. I relaxed even more and, again, the "voice" spoke to me: "No, you are not just imagining......this is *our* place.....the home of the Forest People....the Green People, if you wish." Hearing these words, I immediately could "see" the one who was speaking to me. In my mind's eye there appeared a perfect little elf-like being. He was about a foot high. His skin, which was covered with a soft, brown hair or thin fur, was a lovely green color. His face was perfectly formed and pleasant to look at; not unlike that of a pixie or the leprechans of Irish mythology. His eyes were like human eyes, yet brighter and had more of a sparkle. Atop his head was a "cap" made from a large leaf, I think it was a Lowrie leaf. Smaller leaves were being worn like shoes, but there was no other "clothing" on his little body. Although I am using the term "his", I actually felt that, unlike humans, these little ones have no gender. When I had that thought, he seemed to confirm it by blinking his eyes. I knew that I had intuitively stumbled across a type of Little People of which I had never known about or experienced before. These were the Forest People and this was the hub of their kingdom in this area.

As my vision of the Green One faded, I knew he was still there. I could feel the presence of his watchful eyes. I leaned my head back on the car's headrest and turned to look to my right. Near me, about four to six feet away, there was a steep incline at the base of a mountainous slope. Out of the wet reddish-brown soil grew ferns and several other typical forest plants I could not identify by name. Above them was the ever-present canopy of trees, their leaves still dripping with silvery droplets of the earlier rain shower. My mind still open, I watched as a large drop splashed onto a lacey blade of fern. The clairaudient sound that was emitted by the falling drop striking the fern came across to me like a pleasant "tinkle" that vibrated and echoed through the woods. Drops, one by one, with moments in-between, continued to fall from the trees above, hitting the leaves of the plants and ferns below. Each leaf sent out a different tinkling sound. Some were soft tinkles, while others that fell on the larger leaves made a more hefty "gong-like" sound; chimes, little bells, deep gongs....even notes that could have come from a flute and some sort of soft whistle perhaps. All the sounds vibrated for several seconds after it began. Once again I perceived the voice of the green Forest "Man" speaking to me. "What you are hearing is the sound of 'forest music'. Unlike you.....and in your world....we have no music of our own creation. We only have music when it rains....the raindrops brings us music....myriads of sounds....you are listening to a 'rain symphony'......or something like that." I knew at that moment what it was truly like to smile with my heart. What a lovely thing to know and experience. What beautiful sounds were being made by the forest symphony I was so privileged to hear.....this plant and raindrop concert. "We need moisture here in the forest for the same reasons you do...and .it is always here....it always has been. The rain spirits bring it and, with it, music. Yes, we only have music when it rains."

At that moment, Scott and our friends returned to the car. I must have seemed distracted because Scott asked if I was alright. "Yes," I replied, "but you won't believe what I have been experiencing." Everyone listened intently as I told them of my experience. As we prepared to leave, my thoughts focused again on the Forest People. In a moment the presence was, once again, there. "This area is our home. Others like us dwell in similar terrains all over the Earth. The leaves are our 'clothing'....we use them to make the 'mats' upon which we sit and sleep....we live under the rock ledges and in the little caves....in the crevices of the creekbeds and nestled in the large roots of the big trees....the asters (flowers) heal us....doorways into our world are all around here....just look...you will see them....now you will always be able to see them."

I will never forget that day. Nor will I ever forget the Forest People that I now know exist; my new-found friends. The experiences of that day helped me to lose any fear or unconscious inhibition I might have had of being willing to let my imagination soar.....to let it be the tool by which I can become aware of lives and feelings and thoughts that I might otherwise never perceive or, if I did, cast it aside as mere fantasy. I believe the Forest People are real, perhaps kin to the Little People that the Cherokees know and respect. As with all forms of life, they have purpose and they serve a role in the workings of Nature. They are born from the fertile womb of Mother Nature. They are children of the Earth Mother, the same as me and you. My thanks must go to the Creator for the invisible worlds and helpers created that fit snugly within the Divine Plan.

CONCLUSION:

To the best of my knowledge at the time of this writing, the places given in this chapter attest to the major power spots and vortexes in the Great Smoky and Blue Ridge Mountains. (The water vortexes, sacred sites, and power spots are presented in another chapter of this writing.) I have no doubt that, over time, many sacred sites have been eroded away either by time or by the encroachment of modern society. Time has a way of swallowing the past. Legends fall silent and progress tears away at our values, particularly the value regarding the sacred landscape of the living Earth Mother. It is my hope that this information, even should I learn that I have overlooked some sites known to the locals, will help to restore those much-needed values.

As my readers can clearly see, I believe that ceremony is one of the most valuable tools we have to bring about a change in our consciousness, for healing the earth and ourselves, and for getting into conscious touch with the Spirits and Elementals. In today's society we don't do ceremony much anymore. But, thankfully, those who have an interest in and who have studied and practiced the Native American traditional ways, have come to recognize both the value and the power of doing sacred rites. These are times when we are fortunate enough to have many of the Indian traditional rites open to us. We should never change to suit our own purposes, or otherwise disrespect the rites *or* the opportunity to view and/or participate in them. Such is not only disrespectful, but we have no right to do so. Most of the time, however, we must design our own rituals and carry them out in a sacred way. To help us do this, I think it is important to know as much as we can about the traditional plant, animal, mineral, and terrestrial allies and spirits of the area in which we reside.

In keeping with these thoughts regarding knowing the "allies" in the other kingdoms that live in our area, I came across this valuable information while reading a back issue of Katuah Journal made available to me by David Wheeler, a member of the editorial staff. (Katuah Journal, sadly, is no longer being published, the last issue being Summer 1993) In the Appalachians, the most potent medicine plant is ginseng, which is considered to be the "grandfather" of the underworld of roots, crawling insects, and all plant life. Ginseng is reported to be the oldest plant on Earth and was the first form in which green vegetation appeared. There will be more about ginseng in a later chapter of this book. The rattlesnake is the animal totem of the region; the Elder; "caretaker" and patriarch over all of the terrestrial plane that is above ground, and it is he who guards the entranceways to the spirit and medicine worlds of the animal kingdom. Being in harmony with and invoking the power of these two totems is an important prerequisite to the ceremonies we seek to do in these mountains. They should be honored in our prayers as we visit the various power and sacred sites and live on the land.

It is from the Thunderers that the strongest medicine power

comes. The Thunderers are always in alliance with the lightning spirits. Thunder governs by the power endowed to it by the Great Thunders. When we hear thunder, and especially when the Thunder Beings speak during a ceremony, this is a powerful omen of warning or of blessing, perhaps both, depending upon the circumstances at the time. We should remember to give thanks for The Thunders coming to us; we should utter thanks to their being present when they rumble across the mountains and through the deep green valleys. I feel that the winter Thunders always come for a specific reason, perhaps to bring us a particular warning or prophecy of impending weather in the coming spring and summer season. I remember the voice of The Thunders during the blizzard of Spring, 1993. What might they foretell? I am also reminded that many early Native Americans listened for the first claps of thunder in the Spring to know when it was time to begin their ceremonial year. Without doubt, it is important that we are in harmony with the Thunder Spirits and we should make our peace with them.

Traditional knowledge also tells us that the deer and the pilated woodpecker are powerful totems for the Blue Ridge and the Smokies. They are protectors; the caretakers, if you will, that form the protective power of these mountains. (Katuah Journal; Fall,1983) We are advised never to harm or abuse one of the animal and/or plant totems.

When you visit a sacred site or power spot and decide to do ceremony, keep in mind that ceremony is the manipulation of energy and your rites can add to or take away from the energy that is there. In places that are environmentally challenged or that have been in some way marred by humans, I feel it is good to make a special effort to do earth healing ceremonies to help repair the energy and either begin or advance the Earth's natural healing process. In any case, we must always remember to approach any area with respect. While power spots, vortexes, grids, and sacred sites are indeed special, we must keep in mind that the whole Earth is sacred. This cannot be stressed too many times. I once read a powerful statement by an unknown person that stated that we must not change one stone or even a grain of sand without knowing what good or evil will follow that act. Nothing could be more true or offer better advice. When visiting a sacred or other site, it is a sacred journey and should be approached in a sacred manner. This means that we must go with peace of mind and an open heart. We must not bring harm or do damage to any place or to another other living being who comes to us or who lives in that place. Whether you go alone or in a group, remember, please, that the Earth Mother is alive and will give to you, freely, of her power. You, in turn, can give to her of your power, a power that she can use to heal and sustain herself. Enjoy your journeys.

"Unless the sacred places are discovered and used as religious places, there is no possibility of a nation ever coming to grips with the land itself. Without this basic relationship, national psychic stability is impossible."

Vine Deloria<br>Native American author

\* A useful map appeared in the Spring 1993, Issue 38, of the Katuah Journal of Cherokee mythic sites.

[1] <u>Katuah Journal</u>; Fall Issue, 1983.
[2] <u>When Stars Came Down To Earth</u>: Von Del Chamberlain; Ballena Press/Center for Archaeoastronomy Cooperative Publication; Los Altos, California and College Park, Maryland: 1982.
[3] <u>Where Legends Live</u>; Douglas A. Rossman; Cherokee Publications; Cherokee, North Carolina: 1988.

# THE SPIRITUAL REAWAKENING OF THE GREAT SMOKY MOUNTAINS

## THE PLANT KINGDOM: THE GREEN NATION

### CHAPTER 7

"In all seasons these mountains speak to us of the beauty and sacredness."

Snow Bear

Some of Mother Earth's richest soil is in these ancient mountains. I remember when years ago I heard my first teacher say that the Plant Nation is the "green-blooded kingdom".......a kingdom without *karma* for karma begins with red blood. (Ann Manser, author of Shustah) I have often remembered this statement. More than once it has reminded me of the innate purity of the Plant Nation. It has also resulted in my developing a great love and sensitivity for my green brothers and sisters, and has motivated me to want to know more and to open more to plants, particularly to trees and their powers. I also often think back to the first time I heard Sun Bear speak about when Indians go out to gather plants they never take them all. They always leave some to continue growing and for seed. Sun Bear also taught that each group of plants of the same species, including those in a planted garden, have a "chief" among them and that, when harvesting, one should seek out and ask permission from the elder plant or chief to take from its tribe. This is evidence of the deep respect for the plants native people have. Ultimately, such a practice leads to the same respect for *all* that lives.

I am reminded of having read of the love that Carl Jung had for plants, a love that was spoken about by his close friend Laurens Van Der Post in his book *Jung And The Story Of Our Times.* ......"in Jung's case in both plants and trees he felt himself closer to the act and deed of creation than in any other physical manifestation of life. He was to call them 'thoughts of God', expressing not only the mind of the creator but also the magnetic beauty of the instant of creation."[1] Jung loved all his relations in nature; the mountains, lakes, rivers, snow, the sun and moon....everything....and often said that he could never go along with the concept that only humans were created in God's image. But his special feelings for plants and trees was legendary. One reason he gave for this was, curiously, that plants were stationary, that it was God's will that moved them and not their own. (Van Der Post; pg.69)

The Cherokees showed (and many still do) the same love and respect for their green relations and they used them for food, medicine, and physical nourishment. Out of over 800 species of plants that grow in the Smokies, they use some 400 for medicinal purposes alone. (King; 1988) Cherokee medicine men had a specific way of gathering the plants they used in their medicine (sacred and healing) work. After passing over the first three plants, he (or she) would take the fourth. After digging it up he dropped a bead into the hole as an offering. (King; 1988) The Cherokees, and I would dare say all Native Americans, believe that *every* plant has some sort of power and use if we but knew what it is. The famed healer and discover of the Bach Flower Remedies believed that the Creator taught First Man, Adam, all the uses of plants and that this knowledge has been passed down through the ages.

According to James Mooney, chronicler of Cherokee sacred myths, in the early days the animals, insects, birds, and plants could speak, and they all lived together in perfect harmony and peace. But before long humans expanded their settlements, cramping the others for space. To make matters worse, humans began to kill the animals and birds with increasingly sophisticated weapons. Smaller creatures were crushed without care as humans became more careless and contemptible. Before long the animals had had enough! So they came together in council and decided to reap revenge by bringing disease upon the humans. The fishes, birds, reptiles, and others responded in accordance to the decision which was actually intitiated by the deer and bears.

When the plants, who were friendly to humans, learned of the terror the animals intended to visit upon humanity they were very much against the evil intent and vowed to defeat the plan. Each plant, right down to the least of the mosses and grasses, decided to furnish a cure for the diseases, for they knew that if the animals were successful no human would survive. The indwelling spirit of each plant knew the cure it could provide, and a doctor need only to ask the plant spirit for the answer. As a result the Green Nation averted (and they continue to do so) what could have been the annihilation of all human beings. (Mooney; 1982)

Not only is this a beautiful and interesting story but I feel it also embodies a deep truth. It so clearly illustrates the value of plants in our lives and, in light of the environmental violence that is currently being imposed upon them (and other kingdoms as well) we are truly running the risk of not only threatening the survival of the plant nation, but ourselves along with them. Every day millions of acres of irreplaceable forests....rain forests and old growth stands....are slashed and burned to make way for crops, cattle ranches, and other profitable endeavors. With this destruction, not only do we lose the forests themselves, but who knows what cures along with them? Who can say from where the cure for AIDS, cancer, arthritis, and other life-destroying diseases and ailments may come. What seemingly insignificant weed, leaf, or root may save millions of lives in the future? Has not virtually every cure, thus far, come from the Plant Nation? It is certainly something to think about, and hopefully it will motivate us to take action against such destructive practices before it is too late.

The forests of the Great Smoky Mountains rival any on Earth. In all there are eight distinct forest types, two of which, the heath balds and the cove hardwoods, are unique in the world. (Walker,

1991) The others, beginning at the lowest altitudes, include the yellow-poplar and oak-maple, the pine-oak, the cove hardwood, eastern hemlock, northern hardwood, the unusual heath balds, and the spruce-fir. These green communities of the Smokies have thrived for ages, following a simple life and death cycle. As each fallen log becomes a part of the forest's floor it gives birth to new life from its own decaying body.

Having been born and reared on the seacoast of South Carolina I was accustomed to seeing thick forests throughout my life. The town I grew up in (Conway, S.C.) was so very rich in stately old live oaks with their moss-laden branches hanging heavy, and I have been partial to them ever since. But like others I took the old trees and woods for granted. That changed when I spent almost a dozen years in the desert and high desert of the Southwest. I grew familiar but weary and lonesome with a world devoid of great trees. Even when I lived in the alpine country of northern Arizona where the Ponderosa pine forests are beautiful, the variety and thickness of the tree stands were still short of those back home. When I moved to western North Carolina in the late fall of 1990 the trees were bare. But when Spring came I saw and lavished in the trees and forests I had missed so much! I remembered! All around me was emerald green. The moss-covered logs on the forest floor, the flowering trees and plants, the thickness of the woods, the great green canopies, and the fragrance......ah, the fragrance....the smell of the earth.....the damp, rich soil...was all so sweet. And the sounds.....the gentle, hissing sound of the rain falling through the tree canopy.......the sounds of streams flowing and of the forest alive with the songs of so many birds. It was so good to return to the East, though I will always treasure my time with the desert and rock monuments of the Southwest.

Mooney tells another story of the time when plants and animals were first created. They were told not to sleep for seven nights. (Mooney; 1982) But by the time the seven nights were over, nearly all of them had fallen asleep. Of the animals and birds, it was the owl, panther, and one or two others who were able to stay awake. As a result they were given the gift of seeing in the dark. So their prey became those who must sleep at night. Among the plants it was the trees that triumphed; the cedar, pine, holly, laurels, and spruce. Their gift was that of being green year round. It was determined that all the trees and plants must die away and/or lose their leaves every winter. (Mooney; 1982) It is interesting to note that to the early Cherokees the cedar is sacred. I am also aware that many of the evergreens are sacred to many Native American tribes.

The concept of sacred trees is an ancient one. Perhaps most prominent among the ancient Order of Celtic Druids, tree wisdom (knowledge of the power inherent within various trees) was part of the greater body of Mysteries known only to the Initiates. Passed on through oral tradition, Druid tree wisdom carried tremendous magical implications and trees were often used for divination. They believed that every tree had an indwelling spirit, which they called "dryads", that could easily be communicated with by humans. (Hope; 1987, pg.130) Basically, the Celts systemized tree knowledge in the following way: healers, guardians and protectors, and the "recorders" of and "dispensers" of wisdom. (Hope; 1987, pg.192)

Nowadays there is an intense revival of interest in and seemingly tremendous thirst for the knowledge and practices of tribal medicine people and shamans. But no pursuit of this kind can be complete without one gaining a knowledge of trees and other members of the plant kingdom. Thinking of some trees as being guardians and protectors and certainly as healers is comfortable for most, at least for those who have some knowledge or who possess a belief and experience of tribal spirituality and the ways of the shaman. It is also easy to accept that trees send out their energy to their immediate surroundings and to those who come in contact with them. But when we start thinking of trees as "recorders", this involves something more complex and requires a deeper cognizance. In her book *Prac-*

*tical Celtic Magic*, author and historian Murry Hope reminds us that trees are immobile and that, being rooted in one spot what is for some hundreds of years, they watch and record. This statement is highly reminescent of Jung's observation of plants and trees mentioned earlier in this chapter. Hope wisely points out that "their recordings are totally impartial and uninfluenced by the tides of human affairs."[2] In turn, the dispensing of this and other knowledge makes the "dispensers" extremely valuable to the seeker of wisdom.

The southern Appalachians are a perfect place to study, experience, and interact with trees, shrubs, vines, and many other types of plants, including some ancient and powerful herbs. In fact, the reader will recall that the majestic and ancient Grandfather Mountain is not only said to be the oldest mountain on Earth, but it is also the botanical womb from which all plants in our hemisphere sprang! Many of the trees and their innate power which was known by the Druids live in the southern Appalachians. The following is a nearly complete list of the trees in the area. Those mentioned only in passing and others that I chose to leave out entirely are the exotics which are not natural to the region but were brought here. Whenever possible I have given information about the innate "power" of each specimen. I have also categorized each as being a healer, dispenser, recorder, guardian, or protector. My sources for this information varies. Some is taken from two books on Celtic Magic which are either listed in the Bibliography or have been noted in parentheses within the text. Some comes from knowledge I have learned from the numerous American Indian teachers and medicine people I have been friends with and worked with through my serving as a teacher for over forty of Sun Bear's Medicine Wheel Gatherings over the past 13 years. I have also relied to a great degree upon my intuition and personal experience with trees. But whatever is the case, each source is clearly indicated. For purposes of brevity and space I have chosen to abbreviate the description of each tree. *Each of the botanical descriptions and places that they grow is taken directly from* <u>Trees, Shrubs, and</u>

Woody Vines Of The Great Smoky Mountains National Park by Arthur Stupka. (See Bibliography) I give total credit here for the botanical information to Stupka's work and therefore have not noted that every time in the actual text.

TREES:

FRAZIER FIR: Coniferous needle-bearing; grows at 500-600 feet; small cone-like flowers in Spring; also known as *balsam*; healer (because it is an evergreen). Source: Murry Hope and Albion. I might note that Albion told me that evergreens were healers long before I became aware of the Druid knowledge. I also learned that some Native Americans consider the pine as a healer and a cleanser of the aura. This accounts for why pine is often included in smudging mixtures. In addition, cedar, pine, and juniper are sacred to the Pueblo peoples of the Southwest. Murry Hope acclaims fir to be a remedy for bronchial complaints. (Hope; 1987, pg. 192)

EASTERN HEMLOCK: A large tree common at 3,500-5,000 feet and along streams and cool ravines; small cone-like flowers in late Spring; healer (evergreen). Source: Murry Hope and Albion.

PINE: Several species of pines grow in the Great Smoky Mountains. These include the shortleaf, longleaf, Table Mountain pine, pitch pine, Eastern white pine, and the Virginia pine. Each is fairly common and are found between 2,500-4,500 altitudes, and may be distinguished by the length of the needles and size and shape of its cones. Keep in mind that pine, an evergreen, possesses healing ability. Pine forests are a wonderful source of negative ions, according to author/ Sacred Ecologist, Delores LaChapelle in her book *Earth Wisdom*. (Way of the Mountain Learning Center and International College publication) And it is the negative ions that have a positive effect on the human body and consciousness.

**JUNIPER:** The Eastern Redcedar type of juniper is common in areas below 2,000 feet where limestone prevails. Juniper is a healer and is often used in ceremony by the Indians of the American Southwest.

**WILLOW:** Several forms of willow, some of them uncommon, grow in the Smokies. These include the rare white willow, common weeping willow, the uncommon coastal plain willows, the pussy willow, the common Black willow, the Dwarf greys, and the common shrub that is the Silky Willow. The Druids related willow to the color silver and the Moon and believed it gave a blessing to those who came into contact with it. This makes it a dispenser. Source: Albion. It is also important to note that, traditionally, the water willow is used by most Native Americans to construct the Stone People's Lodge (Sweat Lodge); a sacred rite of purification.

**POPLAR:** White eastern Balm of Gilead, Bigtooth aspen, and Lombary are the poplars found in the Smokies. Most of these are scarce. The poplar is a great source for renewing physical vitality, making it a dispenser and a healer. Source: Albion.

A variety of poplar known as the Tulip Poplar is one of the huge grandfather trees found in the Smokies. A member of the magnolia family, this poplar sports greenish-yellow blossoms with six petals and an orange base that provides one of the most dependable sources of nectar in the eastern U.S. Poplar honey is wonderfully edible and the bark from the smaller of the trees can be used to make carrying vessels. Bark from the larger trees was used by the early Cherokees for lodge covers and dugout canoes. The bark is also said to have several medicinal values, including being a tonic for fevers, stomach cramps, dysentery, gout, and rheumatism. (Katuah Journal; Elliott; pg.11-12)

**WALNUT:** Walnut is an uncommon canopy tree of the Butternut variety found along or near streams at low to middle altitudes. Walnut helps in spirit communication and is a dispenser tree. Source: Albion.

SYCAMORE: The American Sycamore is found along streams and at altitudes up to 3,500 feet. It is a good source of psychological strengthening, making it a healer and a dispenser. Source: Albion.
There is a wonderful Cherokee myth that tells of a time when there was no fire and the world was very cold. So the Thunder Beings sent lightning and put fire in the bottom of a sycamore tree that was growing on an island. Trying desperately to find a way to get the fire to where it was needed, the animals and birds tried everything they knew with no success. Finally, Water Spider agreed to go get the fire because she could scoot across the water. So she spun a thread from her body and made it into a testi bowl within which she placed a hot coal from the fire. Since then there has always been fire. (Katuah Journal; Winter 1991-92, pg.12)

WITCH HAZEL: Witch Hazel is a common shrub or small tree found at low to middle altitudes. The Druids associated hazel with the mind and the color orange. It was also a wisdom-keeper, making it a recorder. (Hope; 1987)

APPLE: Though a small thorny variety of crab apple does grow wild in the Smokies, cultivated apple orchards are plentiful throughout the entire region of western North Carolina. The apple was the most sacred of all trees to the Druids on the Holy Isle of Avalon in Glastonbury, England there are several ancient groves. I have been taught that the apple possesess magical qualities, one of which is the gift of immortality. The apple is a wisdom-keeper that bestows the gift of "sight", making it a dispenser as well as a recorder. Source: Albion.

ASH: The American Mountain ash is a common high altitude

tree found mostly on Clingman's Dome and Mt. Guyot in the Great Smoky Mountains National Park. The White Ash is a fairly common species found in the hemlock and cove hardwood forests up to 5,200 feet. It is a dispenser, a healer, and a recorder. The Druids believed the ash emitted love energy. It was also related to the sea and to the color turquoise. (Hope; 1964)

MAPLE: Several rather common varieties of maple flourish in the Smokies. These include the Boxelder, the Red, Silver, Sugar, and Mountain maples. Most are fairly common except for the Silver, and grow at low to middle altitudes. The maple is a powerful source of life force and will increase vitality, making it a dispenser and a healer. Source: Albion.

BUCKEYE: The yellow Buckeye is common in the northern hardwoods, cove, and occasionally in the spruce-fir forests of the Smokies. It is a dispenser. When carried in a medicine pouch the power inherent within the tree's bark is a source of good fortune and prosperity. Source: Albion.

TUPELO: Commonly known as the Blackgum, this variety of Tupelo is found in the cove hardwoods, oak, and pine stands. It is a good source of strength - physical and/or psychological, making it a dispenser and a healer. Source: Albion.

ELM: Three varieties of Elm......the Winged, American, and Slippery, grow in the Smokies, although the latter two are uncommon. The Winged Elm is found along streams at altitudes below 2,000 feet. The Elm is a source of life force and power. It is a dispenser tree. Source: Albion. I might add that Murry Hope says this tree can help remove frustrations and the difficulty that comes with trying to cope with life's problems that often result in digestive disorders. (Hope; 1964, pg.191-192)

ALDER: The Hazel Alder is a shrub-like tree that is found along streams and other moist environments up to 3,000 feet. It is a recorder tree. The Druids considered the Alder to be a tree of royalty and associated it with the color purple. (Hope; 1987)

OAK: Several varieties of oaks grow in the Smokies. These include the White, Swamp White, Scarlet, Southern Red, Shingle, Northern Red, Chestnut, Post, Black, and Blackjack. Most are fairly abundant, with the exception of the rare Swamp White Oak which is occasionally found in Cades Cove. Oaks are dispensers. The oak was one of the most sacred of trees to the Druids, who considered it to the tree of justice. (Hope; 1987) Albion feels the oak is a tree of strength and courage. This tree can also help us get in touch with the human ancestral "memories" which are held deep within the Collective Unconscious.

BIRCH: The Yellow, Sweet, and River Birch thrive in various forest environments and altitudes in the Smokies. The Yellow Birch is abundant on mountainsides, whereas the Sweet Birch is a high altitude member of the Red Oak, Chestnut, and closed Oak forests. River Birch is fairly scarce but it can be sometimes be found growing along watercourses above 2,000 feet. This tree is a dispenser. The Druids related the birch to Absolute Deity and the color white and considered it a source of pure power. (Hope; 1987)

ELDER: The American Elder is a common shrub found in open woods, clearings, on riverbanks, and low swampy areas up to 5,200 feet. This tree is a recorder. The Druids related the elder to the Triple Goddess and the colors black and dark green. They also looked upon this tree as the tree of fate. (Hope; 1987)

RED SPRUCE: Red Spruce is found at 4,000-6,000 feet and along streams, cool ravines, and north slopes; small cones; healer (evergreen). Source: Albion.

Other species of trees in the Great Smoky Mountains include the rare Hackberry, the uncommon Mulberry, several types of Hickory, the American Hornbeam or Ironwood, the fairly common Black Cherry, the common Persimmon, the common Sassafras, and several types of Beech, of which the American variety is the most common. (Stupka; 1964) Murry Hope states that the beech helps one to learn the lesson of tolerance. We can all use more of that! Chestnuts are also good for relieving worry and fears. (Hope; 1987, pg.191-2)

Spring in the Smokies brings the beautiful white and pink blooms of the Silky and Flowering Dogwoods. The mountains seem to come alive with the millions of beautiful blossoms that make the woods look like they are filled with bridal bouquets! To Christians, the dogwood flower represents the crown of thorns placed on Jesus' head at the time of the Crucifixion. Flame azaleas, which flower in late April through July, and the Mountain Laurel which blooms in May and June, add vibrant violets, pinks, and purples to nature's already spectacular Spring palette. The lovely Catawba Rhododendruns, mentioned earlier in relation to Roan Mountain, are a variety of the Flame Azaleas; an endemic shrub found at the higher altitudes above 4,000 feet. (Stupka; 1964) These add a soft pinkish color to the forested slopes and makes a late Spring journey across the Blue Ridge Parkway a memorable experience indeed.

Some time ago Albion gave some information on trees that I choose to share with my readers in the hopes that it will shed some further light on the subject. "It is our intent to speak about the nature of trees and to give some basic instructions as to how one might draw upon their energy. Trees are an integral part Nature. They are considered by some to be the strongest, most vital among all plants."

"Tree Wisdom is a subject that is far more complex than one might assume. It is a body of knowledge that contains several fundamentally profound truths. The first involves a tree's *roots*. Roots anchor the tree and is the system through which trees receive nourishment. According to ancient esoteric teachings, trees bridge the gap between Earth and Sky. Their roots go deep into the Earth and co-exist with the minerals; its trunk lives on the surface of the Earth with the animals and humans, while its branches reach up to Sky Country, making the tree a manifestation of Heaven and Earth in physical form. Because of this the tree is rooted in the physical dimension and, therefore, it partook of the Earth's mysteries and lived by the Earth's breath. But by and through its branches, the tree, symbolic as it may be, embodied the powers of the earth and heavens in one form."

"Throughout history trees have served animals, birds, reptiles, and humans. They have provided shelter, food, fuel, and protection from the elements. Because of this trees are an integral part of the Law of Cycles involved in planetary evolution. Life on Earth would not, could not, exist without them."

"Since ancient times shamans have possessed special knowledge about trees. Priests and priestesses of various orders the world over have known the medicinal value in flowering and non-flowering plants, vines, trees, and vegetables. Many have been highly skilled healers and have known the vast body of tree wisdom. Though much of this knowledge has been lost, interest in tree wisdom is being revived today. Taking some knowledge from the Druids, some from the American Indians, and some comments from ourselves, (Albion often refers to himself as "ourselves") let us consider the power inherent within seven different trees, all of which are found in your immediate vicinity [Smokies]. We begin with *cedar.*"

"The people who came long ago to this area knew the cedar as the most sacred of all trees. This was due, in part, to its aroma. It was also green year round, indicating its powerful life force and its victory over the elements in Nature. Its wood was never burned for fuel or even for ceremonial purposes. Its wood was believed never to decay for the time required for such decay was far beyond a human's life. Cedar thus possesses the power of longevity."

"Now let us speak about the oak. This tree has the power of strength, courage, stability, and steadfastness. And then there is the *hawthorn* (another sacred tree to the people of the Eastern tribes) which embodies a power that protects a human being and those within a given human household. Oftentimes a hawthorn log was placed in the home for just such a purpose."

"Ah......the ash. Shamans know that ash wood enhances ceremony and was often used to make ceremonial objects by various people. The fifth tree, hazel, has an ancient and powerful relationship with water and the water spirits, as does the sixth tree, *willow*. Willows possess the power of cleansing. Also.....hazel branches are often used to make dowsing rods for the wood is naturally drawn to water. When one is in their presence, both the hazel and the willow can help one to turn within and tap their inner resources. Hazel encourages vivid psychic experiences, past life recall, and unlocks the sorts of things that are locked in the human unconscious. Being with the willows can help one to gain a firmer grip on reality. It also helps abolish deception and delusions within the human mind."

"The seventh type of trees we wish to mention are the *spruce* and *fir......the evergreens*. It is a miracle that these two trees live so far to the south; a gift deposited here by the glaciers of eons ago. Evergreens are healers. They give harmony and balance to the areas within which they live. They are also cleansers, as is the holly, the catawba, the laurel, and the rhododendrens. They can detoxify the emotions by your being in their presence."

"With this information in mind, let us consider a simple way to draw upon the energy of a tree. To do so you must personally interact with the tree. First, you must gain permission to make physical and psychic contact with the tree. If, for example, you need physical vitality, go out into the forest and seek out an oak. When you have found the tree or grove of your choice, announce who you are and why you have come. Then stand or sit and be quiet and still. Ask, especially if you are in a grove, that the tree give you a sign to let you know it is open to having its energy tapped. A sign might be that, on a still day, a breeze begins to blow. Or a leaf might fall at your feet, or a bird or other animal might light or climb onto the tree. When you have received a proper omen, give the tree(s) your offering which can be anything you choose it to be. Next, center your attention on your solar plexus. Imagine that 'threads' made of pure light are going from your body into the ground to the tree's roots. See the threads wrapping around the roots completely. Then, with your breath, pull the moist, sticky astral life force of the roots into your solar plexus. You may experience some reaction such as a slight smell or taste of chlorophyll, or a strong 'earthy' fragrance. You might also experience a mild sweat, even in cold weather. None of these reactions should result in any long-term physical or emotional discomfort. Take only what energy you need from the tree. You should feel the charge of energy almost instantly. When you are finished, withdraw the 'threads'. Afterwards, spend three to five minutes sitting at the base or leaning against the tree in order to 'ground' yourself and allow the tree's energy to flow through your conscious mind and physical body. This exact procedure may be used for drawing upon the inherent energy within all kinds of trees and plants. However, the only time of year the energy of the trees is low and, therefore, not the best time to have their energy drawn upon is when the pigmentation is changing (Autumn). Once the leaves begin to drop it is alright to go ahead, the tree permitting of course."

"Finally, we wish to share some thoughts that also concern trees; thoughts that were part of ancient tree wisdom. A tree that has been struck by lightning is a powerful one indeed.....especially if the tree survives the strike. Its wood must never be burned. Such trees can be tapped for enhancing and empowering your spiritual and shamanic activities such as prayer and ceremony. To the Druids, an oak that had been struck by lightning was considered an *avatar* among trees. A small piece of its wood was the most precious of all sacred objects for it held special sacred powers. When one becomes truly observant of trees, one can look at the body and shape of a tree and *know* intimately the energy of the place where it grows. A tree's shape and distortions will always reveal the energy of the land. Stunted trees, for example, will always show that the water source is either not good or is sporadic. Trees that have been distorted by the wind indicates strong wind phenomena in the area that might be harmful to humans and not be a suitable place to live. Truly *see* the forest the next time you go. Do not just look. Observe the dignity of your plant brothers and sisters. See the diversity of the trees. Take note of the the textures, colors, and forms of the trees. Trees and other plants do not move around like animals and humans do, thus they know their environment intimately. And as you walk among the trees, if you should come across two or more that have come together to form one tree, know that you have come across a sacred phenomena. The Druids called them 'fairy trees'. Where these are present there is an 'opening' into another dimension......an 'opening' into the world of the fairy folk. Such a tree is the gnarled *guardian* of that special place."

Albion's words brought me into a deeper sense of kindredship with trees and with the forests. It is to the forest I go for refuge, prayer, and strength. It is to the trees I turn for companionship when all else seems to fail me. Collectively the trees in these old mountains form some of the most beautiful and powerful forests on Turtle Island. In fact, some of the plant life in the region is extremely rare. The incredible variety of plants found in the Smokies is due, in part, to the abundant rainfall; about 80 inches a year, providing some 900 million gallons of water to the area. (Walker; 1991, pg.31) As stated earlier, "the Great Smoky Mountains are home to more than 1,570 species of flowering plants, 10 per cent of which are considered rare, and more than 4,000 species of non-flowering plants."[3]

The blue haze that gives the Smokies their name, the varying elevations, and the orientation of the mountains provides conditions that also play an important role in the way things are here. Each season offers spectacular beauty we can both see and *experience*. Old growth forests, one of our most valuable natural resources and one of the most threatened, are generous to humans in their gifts of food, shelter, medicine, and counsel. (Katuah Journal; Fall, 1991) In fact the old growth forests in the Smokies are some of the best and most renowned of their kind in the world.

The technical definition of an old growth forest is that it is a pristine woods with large trees and an uneven canopy, as well as an abundant floral counterpart and the presence of logs in various stages of decay. Such woods are relatively free of human disturbances and human "vibes", if you will. Examples of old growth stands in the area include the Gregory Bald Trail which starts at the Parson's Branch Road leading out of Cades Cove, and the Jellystone Park Campground area between Gatlinburg and Cosby, Tennessee. Remember........spending time in any forest is a relaxing, cleansing, healing, and all around empowering physical and spiritual experience. And when you go into the woods don't forget to take an offering of your choice to the Green Spirits of the Forests.

According to Albion's teachings the plant kingdom is purely *magnetic* and therefore possesses *all* the qualities of magnetism. These include increased perception, intuitiveness, receptivity, femininity, natural healing energy, as well as calming and relaxing capabilities. Physically, it will lower the blood pressure, calm the nerves, slow the heart rate, and generally relax the body. Magnetism operates primarily on the alpha level and during the dream state. Being in the forest promotes relaxation of the mind and body and this allows us easier access to the soul. It "opens" you up, so to speak. When one is open, one can receive information, be taught, be healed, and get into more conscious contact with the inner feminine and become much more *aware* of not only what is within ourselves, but also of that which is in our environment which we so often overlook and/or simply take for granted. When we are in this frame of mind and feeling we recognize that we are a part of the environment and it is part of us. We are no longer negatively objective. We can experience being brother or sister to the trees, the animals, stones, sky, and the mountains themselves. It is this level of conscious awareness which also tunes us in to the forces and spirits of Nature and is one of the, if not *the*, first steps towards becoming a true shaman. This state of awareness also allows us to not only listen to the voices of Nature, in this case to the trees and plants, and allows us to transmit and receive knowledge and feelings from the same. How else are we to benefit from the "dispensers"? The magnetism of the Plant Nation helps us to be able to intuitively recognize the "protectors" and "guardians", and which plants and trees will give us the healing we need on whatever level we need it most. Certainly such "knowing" and healing occurs, to some degree, no matter what. But when we are consciously open and intuitive, then the intensity, depth, and power of what can transpire is greatly increased.

Cherokee shamans were the possessors of a natural and/or acquired ability to communicate with the Great Spirit and other spirit beings and forces in their environment. Plant medicine, along with certain ceremonials, affected successful treatments. The sacred formulas were known only to the medicine people who were called upon when a particular condition became extremely serious or prolonged so as to warrant "divine intervention". Plant Medicine is a practice that is difficult to find available among today's Cherokees, but I know it is not totally extinct. A complete guide to Cherokee plant lore may be found by studying the booklet <u>Cherokee Plants: their uses - a 400 year history</u> by Paul B. Hamel and Mary V. Chiltoskey. The following are a few comments I would like to share concerning certain plants that serve extremely valuable purposes to tribal peoples and that play a role in their spiritual life.

Though not all that common, *mistletoe* is found at altitudes below 2,500 feet throughout the Smokies. (Stupka; 1964) A parasitic evergreen, mistletoe usually grows in the high branches of oaks, blackgum, and other deciduous trees. The plant flowers in late autumn but caution must be taken because the white sticky berry-like fruit is poisonous. I have known for a long time that the Druids considered mistletoe to be sacred and an intimate part of their spirituality. In addition, according to author Murry Hope, (Hope; 1987, pg.143-144) tells us that the plant was related to the color white, probably due to its potent berries, and was gathered during a rather complex ceremony. On the sixth day of the Moon two white bulls were sacrificed. After a feast the mistletoe berries were then received by "a white-clad priest who held out a white cloak for its reception."[4] When drank, the Druids believed the mistletoe made barren animals fertile and that it was an antidote for all poisons. Some say that mistletoe also served as a phallic symbol, (Hope; 1987, pg.144) while still others suggest that it signifies the end of an age and therefore" the inevitable hand of time that decides all."[5] I find this latter comment most interesting, especially in light of the intense, changing times we are living in today. I have often gathered mistletoe to use for ceremonial purposes, particularly in rites that have to do with fertility and prosperity. I simply lay a sprig on my altar. I also feel that due to its phallic connotations, mistletoe would be a good plant for men to use during ceremonies and/or place on their altars for the purpose of personal empowerment and for increased power and fecundity. Of course the plant should never be ingested without proper knowledge or instructions for its internal use from a qualified herbalist. One last thought regarding the sexual energy inherent within mistletoe is its relationship to the kissing tradition at Christmastime, a tradition that probably originating at the old Yule and winter solstice.

    The *apple* is another plant that has long been associated with the Druids and ancient Celts. Remember; the word Avalon, the age-old name for the Holy Isle in Glastonbury, England means *apple*. Apple farming is a main industry in western North Carolina and surrounding areas. If the apple does indeed possess magical qualities and powers in its core and seeds which when cut form a five-pointed star, then the abundant presence of the numerous orchards here must surely add a enchanted air and magical energy to the area.

While this book is not intended to be a complete herb manual, I do feel it is important to investigate the fact that the southern Appalachians, namely the Smokies, are rich in edible plants. If my Spirit Teacher's prophecy about the reawakening of these old mountains is true, and I believe it is, then the effect this resurgence of power will have on the plant kingdom bears repeating. Albion said the plants' potency will increase tremendously. Those that have medicinal value will heal the body more thoroughly, and their power will be quick and sure. Those plants that have magical properties will have those properties increased, resulting in their magic becoming much more effective. Ceremonial plants will lend their energy toward empowering rites and rituals in ways unknown and unexperienced for many generations. Surely the plants we take into our bodies will nourish and heal us and, yes, physically empower us in stronger and perhaps more definite ways.

From an informative article in the Katuah Journal in the Spring, 1990 issue, I learned about some of the edible plants in the Great Smoky Mountains. Credit for much of the following information must go to the article *Food From The Ancient Forest* and its author Snow Bear.

Available in April and early May, the Trout Lily is a yellow lily that emerges from two greenish-brown mottled leaves. The leaves, preferably those with no blossoms, may be added to salads or steamed as a green. The same is true for Toadshade Trillium whose blossom-free leaves are said to have a sweet taste.

Spring Beauty and Rue Anemone are often found together in large patches on forest slopes. The tubers are small and may be used in soups and stews or simply steamed. Solomon's Seal is available through August and both the leaves and roots may be eaten. In the Spring the lower leaves are advised, while the higher leaves are best later on. They too are supposed to be good in soups and stews.

Ramps, or wild leeks, are the only vegetable I have known festivals to be centered around. (Ramp Festival is held in the Spring in Waynesville, N.C.) Having a pungent garlic-like fragrance and a taste that is similar to a very strong onion, ramps are good in soups or as simply eaten as greens. They are also said to be good blood purifiers.

Broad Leaf Toothwort may be found growing on creekbanks. Its leaves have a taste similar to horseradish and may be used to flavor other foods or eaten alone.

Sun Root is a perennial sunflower with large edible roots which may be eaten or ground into a high-protein flour. The roots can be harvested at any time when the ground is not frozen. (Katuah Journal; Summer, 1986, pg.14) Other edible plants surely grow in the area and the reader is encouraged to learn all you can by researching available books and by seeking out classes. Snow Bear advises that plants for food should not be taken from hiking trails or other heavily trafficked areas. When digging for plants, one should also take great care so as not to cause any damage to the environment. Again, it is important to keep in mind that when we eat the plants from any region, we are ingesting the energy of the land and, to quote Snow Bear...."in the mountains where the beings of nature live in undisturbed patterns of the long-ago forest attunes our bodies with the seasons and climate of Katuah, our minds with the beauty of Katuah, and our hearts with the nature spirits of Katuah."[6]

Since embarking upon the Native American spiritual path, the good Red Road, over a decade ago, I have been fully aware of the tremendous importance Indian people place upon tobacco. Aside from its being used as part of the smoking mixture for sacred pipe ceremonies, I have seen it used for offerings in the holes where the willow branches are placed during the building of the Sweat Lodge, and for offerings to the land, the Sun, and to the Spirit Keepers of the Four Directions. I have also seen it made into tobacco "ties" that are used for speaking prayers into prior to or during the Sweat and Medicine Wheel Ceremonies. Sun Bear taught that tobacco, the most sacred of all plants, has the ability to absorb negativity. Many people like to hang a "hand" of dried tobacco leaves on a wall in their home, or place some in each room in a bowl of basket for that purpose. After a few weeks the tobacco should be removed and replaced with fresh dried tobacco leaves. The old leaves may be given to the Earth as an offering, or simply buried so the negativity can be absorbed into the earth's body and recycled.

When you think about it there may be no other plant, with the exception of those used for food, that has had a greater, more profound effect upon humans than tobacco. And that affect has been both positive and negative. We are all painfully aware of the negative results of using chemically-treated tobacco products such as cigarettes, cigars, and snuff. I once heard Sun Bear say that the white man's sacrament (wine) is killing Indians (alcoholism is rampart among Indian people), while the red man's sacrament (tobacco) is killing whites. We must be ever mindful of tobacco's power when that power is abused. This is true, of course, for all plants, minerals, sacred objects.....in all things.

Like all Indians, the Cherokees believe(d) tobacco to be an ancient and powerful plant. They called it Old One or Tsal Agayun'li. (Katuah Journal; Summer 1986, pg.12) Although there are two types of tobacco, one with yellow blossoms and the other with pink, it is the old plant with yellow blossoms that was used for ceremonial purposes. This is an extremely potent plant that some say contains as much as ten times more nicotene than the commercial tobacco used today. Yet another account says there is no significant chemical differences between the ancient and modern commercial tobacco, and that any mind-altering effect involved is probably due to the Cherokee practice of mixing the Old One with sumac. (Journal of Cherokee Studies, Spring 1978, pg.76)

The Old One was grown in a sacred manner that, as far as I know, is unique to the Cherokees. "A medicine person would go into the woods and plant the tobacco seed in a spot he would clear by burning. They might plant eight or ten of these patches so that no one would see the tobacco. The tobacco would lose its power if someone else saw it growing."[7] That tobacco was then used by medicine people for both medicinal and magical purposes. Smoking prior to rituals, councils, vision quests, or Sweats, petitioned the smoke to carry the people's prayers to the Great Spirit. The Old One was also used to help the Cherokees fast because it suppressed the appetite and helped ward off sleep, which must have made it particularly useful prior to and during vision quests. But the Cherokees and other tribes used tobacco for many purposes which included sacred incense, a cementer of oaths and promises, binding the warrior to the war path, confirming sales, for seeking omens, and prior to and during sacred ceremonies. On these occasions, I assume the tobacco was smoked.

Tobacco was also used as an agent of curing, the Cherokee term for healing. An interesting example may be seen in its being used in treating snakebites, *whether the bite occured in reality or in a dream.* (Journal of Cherokee Studies, Spring 1978, pg.77) I have heard all my life that chewed tobacco, when applied topically, would treat insect bites as well as muscle and joint pains. Also, a pipeful of Old One can help a toothache. (Journal for Cherokee Studies, Spring 1978, pg.78) Other uses include its being used as a diuretic, an antispasmodic, expectorant, and for treating ramps, locked-jaw, colic, dizziness and fainting, as a poultice for boils, and many other ailments. (Hamel and Chiltoskey; 1975, pg.59)

When tobacco is to be used in a sacred manner, not only is it planted in a special way, but after harvest, the Cherokee medicine man put the plant through a special process called "re-making". (Journal for Cherokee Studies, 1978, pg.80-81) This process involves working a special medicine on the tobacco to further "charge" it so it can be used for healing and/or some other sacred purpose. At dawn the medicine man takes the tobacco to a creekbank and, facing east, recites a secret text over it. He then chews the plant to give it his own medicine power. Next, he spits the cud into his left hand and kneads it in a counter-clockwise rolling motion with the right. On occasion, cedar leaves or seeds, or shredded grapevine might be added to the tobacco so it might be used for other specific purposes. The "remade" tobacco is carefully guarded by the shaman who considers it useless if it is smoked by anyone other than the person it was remade for. (Cherokee Journal; Ethridge, 1978, pg.76) If there is a plant that is used more among Indian people, I cannot imagine what it is. Robert F. Ethridge, in an enlightening thesis on tobacco and its use by the Cherokees, eloquently carries the use of tobacco out of the physical world and gives us a glimpse of the higher realms of "medicine" when he states: "As a person turns, in the smoking ritual, and faces each direction, he addresses and shows his recognition and awareness of the universal essence which is symbolized by that cardinal direction; and as he emits the sacred smoke towards that point, he strengthens the spiritual umbilical cord to the universe thus linking his power of thought and being to the overwhelming and omnipotent powers."[8]

Having clearly established the importance of and uses of tobacco, there is another ancient one that cannot be overlooked. That one is *ginseng*. Although usually associated with the Chinese and the East, ginseng does have a western home in the shady parts of the forests in the Great Smoky Mountains. Acclaimed as the oldest of plants, ginseng is clearly a "grandfather" plant; the elder plant, if you will, that some have named "the old man of the mountains". (Katuah Journal; Fall 1984, pg.19) Like other Indian people, the Cherokees saw ginseng as having a human shape, thus it's being called *a-tali-kuli*....."little man, powerful healer". (Katuah Journal, Fall 1984, pg.19)

Ginseng is rivaled only by the oaks and the giant trees of other species in terms of its age. And not only did the Indians respect and cherish their human elders as wisdom keepers, but they also afforded the same respect to the elders of all kingdoms, including the plants. With pale roots that branch into an uncanny human likeness, each ginseng plant reveals its age through its leafy top that grows above ground. Each year a new stalk is formed off the "age stalk" of the previous year, leaving a small scar that is shaped like a horse's hoof. (Katuah Journal, Fall 1984, pg.19) The uses for ginseng are many and varied. Among them are its reputation for relieving anxiety, decreasing susceptibility to infection, and fatigue. All of these are of interest to herbalists whose task it is to use ginseng and other plants to doctor and heal. Whenever I encounter the Old Ones, no matter what kingdom within which they reside, I am reminded of them as "Wisdom Keepers". These are our teachers. Another of the elder plant and tree teachers is the sturdy bristlecone pines. I learned about them some time ago and saw them growing in solitude atop the San Francisco Peaks; sacred mountains to the Hopi and Navajo people in northeastern Arizona. First and foremost, such ancient plants and trees have the power of *longevity*. They are *survivors*. And to me this is the most obvious lesson they can teach us; steadfastness, commitment, longevity, and survival. Ginseng calms and in today's world that is a state that many of us find rare. Our lives are filled with schedules, deadlines, and obligations to the point that relaxation has become a rare commodity that is, sadly, often pursued with the aid of alcohol and other dangerously addictive drugs. Just think, ginseng has chosen these old mountains as one of only two "homes" on Earth. For me mountains have always embodied energies that only words like "majesty", "glory", "strength", "power", and "freedom" can define. Ginseng's roots go deep into the soil here. It has undoubtedly found a way to absorb the energies embodied within these great mountain peaks......a way to store these energies and the power of the soil of the Earth, and the light from the Sun, and to give them to humankind. We receive the energy of the plant by experiencing its healing effects from the plant's subtle power. As it goes into our bodies we are blessed with its calming power......with a restoration of health......we are assisted in being vital and completely alive. We must give thanks to our brothers and sisters in the Green Kingdom. We must give thanks for the nourishment and healing they give to our bodies, and for the ecological role they play so that all others might live. Plants give us our breath. Without them we could not be.

*Corn* is another plant that has long been and continues to be of tremendous value to Native Americans. Called Mother Corn by the Hopi and other Pueblo tribes, cornmeal, corn pollen, corn husks, and the kernels themselves have found their way into both the practical and spiritual lives of tribal folks.

Among the early Cherokees there were those shamans who could, like many Earth and Nature-sensitive people today, speak the elemental language of the plants and minerals, as well as that of the thunders, the wind, and rain spirits. To the Cherokees the corn spirit was the ancient goddess they called Selu (pronounced Seh-loo); the same Old Woman who is known and honored by people the world over. In Africa she takes the form of millet; in the Orient she is rice. She has been called by many names; Ishtar, Demeter, and Ashtoreth, to name but a few. In the Americas and Great Britain she is corn. Wherever she grows Mother Corn is an incredibly adaptable and enduring plant. Whatever the conditions with which corn is faced, it will adapt and grow. Remarkably, maize (another name for corn) has been reported to retain its food value for over a thousand years! (Katuah Journal; Spring 1984, pg.1) When I read this I was reminded of a gift of anasazi beans that were given to me some years ago by my friend and colleague, Brooke Medicine Eagle. Brooke said these were beans that had been retrieved from an ancient village site and that could still be planted and grow into the same plant that were put into the soil by ancestral hands so long ago! I kept them in a sacred bundle and think of them as sacred.....as a link to the dim past that is a part of the human collective memory that is common to us all.

Called Agawela (pronounced ag-ah-WAY-la) by the Cherokees, corn is one of what most Native Americans call the "three sisters"; corn, beans, and squash. The Cherokees planted these three in a symbolic manner; corn first. This allowed one plant to rely upon the other in providing proper environmental and growing conditions, and so that each might encourage the other's growth, and to protect each other from the harm of insects and disease. (Katuah Journal; Spring 1984, pg. 84) Corn was always planted in sevens and the planting was done by women. (Katuah Journal, Spring 1984, pg.84)

In the overall life of corn.....the planting, growth, and harvest.......the Cherokees, like other tribal people, saw the natural cycle of life reflected. Planting and harvest times were (and are) the most important occasions in the life of the people, and were always marked by sacred ceremonies and social festivals. With the Cherokees it was the Corn Dance. Held for the purpose of giving thanks for a good corn crop, the Corn Dance was done by both men and women, and was/is highlighted by a pouring of corn from a basket or bowl which, like the cornucopia, symbolizes plenty. (French and Hornbuckle; 1981; pg.133) Through our spiritual relationship with Mother Corn, we come into touch with the powers of fertility and growth. For humans, these include the power of such things as motivation, action and activity.....doing and being....the will to survive, to achieve, and to press forward and to create.

In an issue of Katuah Journal (Spring, 1990), I came across a beautiful commentary which stated that "plants have been in communion with the human species for thousands of years. Only recently with the advent of the mechanical age have we relegated them to muteness. In the past, plants have shared their information with us. They have told us which of their species is good for medicines, for healing, for food, for making musical instruments. They have whispered songs to our ancestors...and poems. They have sent dreams our way...and visions. We share a sacred bond with plants. Our 'world' depends on their world. Even from the beginning, photosynthesis was essential in allowing our species to eventually occur. Today, sharing the earth's atmosphere....exchanging oxygen and carbon dioxide with each other....reflects how intimate our connection is. In fact, at the heart of the relationship is 'exchange'. We receive nourishment from plants...not only for the physical body, but also for the psyche. They daily reveal to us visions of rootedness, stillness....vibrancy and life. The plant world holds the memory of what a bioregion is...what it looks like in its wholeness. By listening to the plant world, we can tap our own underlying sense of what this region could be...how to re-inhabit Katuah. As we begin to become more conscious, we see how power and creativity can be used to enhance and celebrate the heartbeat of the ecological processes here rather than disrupt or destroy it. The plant world can participate in a vital way in this internal reawakening. Plants can partner with us as we explore integrating the human species into the ecological symphony of this place. Whether in a garden, in a grove....or in wilderness, we can begin to develop a co-creative partnership with plants, where once again, they speak to us." (Author unknown)

We must give thank to the plants whose leaves, stems, flowers, berries, and roots contain the ingredients of those wonder drugs that heal the diseases of the body and mind. Yes; we must remember to thank them all; the members of the great forest communities.....trees, shrubs, woody vines, flowers, fruits, berries......all plants that live in the water and on land.....we give thanks to each one.

[1] Jung And The Story Of Our Time; Van Der Post, Laurens; London, England: 1976.
[2] Practical Celtic Magic; Hope, Murry; Aquarian/ Thorsons; London, England: 1987.
[3] Great Smoky Mountains: The Splendor Of The Southern Appalachians; Walker, Steven L; Elan Publishing; Scottsdale, Arizona: 1991.
[4] Practical Celtic Magic; Hope, Murry; Aquarian/ Thorsons; London, England: 1987.
[5] Ibid
[6] Katuah Journal, Issue 27; Spring 1990.

[7] Journal Of Cherokee Studies; Vol. III, No.2; Museum of the Cherokee Indian/Cherokee Historical Association; Spring 1978.
[8] Ethridge, Robbie F.; Journal Of Cherokee Studies, Vol.III, No.2; Spring, 1978, page 84.

# THE SPIRITUAL REAWAKENING OF THE GREAT SMOKY MOUNTAINS

## FOREVER FLOWS THE SACRED WATERS

### CHAPTER 8

"In the beginning, there was no water. Earth was too hot to let it happen. But as the molten core of the planet slowly settled, producing a viscous mantle and a thin outer crust, it covered itself in a dense cloud of methane, ammonia, and carbon monoxide. In time, this poisonous early envelope boiled off into space and a new atmosphere began to develop - one dominated by hydrogen and carbon dioxide and, eventually, by water vapor. Then it rained."[1]

Lyall Watson
The Water Planet

Water is the physical manifestation of pure *magnetism* on our planet. It is the life-giving, life-sustaining power that touches the human psyche in unique and profound ways. It soothes our jangled nerves and tranquilizes our souls. Renowned author and philosopher, Lyall Watson, tells us ..... "water, one of the simplest and most common chemical compounds on our planet, is also one of the most mysterious and awe inspiring substances we know."[2]

Water manifests in a variety of forms: snowflakes, raindrops, sleet, hail, the morning dew, and as the misty, enigmatic fog that gently caresses the landscapes shrouding it in mystery and turning its forms into enigmatic shadows that both frightens and makes us curious as to the structures they conceal. It is water that comprises the great seas..... and water that rushes over precipices to form roaring waterfalls like Yellowstone and the magnificent Niagra. Water can be both gentle and violent. It can give birth to and destroy life with equal power. Yes.....water is most often pleasing to our eyes, and both soothing and troubling to our hearts.

It is water's task to flow. Stand by a rushing stream sometime and watch. Whatever may be in its path....limbs, boulders, tree trunks....still the water makes its way. Water will go over, around, under.....whatever it takes...it continues to flow, bound to an urge to return to the ocean....an urge that is as ancient as the Earth herself. Water teaches us the lessons of continuity, of commitment to our course, of action versus stagnation, and of flexibility. As water flows it carries everything downstream. Indigenous people point out that this constitutes a cleansing and purification. Flowing water brings change........and......water heals.

As one drives or hikes through the Great Smoky Mountains, water is omnipresent. It is not uncommon to see massive rock walls leaking with life-giving fluid. Little cascades trickle playfully over rocks that wear garments of emerald-colored moss. Large cascades flow.......waterfalls thunder.....everywhere there is water. There are springs where water bubbles up from deep within the earth, and according to those who are most sensitive to Nature, these springs bring spirit power up to the world. And as an unknown author stated in the Katuah Journal (Summer, 1984, pg.18)...... "water rises from the Underworld of our own subconscious....plunge into the inner parts of ourselves and explore the deepest pools within...." Water helps us to get in touch with the soul of all that lives in Nature; it is the very blood of Mother Nature herself.

Throughout the Blue Ridge and the Great Smoky Mountains the waters flow, countless drops joining together to form mighty rivers and peaceful creeks and rushing streams. Some of these drops of liquid nature meander lazily through the forested valleys, while others roar triumphantly over ancient boulders and through scenic gorges, creating mischievous white rapids whose voices sing the endless songs of erosion and time. Beautiful waters fall over gaps and moss-laden ledges, creating numerous waterfalls that are the generators of powerful natural healing energy. Lakes and pools lie still and silent in the fragrant woods that delight our senses and repair our wounded bodies, minds, and hearts with their peace.

As one might suspect, the Cherokees valued certain water sites and held them sacred or special in some way. In a monthly cleansing that was somewhat symbolic of a woman's menstrual cycle, Cherokee men use to strip and plunge into the cold waters of a river or stream as an act of healing and purification at the time of the new moon. (Katuah Journal; Fall/Winter, 1990) In Cherokee tradition streams were believed to be *trails* that led into the Otherworld or Spirit World. The reader will recall that the Cherokee say that, following seven days of fasting and after obtaining a qualified guide from within the ranks of the Little People, humans were allowed entrance into the other dimensions of reality. Streams formed the roadways they followed. Also, most of us have had the experience at one time or another in our lives of going to the coast and being soothed as we listened quietly to the rhythmic crashing of the waves upon the seashore, or knowing the peace that came over us as we sat by a bubbling stream or quiet pond. Water has a tranquilizing effect, so it would seem, on the human psyche and that can translate into balance on all levels of our being. Those of us who have grown up near water, especially the ocean, will remember the constant background sound of the sea. I remember that when I left home to go to college, it took me a long time to be able to fall asleep, a fact which I soon realized was that I missed the resound of the Atlantic that had so long been a part of my world. Jung believed strongly in the affect one's environment had upon the human psyche, himself having been born and reared on the banks of one of the tumultuous falls along the Rhine.

Water has always held an integral place in the performance of sacred ceremonies. In many tribal cultures babies were (are) taken to the water to be named. In Tibet the greatest of the prophets looks into a small sacred lake to see into the future. Shamans and medicine people have gone to the water over the ages for divination. Since the time of Jesus, Christians have been submerged in a act symbolic of rebirth in the baptismal pools of churches and in natural rivers worldwide. Water has moistened the tips of the fingers of many priests and priestesses who, in turn, touched many a human brow in blessing. The Cherokees say that water was the second to be created after fire; evidence of its being one of humankind's most ancient helpers. (Katuah Journal; Fall/Winter, 1990, pg.18)

Bodies of water were treated with great respect by our ancestors. In ancient Egypt there is the Nile; in India the sacred Ganges; in the American Southwest the mighty Colorado, sacred to the peoples who live along its banks; sacred rivers all over the world that embody the divine Water Spirit.

I encountered one of the most intriguing and unique water myths in the Fall/Winter 1990 issue of Katuah. Referred to as the "Long Human Being", the collective waters in the Great Smoky Mountains is believed to form a human-like figure. The head of the figure is in the mountains, the torso spreads across the bottomlands, and the feet stretch into the ocean. The Long Human must be kept whole at all cost, or otherwise the damage done will reflect damage to the ecosystem's chances for survival. Needless to say, if the land goes, we go with it. There *is* already environmental damage be done to the Smokies. All the better reason that the source and extent of that damage must be faced and turned around before it is too late.

In addition to those of the Cherokees, the worldwide body of myths is filled with stories of the supernatural and sacred powers of springs and wells. One of the most interesting studies I have ever undertaken involves the so-called *"water cults"* which are believed to have originated over 5,000 years ago. "Water symbols have been found on many goddess and other figurines from south-eastern Europe, dating from the period 6000-4000 B.C., this probably being the earliest evidence for water cults so far discovered. Researchers have found examples for water worship in most of the major civilizations of the world, including ancient Egypt, classical Greece, Troy,

Babylon and ancient Rome; and there is ample evidence of water worship continuing until the recent past, and perhaps even being practised in the present, among many groups of people, such as the Australian Aboriginals, the American Indians, and by some African peoples."[3]

There can be little doubt that our general attitude regarding water has degraded into one of abuse and taking it for granted. Like with our relationship with the land, we seem to have lost touch with water. Wells and springs that were once considered sacred have been abandoned to fall into ruin and decay. The oceans and rivers are being polluted by industrial wastes that are being dumped into them without conscience at an alarming rate. We have lost our sense of awe towards water. Not only do we think that an ever-constant, clean supply will always be there, but that in fact having clean water is everyone's right! We want clean water to be guaranteed while we continue to vote in candidates, buy products, and endorse industrial behavior that guarantees that we will not have the very thing we demand! Is there a better definition of insanity? I think not. It is only during times of drought or the breaking of a water main do we realize how dependent we are upon water and how absolutely essential it is for our crops, animals, and our own human lives.

But, again, we have not always been this negligent or apathetic. Strong evidence exists which indicates that in times past our ancestors sited their various temples, standing stones, and stone circles such as Stonehenge, near water. Famed author and megalithic site historian Aubrey Burl pointed out that ......"Where an avenue of stones is associated with a stone circle it almost invariably leads from a source of water, indicating the importance of water in the ceremonies that took place in the rings."[4] The tradition of giving gifts to the "spirits" of wells and springs was always a part of the sundry rituals that were once performed at sacred water sites, wells in particular. Thankfully this practice has never ceased completely, as it is still a rather common practice in the British Isles and with various tribes of

Native Americans to this day. Water has also often been associated with the ancient Mystery Schools and priesthoods known to the ancients, as well as with magical worlds, many of which were said to be islands that were known by a variety of names. One of the most celebrated examples is the ancient Isle of Avalon and its priestesses who were called the Ladies of the Lake. The enchanted lake was a "doorway" into the Otherworld; the World of Anwynn. Along with otherworlds, priests, and priestesses, water has long been linked with the Moon, no doubt due its effect upon and relationship with the earth's tides. So it would seem that water is, at least in part, a major part of the "key" to our being able to enter into other worlds beyond our own; magical worlds.......timeless......eternal worlds where the Supernaturals reside.

In all of Nature I find nothing more empowering than the sight and sound of a thundering waterfall! Throughout my travels I have sought them out; Yellowstone, the mighty Niagra, the turquoise falls in the Grand Canyon, the powerful Dry Falls in the Cullasaja River Gorge, and the sacred Snoqualmie Falls in Washington state. Each has it own unique character and setting, but they all have something in common: *power.*

Some three years ago during a visit to the sacred Snoqualmie Falls I was "shown" a vision of one of the most magnificent sights my psychic sight has ever afforded me. While making an offering of sage to the slender, misty falls, the image of a magnificent golden Water Deva unfolded before me. Its body stretched the entire length of the high falls and appeared as if it were clad in a "robe" woven from flaxen-haired threads saturated with glistening water droplets. The willowy undulating Being's eyes were like dark yellow discs that flashed beams of light all around the immediate vicinity of the waterfall. Never had I perceived such a creature. I knew it was the indwelling Spirit of the Falls. Since that time, when visiting any waterfall, I have been able to "see" the deva there, and have found them to seem to be open to my presence. They are healers. They are the distributors of and the regulators of the energy of the falls they inhabit.

The early Cherokees believed in the power of waterfalls. The people went to the waterfalls for fasting and, after a time, were said to be able to pass through the falls. Falls were known to be "doorways" that opened into a world called Nunnehi (pronounced Nuh-NAY-ha). (Katuah Journal; Fall/Winter 1990, pg.18)

Keep in mind that *all* waterfalls are *electromagnetic*, and often constitute extremely powerful vortexes. Even though the water itself is totally magnetic, the kinetic energy generates a tremendous charge of electricity in the water that results in the entity that is the waterfall being electromagnetic. Also, because the element of water is involved and the fact that most water sites are magnetic, waterfall sites are excellent places to go for cleansing and purification ceremonies, and for assistance to look within yourself for the purpose of meditation, prayer, and self-discovery. Spending prolonged periods of time near water can produce vivid dreams and intensify other types of psychic experiences such as astral travel, guided imagery, vision quests, and creative visualization. In addition, some have reported having experienced past life recall at magnetic sites.

Cherokee legends are filled with many incredible tales of water monsters. With the possible exception of the Indians in the Pacific Northwest and the ogres of the Hopi and Zuni in the Southwest, I have not encountered so many monster stories among any Native Americans. Cherokee water monsters included Dagwuh-i, a giant fish (Rossman; 1988, pg.40); Dotsiye or Dotsi, a water serpent who lived in a deep hole (Rossman; 1988, pg.37); and several Uktenas who frequented a deep hole in the Oconoluftee River (Rossman; 1988, pg.35), to name but a few. Available sources suggest that most, if not all, of the specific sites associated with these aquatic ogres are either a part of lost knowledge, or have been covered up and/or destroyed by modern dams, man-made lakes, and the like. But they did exist if in no way other than in legend. Perhaps, at some time in days long past, these mythical beings were real. Or maybe they were actual life forms whose size was exaggerated to make the point that they embodied power of the rivers, lakes, and streams of these old mountains. Maybe both. It is difficult to know. But what can be known for certain is the respectful relationship all tribal peoples have had for ages with the waters of their regions. Water cleansed and healed, purified and baptized. It flowed into and touched every life in every kingdom. It gave life. It gave power. Now, as then, it falls to upon the earth as gentle summer rain and as the torrential downpours that have washed the land clean since time began. Sadly, many of the legendary aquatic sites known by the Cherokees have been the victims of dams and other forms of "progress" imposed upon the land by human development activity.

Unless otherwise stated all the water sites listed below are good places to go for meditation, healing, earth healing ceremonies, cleansing and purification rites, prayer, assistance for entering into altered states of consciousness, and simple quiet time. As with terrestrial power spots, vortexes, and sacred sites discussed earlier my list is not necessarily complete. It reflects the places I have been drawn to over the last three and a half years. Other aquatic sites that my readers may be aware of should be added to the list and I would appreciate being made aware of them. For assistance in directing readers in the most concise way possible to reach the water sites listed I have relied on maps and two books I used for research: <u>Waterfalls and Cascades Of The Great Smoky Mountains</u> by Hal Hubbs, Charles Maynard, and David Morris (Panther Press) and <u>Touring the Western North Carolina Backroads</u> by Carolyn Sakowski (John F. Blair, Publisher) I have put the locations in my own words. The physical and spiritual descriptions are the result of my own excursions to these places and my experiences there.

SACRED LAKE:
In a delightful little booklet entitled <u>The Magic Lake: A Mysti-</u>

cal Healing Lake of the Cherokee, author Tom Underwood retells the ancient story of a magical lake whose location was secret except, perhaps, to some of the medicine people. It seems that a hunter shot and wounded a black bear. Realizing the bear would soon die, the hunter tracked the wounded bear for several days. After finally spotting the bear, the young man fell asleep. Shortly, he awakened to see "a beautiful lake from which a gray mist was ever rising."[5] The bear, who was swimming in the lake, was immediately healed of his wound. The boy knew he had found the magic lake the Cherokee storytellers had told about. He was instructed by the Creator never to reveal the lake's location, and if he did the bear and deer would vanish forever!

We can, of course, accept the story of the lake that heals animals as just that; a story. Or we can stretch our imagination a bit and believe it is a real place. After all, magical places of all kinds have long been a part of historical, cultural, and spiritual lore all over the world. Perhaps there is an element of truth contained within these myths that we are not aware of or simply overlook. Certainly to think that they are real is relegated to mere superstition these days. But in the conflict that arises between arguing about what is real and what is myth often causes us to either miss or deny the reality of the *energy* or *spiritual power or entity* the myth defines. Whether this or any other sacred lake exists now or ever did exist is something readers must decide for themselves.

Versions of the Cherokee sacred lake story vary. I heard one which is likely an account of the same lake that Underwood describes but that has a decidedly different twist. The story tells of a invisible sacred lake, Atakahi' or Adagahi; a healing lake of purple water where the animals went to be healed of their wounds and illnesses. No humans were allowed to go to the lake except for one wounded warrior who was so pure in his heart, he was allowed to there to be healed. Even so the warrior was instructed never to reveal the lake's location. But he did not keep quiet and as a result the lake was rendered forever invisible to human eyes. Yet another slightly different version does not tell the warrior's story, but says that the lake's purple waters can be seen....."at dawn by one who has fasted and keep a night-long vigil."[6]

The location of the astral lake is said to be on the northern boundary of Swain County between the headwaters of Bradley's Fork and Eagle Creek. But another direction has it being "westward from the headwaters of the Oconoluftee river in the wildest depths of the Great Smoky Mountains, which form the line between North Carolina and Tennessee, is the enchanted lake of Atagahi."[7] Two lakes? Two opinions? Most likely the latter is true. I for one believe that the lake did and still does exist on the astral plane. I feel its *energy* can still be detected. Going to the areas mentioned or an area that you feel drawn to and spending time, particularly overnight, could very well result in one being able to travel to the sacred lake in the dream state. I must say that I have felt the energy presence of the sacred lake whenever I have gone anywhere near Clingman's Dome.

Another similar water site, also reported to be a pond of purple water that has now disappeared, is supposed to have been located at Raven Ford on the Oconoluftee River in Swain County. It too was known as a healing site. (Rossman; 1988, pg.44)

DRY FALLS:

From the astral plane to our physical journey, we begin at a powerful waterfall which is easily accessible. Located off U.S.64 in the Cullasaja River Gorge in Macon County, *Dry Falls* is one that you can walk behind on a paved walkway provided to view the falls closeup. Unless crowded, it is also a great place to do prayer and ceremony. Although every effort has been made to make the area safe for visitors, caution should be exercised. Waterfall areas are extremely slippery and one should never climb or go outside protected walkways or paths. Keep in mind that most falls sites are crowded during tourist season, particularly this one.

On the first of my many visits to the Dry Falls *electromagnetic vortex*, I had a vision of the powerful Water Deva, the indwelling spirit who embodies the energy of the falls. This wonderful, ancient Being appeared before me in a human-like form that looked like an undulating mixture of gentle pink and lavender light that towered well above the falls. Its eyes were like deep blue crystals afloat in pools of clear blue water. A lovely iridescent pastel-colored rainbow swirled in a rotating spiral that seemed to come from the base of the falls, swept up to enshroud the Deva's entire body. I felt a tremendous sense of compassion emanating from this wonderful Being who emitted a soft, gentle sound that reminded me of raindrops falling upon the leaves in a forest; a sound that, although distinctly less audible I could hear it above the physical roar of the falls themselves. When visiting a waterfall perhaps you will "tune in", and within the quiet of yourself allow space for the devas to appear to you. I have found that my relationship with these Great Ones enhances my sense of kindredship with all in Nature.

ARAKA FALLS:

I first learned about *Araka Falls*, also known as <u>Raven</u> or *Kalunu Falls*, from Cherokee elder Walker Calhoun. He did not tell me of its specific location, saying only that the falls and the area surrounding them are sacred. It did not seem that Walker was reluctant to reveal the location of the falls. It was more like he assumed that I knew. I, on the other hand, was hesitant to ask where the site is, assuming that if it was something I should know he would tell me. He did mention a place which he called the Raven Cliffs as being nearby; a place where "bad stuff" was taken and buried or was sent, he said. It doesn't sound like a place where one would wish to go unless it would be to do an earth healing ceremony and, even then, one should be given permission and guided by an elder or someone who is familiar with the place. Interacting with such places, though well-intended, can get you into more trouble than you might be able to handle! I chose to mention this place only to let readers know that there are places that are not positive and special knowledge and caution should be gained before going to or interacting with them.

## BRIDAL VEIL FALLS:

Located on U.S.64 near Dry Falls, *Bridal Veil Falls* is a place where I feel very close to the nature spirits; the earth, air, and water Elementals. There is a small shallow cave just beneath the falls, but it is not big enough nor is this a very private area for meditation or for doing ceremony. I do not feel that Bridal Veil is strong enough to be a vortex but it is an electromagnetic spot from which you can get a good dose of healing energy.

## CONESTEE FALLS:

*Conestee Falls,* a rather unique double aquatic electromagnetic vortex, consists of two 110-foot waterfalls. The falls are located on private property about 7 miles south of Brevard in Transylvania County. This is a marvelous healing site.

## ELK FALLS:

*Elk Falls*, which I feel constitute a very ancient *electromagnetic vortex,* are located on S.R.1305 on the N.C./Tennessee state line at Elk Park, N.C.

## ENLOE CREEK AREA:

This is a small but highly *magnetic grid* located in the Great Smoky Mountains National Park between the Oconoluftee and Raven Fork areas.

## INDIAN CREEK FALLS:

*Indian Creek Falls* is located in the Park near the Deep Creek Campground.

KATHEY FALLS:
*Kathey Falls* is located on Bear Wallow Creek just south of U.S.64 in Transylvania County.

LOOKING GLASS FALLS:
Located on U.S.64 in Transylvania County, *Looking Glass Falls* is usually crowded with visitors year round. A walkway leads down to the base of the falls. Trying to view the falls from other areas and climbing through the woods above them is dangerous and is strongly discouraged. This is a powerful healing site and a place I go often to pray.

MOUNT TOXAWAY FALLS:
Located off U.S.64 near the road to Mount Toxaway Lookout Tower in southern Jackson County, *Mount Toxaway Falls* falls slide down a 300 foot series of smooth rocks and small ledges, creating a rather spectacular and beautiful sight.

NICHOLS COVE BRANCH FALLS:
The area around *Nichols Cove Branch Falls* comprises a small *magnetic grid* within the large Slickrock Wilderness grid in Graham County. The larger grid contains several waterfalls and cascades, all of which are good places for prayer and quiet time.

QUEEN FALLS:
*Queen Falls* is located in the northeastern-most corner of Macon County in the Nantahala Gorge area.

RAINBOW FALLS:
*Rainbow Falls* is located in Transylvania County on the Horsepasture River. (There is also a Rainbow Falls that is inside the Great Smoky Mountains National Park that is equally powerful) The trailhead leading to the falls is a 5 and a half mile round trip hike

along Cherokee Orchard Road near my favorite place in the Smokies, *Roaring Fork*. Roaring Fork, Rainbow Falls, and Grotto Falls may be reached from the Tennessee side of the Park. Roaring Fork is *the* most powerful *terrestrial magnetic grid* I have ever experienced. It is also the sight of the Place of Ten Thousand Drips, an incredible cascade that falls some 80 feet over and through various rocks and crevices before emptying into the Roaring Fork creek.

STILL HOUSE FALLS:

*Still House Falls* are located just north of Lake Toxaway. You can get behind these falls which form an *electromagnetic vortex*. Again, exercise extreme caution.

WHITEWATER FALLS:

Located on the Whitewater River off N.C.281 near the Jackson and Oconee county lines, this area around *Whitewater Falls* comprises a small *magnetic grid* that contains several cascades. The falls themselves constitute a 411 foot high *electromagnetic vortex* and are said to be the highest waterfall in the eastern U.S.

YELLOWSTONE FALLS:

*Yellowstone Falls* is located near milepost 418.3 on the Blue Ridge Parkway.

MOONEY FALLS:

*Mooney Falls* is located on F.R.67 near the trailhead for the Timber Ridge Trail in Macon County.

BIG LAUREL FALLS:

*Big Laurel Falls* is also located on F.R.67 near the Timber Ridge trailhead in Macon County.

LOWER and UPPER CULLASAJA FALLS:
Both of these fantastic falls are located in the beautiful Cullasaja River Gorge along U.S.64. The gorge has become a special place for me. Its energy relaxes my body but stimulates my mind. The reader will recall that the gorge was a sacred place to the early Cherokees and one need only visit once to know why.

SLIDING ROCK:
Located on U.S.276 in Transylvania County, *Sliding Rock* is an unusual waterfall that flows happily over a 60 foot long granite water slide into a 6 foot deep pool. This is a good place to get into the water and flow with it! Here you can get in closer touch with the water spirits. Don't forget to take an offering. Sliding Rock is a power spot but it is not a vortex.

Sliding Rock near Brevard, NC

## MIDNIGHT HOLE:

*Midnight Hole is* a place I feel is an especially powerful *magnetic vortex* site. It is a huge pool that measures some 80 feet across and is 15 feet deep, and is actually composed of two falls. You can get to Midnight Hole by following the Big Creek Trail at the Big Creek Campground which can be reached by taking the Waterville exit off I-40.

## RAMSAY CASCADE:

Located in the Park, *Ramsay Cascade* is 105 feet in height! It is a difficult 8 mile hike to the falls which I feel is an *electromagnetic vortex*.

## ABRAMS FALLS:

Located in Cades Cove in the Park, *Abrams Falls* is an powerful *electromagnetic vortex*.

## MINGO FALLS:

This magnificent waterfall on the Qualla (Cherokee) Indian Reservation. It drops 180 feet, splashing over many ledges and rock shelves as it goes. Located off the Big Cove Road to the Mingo Falls Campground, Mingo Falls is a powerful *electromagnetic vortex;* a special place to go for healing and meditation. Be open for the Water Deva there. It is an especially beautiful one.

## INDIAN CREEK FALLS:

Located above Deep Creek Campground, *Indian Creek Falls* forms a strong *electromagnetic vortex*. It is a good place to go for ceremony, particularly ones that have to do with healing and re-centering yourself.

CONCLUSION:

I remind you that this is a list is of the waterfalls I have either visited and felt a special connection with, or sensed through map dowsing their particular power. A complete list of waterfalls and cascades in the region of the Smokies may be gleaned from a thorough reading of the two books mentioned earlier in this chapter.

RIVERS:

The early Cherokees held the rivers in high esteem and believed them to be, in some ways, prophetic. Let me explain. As I related in an earlier part of this chapter, I discovered in an issue of the Katuah Journal that a Park Ranger tells about what the Indians said regarding the rivers being the "Long Human". What I neglected to tell my readers then is that the legs, arms, and torso of the Long Human are very now diseased. But thankfully the head is still alive! The "disease" no doubt refers to damage humans have done by the polluting and plundering of the air, land, and waters in the area. The people who tell of the Long Human say that at all cost we must keep the head alive for when, and if, the head dies we all die! We would do well to keep this prophecy in mind when we see the rivers, and remember to visit them and use them in a sacred manner. I feel that most of the rivers mentioned here form *magnetic grids*. Some were considered sacred by the Cherokees.

NANTAHALA RIVER:

The beautiful *Nantahala River* was revered by the Cherokees who associated it with several creatures who are prominent in their legends. (Rossman; 1988)

HORSEPASTURE RIVER:

The *Horsepasture*, unlike some others, forms an *electromagnetic grid* due to the presence of its numerous waterfalls and cascades that include *Rainbow Falls, Drift Falls, Stairway Falls,* and

Windy Falls. The river itself and the immediate area around it is a wonderful source of healing energy. I feel its water can heal when applied to the physical body.

## OCONOLUFTEE RIVER:

The powerful, yet gentle *Oconoluftee River* runs through the Cherokee Indian Reservation and the Great Smoky Mountains National Park. It constitutes a strong *magnetic grid*.

## PIGEON RIVER:

The *Pigeon River* crosses the boundaries of both N.C. and Tennessee. Sadly, ecological reports claim that the river is being polluted and legal action has been filed to force a cleanup before it becomes permanently damaged. I feel this river is a *magnetic grid*.

## SPRINGS:

Keep in mind that springs bring water up from deep within the body of the Earth Mother and from the mysterious invisible Underworld. This brings the supernatural and spirit power into our world so we might have access to it. Readers are advised to take measures to make sure that the water in any of the springs you visit is safe to drink and/or get into. The location of any springs, particularly sacred ones, that are not mentioned here would be appreciated.

## SHATLEY SPRINGS:

Located off Shatley Springs Road off U.S.221, the water from *Shatley Springs* has been claimed to work miracles on the physical body.

## HOT SPRINGS:

The *Hot Springs* is located in the town of Hot Springs in Madison County on Highway 25/70.

MILL SPRINGS:
*Mill Springs* is located where U.S.108 intersects with N.C.9 in the town by the same name.

MOODY SPRING:
*Moody Springs* is located off S.C.107 near the Moody Springs Picnic Area. Visitors can still use the springs.

RAINBOW SPRINGS:
*Rainbow Springs* is located off U.S.64 in the Standing Indian Campground area.

CREEKS:
SHOOTING CREEK:
Located on U.S.64 in Cherokee County, *Shooting Creek* was sacred to the early Cherokees who said it was once a place where they went to fast so they might be able to see the Little People and go beneath the waters to be with them. (Mooney; 1982) I feel that the creek is a rare *magnetic* "sound" vortex (a place where spirit voices may be heard) and that the voices of the Nunnehi can still be heard there today.

POOLS:
BOTTOMLESS POOLS:
Located in the area of Lake Lure in the scenic Hickory Nut Gap, these three sacred pools are a powerful *magnetic vortex* site. The pools are bored deep into one of the earth's most ancient rocks. This is one the most potent magnetic site I have encountered in western N.C., even though I feel the pools' power is being drained off by tourists and the fact that a fee is being charged for admission into the pools area.

The location of other eddys and pools may be gleaned from Douglas A. Rossman's book <u>Where Legends Live.</u> (Cherokee Publications; 1988)  I again propose that there must be many more pools and springs in the Blue Ridge and Smoky Mountains of which I am not aware. All of them, unless known to be polluted by some sort of industrial or agricultural wastes and toxins, should be good healing sites. Keep in mind that in these times of major planetary change, and because so much of our waters *are* polluted, it is advisable to know the waters of a given area before you drink of or bathe in them. Being in touch and in harmony with the water spirits is a necessity if we are to have a better relationship with and understanding of our Earth Mother. This includes our being thankful, daily, for the water that flows into our homes to serves our human needs. Above each of the water faucets in our home my husband has placed a small sign to reminds us and our guests to remember to give thanks to the water spirits here. Always remember to take an offering to the water spirits of all the waterfalls, creeks, streams, pools, and rivers. And it is always good to keep in mind that when water flows, it takes with it the negative energy we have asked to be removed from our bodies, minds, and souls. With the water flows away our troubles and pains; downstream with all the other debris. I believe that the Full Moon is a very potent time to go to the waters for healing. Make prayers whenever you go for the replenishment of the waters and to the Spirits of the Waters for the health of the Earth Mother, and for your own healing and balance.

[1] The Water Planet: A Celebration Of The Wonder Of Water; Watson, Lyall; Crown Publishers, Inc.; New York, New York: 1988.
[2] Ibid.
[3] Scared Waters; Janet and Colin Bord; Paladin Books; London England: 1986.
[4] Ibid.

[5] The Magic Lake: A Mystical Healing Lake Of The Cherokee; Underwood, Tom B.; Cherokee Publications; Cherokee, North Carolina: 1969.

[6] Sacred Myths Of The Cherokee/Sacred Formulas Of The Cherokee; Mooney, James A.; Charles and Randy Elder-Booksellers; Nashville, Tennessee: 1982.

[7] Where Legends Live: A Pictorial Guide To Cherokee Mythic Places; Rossman, Douglas A.; Cherokee Publications; Cherokee, North Carolina: 1988.

Table Rock

Mt. Mitchell

## CONCLUSION:

For the past thirteen years I have pursued knowledge and empirical understanding of Sacred Ecology from several perspectives; as student, writer, and teacher. During that time, with the loving and informative efforts of my spirit teacher Albion, I have written three books on the subject and taught numerous seminars and workshops throughout the United States and England. I have also led sacred journeys, which I think of as *pilgrimages,* to power spots and sacred sites throughout the American Southwest, Alaska and Hawaii, England, Scotland, and Egypt. Two of the trips I made in partnership with the late Sun Bear, famed Chippewa medicine teacher who passed into spirit in June of 1992. Sun Bear and I had many things in common, but none so pertinent than our love for Nature. And no single person did more than Sun Bear to draw attention to the pressing need humans have to re-connect with the Earth Mother. Sun Bear felt deeply that time is running short for us to regain a better understanding of our planet and all our relations with whom we share a home. He believed that our very survival hangs in the balance. My personal focus and contribution, however great or small it may have been thus far, toward helping to fulfill this need has been to explore and teach of the earth's living energy as it manifests at and through the many power spots, sacred sites, vortexes, grids, and ley lines, worldwide. *The Spiritual Reawakening Of The Great Smoky Mountains* is offered in the spirit of serving as another contribution to that end.

During the early years of my study of the *soul* of the planet I quickly realized that it was of primary importance to recognize and identify sacred sites, vortexes, and leys so that when we make special trips to these places or encounter them in the normal course of daily living we might truly experience the Earth Mother's living power. As time went by, however, I came to realize that the *whole earth* is sacred and the importance of this truth. Understanding this helps cultivate an attitude that helps change our values regarding all in Nature. I felt a strong need to devise a single, workable system of knowledge and practice that could serve the purpose of enhancing human awareness of special energy sites and the "ordinary" landscape no matter where on earth we may be at any given time. I knew that system must enable us to open our inner eyes and hearts to the earth and all the lives who live upon her skin. The system I devised and its practical application is recanted earlier in this writing, and it is hoped that the reader will use it to construct a quality relationship with the land.

When my husband Scott and I moved from Sedona, Arizona where we lived for over ten years to western North Carolina in November of 1990, I began a study of the Cherokees and other indigenous peoples of the area. I have long had a tremendous interest in the beliefs and relationship with the other kingdoms of life held by Indian peoples. What I have learned about the Cherokees, thus far, I find to be extremely compelling. Although their traditions were/are similar to other tribes with whom I am familiar, there are some Cherokee spirits and legends I find unique. I have made every effort to share what I have learned about these people and their spiritual/religious tradition in this book and to inform my readers of the sources of that knowledge. I am certain that because my time here is relatively short, my knowledge of the Cherokees and their old ways but scratches the surface of what there is to be known. It is my hope that what I have learned and shared here will inspire readers to pursue a greater, more in-depth knowledge and, most importantly, to seek a true *understanding* of what is learned. Gaining an awareness of the Cherokees and honoring that knowledge can go far in helping to assure that the tradition will not die.

My personal relationship with the Great Smoky and Blue Ridge Mountains began in my early teens when I attended summer camp and vacationed here. At that time I did not have the appreciation for nor the understanding of the Earth that I have now. Returning to the east and living in these old mountains has truly been, and I trust will continue to be, an opportunity and a blessing. I have come to know these mountains intimately. My relationship with them is a direct result of the application of Albion's system of knowledge that I call the *Life Energies*. My putting this system into practical use has helped me gain special knowledge of the land, waters, and the ability to identify the nature of the natural planetary energy that is here. In short, it works for me and it can work for you.

Yes, the mountains here are beautiful. They stimulate our senses and inspire our souls. But, physical beauty aside, these ancient ones possess a special essence, an essence that reaches deep inside and stirs the human psyche in their own unique way. The Smokies are our *Grandfathers;* the oldest mountains on Turtle Island. Tribal peoples the world over have a deep and abiding respect for their elders. From the elders there is much to learn. And as we learn we grow as human beings. We become better people; more aware, more conscious, and more conscientious.

Now, in this time of planetary change, these Old Ones, these elder mountains, are once more awakening to their full physical and spiritual power. For all who live here, in each individual kingdom, this is an auspicious and fortunate time. Those who visit here can also participate in, albeit short term, and contribute to the *awakening* and come to know these Grandfathers in an intimate way.

Most people tend to view earth changes as a fearful, negative time. Perhaps this is due, in part, to our tendency to focus primarily on the geological upheaval and fitful climatic shifts, some of which can be frightening, that occur during such times. But this is only the physical part of what is going on. Certainly physical events trigger psychic and even archetypal events that affect us on every level of our being. But the fear subsides when we shift our focus from the purely physical events that earth changes involve, and come to view these current planetary changes for what they really are: *a positive process of events that will ultimately result in the dawning of a new day and time for ourselves and the Earth Mother.*

Once Albion made me aware of the *awakening* that is presently occurring in the Great Smoky Mountains, and after my move to the area, I began the research and explorations that led to this book. What I have written upon these pages reflects my own personal awareness and understanding, to date, to the geology, history, and culture of the area. As stated earlier, my knowledge is far from complete. My relationship with the Smokies and Blue Ridge Mountains is an ongoing affair. In light of this I feel that what is shared in this writing represents only a prelude to more knowledge and experience yet to come. It is my hope that I will be further informed by those who read this work and by those who have lived here longer than I about the land, the history, and legends of the places I have mentioned and others of which I am not yet aware. We learn from each other. This book is not presented in the spirit of its being the only or last word. Rather, I offer it as *a travel handbook that contains a way* that one might approach a better awareness and understanding of these grandfather mountains. It is my sincerest hope that my readers will take the Life Energies information and apply it to other places in the world for the same purpose: *the cultivation of a closer more intimate relationship with the Mother Earth and Nature.* Time is critical. We have no time to waste. We must not allow ourselves, as individuals and as the collective human family, to remain in ignorance of the vital life force of our planet. Is it time for us to learn and to take the fullest possible advantage of the knowledge of the traditional ways of the American Indians. We must come to understand that *all* life is sacred. We must begin now to cast aside the political, social, and individual values and policies that place the earth and all that lives in danger of extinction. We must begin to apply the *"right to life"* consciousness to all our relations and, in doing so, come to understand how each life form is a vital and necessary part of the ecosystem that is Earth. Is it not time for us to abandon the orthodoxy that places humans in *dominion* over all the kingdoms of life and that insists that humanity and human life be valued above all others? Is it not time for us to cease the oftentimes blind sanction of the reckless abuse of our natural resources for the idol of profit?

Throughout this writing I have stressed the importance of our doing earth healing ceremonies at every opportunity that avails itself for us to do so. By extending ourselves in this way and by holding healing, reconstructive thoughts, we and Nature can begin to live in harmony again. Perhaps there are those who will read this work who know precisely how to go about doing such a rite. Others will not. For them I offer the following instructions how one might perform a simple ceremony designed to help you get in touch with and pay honor to the Spirit Keepers of the Four Directions, how to invoke the spirits of the various places you visit, as well as the entire bioregion. Conscious communication with the living forces of the land is a prerequisite to healing. Although I have learned about and done several such ceremonies, I have chosen one that was presented in the Katuah Journal (Issue 6; Winter 1984-1985). My heart-felt gratitude goes to the staff of Katuah for allowing me to reprint this beautiful and powerful earth awareness, earth healing rite. I have taken the liberty to add comments to the instructions that I felt would help the ceremony go even more smoothly. The rite may be done alone or in a group.

## INVOKING THE SPIRITS OF THE BIOREGION

We gather here in Katuah in the southern heartland of the Appalachians.

Facing each of the four directions, beginning in the east and moving sunwise (clockwise), offer a prayer to the land and the spirits that inhabit and embody the land's power: East/the Blue Ridge; South/ the Foothills; West/the Smokies; North/the Shenandoah Valley.

In silence or aloud, individually or in unison with your group, repeat:

> *We invoke the ancient spirit of Katuah whose energies sustain and embrace us. We call upon the depths of the Linville Gorge, the mystery of the Brown Mountain Lights, the majesty of Looking Glass, the massiveness of Stone Mountain, the ancient power of Grandfather Mountain, Mt. Mitchell, and Mt. Pisgah and the richness of the Great Smoky Mountains. We call on the winds that live in this place...the winds that bring the changes of the seasons. In the heart of these mountains are born many rivers which flow in all directions. We call upon these rivers: the New, the Green, the Tuckaseegee, the Pigeon, the French Broad....these rivers that carry life through this region and to lands far beyond these mountains. For these presences and for this water that strengthens, cleanses, and gives us life, we give thanks."* [1]

At this point you may wish to give an offering to the Earth Mother.

After the invocation you may wish to drink from a cup of the water (being sure it is pure) of the area. If you are in a group you may wish to pass the cup around among the celebrants.

Next, invoke, silently or aloud, the animal and plant totems of the area. Rattlesnake, black bear, ginseng, tobacco, deer...to name a few. And finally, stand alone or in a circle and return to the earth by kneeling. Place both hands flat on the ground and bow and kiss the Earth Mother.

Individual prayers may be made during or after this type of ceremony for the healing of the earth. I might also mention that it is a good practice that when we know of or come across a place that has been damaged by fire, flood, drought, pollution, or some other man-caused trauma, it is good to take a few moments to make prayers and/or do a simple earth healing rite, as such places are in need of positive input and vitality. This gives us an opportunity to share with the Earth Mother and give away of our energy. It also helps to become more aware of the condition of our environment and get us into the *habit* of thinking positive, healing, vital thoughts for the planet.

Please feel free to make any changes in this basic ceremony you wish. You may even want to make the effort to get a group together for the purpose of going out to different sacred sites and vortexes each Full Moon or on each solstice and equinox day (or other times of your choosing) to do this or another rite for planetary and personal healing. When we reach out to help heal the Earth Mother, we help heal ourselves. "Protecting and maintaining the life of the mountains is a very practical sort of wisdom, for our well-being and the spiritual health of the land are ultimately linked."[2]

On numerous occasions throughout this writing I have suggested that certain places are especially conducive to healing our own bodies, minds, and emotions. For example, there are healing springs, places that are highly magnetic, and old ceremonial grounds sprinkled throughout the area. Going to such places when we have a need for physical, emotional, mental, or spiritual healing can go far in establishing a rapport with natural planetary powers and forces.

Thinking about emotional healing in particular, I would like to share something that Sun Bear taught all of his apprentices. He called it "digging a hole". Based upon his belief that the Earth Mother can and will take our problems and pains into her body so that we might be rid of them, and that the planet can transform negative energy into positive power, Sun Bear suggested that one go alone to a place of your choosing and where you can be in private. With your hands, dig a small hole. Then, lay on the ground and hold your head, face down, just above the hole. Talk to the Earth Mother; speak your troubles and feelings into the hole. Say it all....leave nothing out. When you have finished, cover up the hole by refilling it with the soil that came from it, and give thanks to the Earth Mother. This ceremony can be repeated as often as you like and in any place that is appropriate.

When Albion first told us about the reawakening process currently taking place in the Great Smoky Mountains, I had no concrete evidence that the information was true. This was due not only to my not having actually lived in the area, and the fact that I was not entirely clear about when the reawakening had really begun. I was under the impression it had begun just shortly before he gave the information. However, after being here for over three years (at the time of this writing) and what I intuitively felt and experienced during the time I spent researching and writing this book and being out on and with the land, I now realize that the process began in the early 1980s. I feel it will be complete by the end of the 1990s, actually peaking in 1995 and 1996. Albion agrees.

In addition to the evidence of the first Pow Wow in almost a hundred years, the return of the sacred fire from the Western Cherokee to the Eastern Band people, the re-establishment of the Green Corn Ceremony and the Stomp Dance, I also discovered evidence that involves certain animals. From reading numerous back issues of Katuah Journal I came across some exciting information which of course can be viewed literally. But when viewed symbolically it is quite revealing indeed.

In March of 1990, at about the exact time that Albion gave us the reawakening information, three pairs of red wolves were released on the Tennessee side of the Great Smoky Mountains National Park. Being no threat to humans, the red wolf had been extinct for over ten years and the release is hoped to lead to a population of 50-100 wolves. (Katuah; Spring, 1986) It is also hoped that the reappearance of the wolves will help to drive out the smaller coyote who have migrated into the area since 1985. If this is nature's natural course, so be it. Mother Nature does, after all, have her own ways of restoring and maintaining balance.

You might wonder why the reintroduction of the wolves into the Smokies caught my attention. The reason has to do with the ancient concept of *totems;* the belief that animals possess powers that embody skills and qualities from which humans can learn and benefit. Wolf is a powerful totem to Native Americans. "In reality, each animal in creation has hundreds of lessons to impart, and all of those lessons are powers that can be called upon."[3] And....."when you call upon the power of an animal, you are asking to be drawn into complete harmony with the strength of that creature's essence."[4] Knowledge of totems is an integral part of the wisdom to be gained by walking the Native American path of power. Through totems we can come into an increased awareness of our animal relations, including birds, reptiles, water mammals, fishes, and, ultimately, our own selves. When we view the wolf as a totem we find this four-legged to be one of our greatest teachers. By example wolves teach us a strong sense of family, as well as the value of strong personal individuality. (Sams and Carson; pg. 97) The wolf has long been associated with the moon and, therefore, the psychic realms of the human mind that gives birth to visions and dreams, and gives us access to the deepest recesses of the personal and collective unconscious. Having the wolf returned to these old mountains restores an energy that can go far in helping us come to realize, consciously, the value and power of having vision in our personal lives. It can help us seek a greater vision for the future of this land, a vision that can and will become more and more prominent and stronger as time goes by.

In addition to and beyond the value we place on our human family units, we must come to realize the fact that the members of *all* kingdoms comprise a *global family*. Learning to value and respect the right to life of each member of *that* family will occur here again. Teachers will share their insights regarding the reality of global consciousness. New light centers will be founded upon these principles. More teachers and teachings that involve archetypal psychology will spring up. As the mountains' power elevates, people will be drawn here from all walks of life to embark upon their own personal vision quests. Organizations will move here and be formed here that will have as their aim to preserve the land and others that will teach Sacred Ecology. A renewed interest in the spirituality of the native peoples will continue to grow. People who possess healing skills will come here in great numbers, as will light workers who hold in their hearts a vision of world peace. This is what I see. But whatever happens, we can be sure that the renewed presence of the wolves onto this land will affect the overall energy here and I, for one, feel that will only be for the better.

A thought occurs to me. Whether we happen to be talking about the wolf or any other totem, when we use the word *teacher* we are making reference to someone, something, or some place serving as a *pathfinder* or *wayshower*. Teachers are empirical; they share information based upon not only their *intellectual knowledge*, but also upon their individual *experience*. Perhaps the most important thing teachers share with those who seek to learn is how we can be a *conscious* part of the greater whole of society and the planet, while retaining our sense of individuality in response to our strong archetypal urge to be who and what we are. Each of us, whether we are conscious of it or not, are teachers. The way we live our lives, how we think and feel, what our values are, and how we react to one another, affects all around us.

I am reminded of a question posed in an article about climate in an early 1980s edition of *Smithsonian* magazine, as to whether the flapping of a butterfly's wings on earth affects the most distant of stars? The answer was emphatically *yes*! It is simple. All affects all else. How different our behavior might be if we were to take this truth to heart and actually live it in our daily lives. How would our world and our individual and collective lives be different if we consciously realized that every thought has some affect upon everything that lives......that our tears and our laughter are both contagious....that our unaddressed fears make for a fearful world.....that war and conflict harms the psychic health of all? I recall reading an account by Laurens Van Der Post who told of going into the African jungle carrying a gun, but with no intention of hunting or killing. He observed animals and birds having little or no reaction to his presence. Yet, on the day he took his gun and went into the same jungle intending to hunt for food, the animals hid and took on other self-protective postures that had otherwise been virtually non-existent! Obviously the animals sensed his intent! It is time to re-learn and remember to honor the sort of natural telepathic exchange that exists between the members of all kingdoms of life. And we must remember that we are teachers to one another. It can be a sobering experience when we take a moment to reflect upon what we have taught, through our behavior, plants and animals and the Earth Mother herself. Surely we have taught the great whales, for example, that humans are dangerous and cannot be trusted to live in harmony with them. We have taught the old growth forests that profit is more important than their beauty and the value of their role in insuring we have air to breathe. We have taught the Earth Mother that we are willing to pollute and destroy our planetary home.

In addition, Sams and Carson (*Medicine Cards*) tell us that "wolf medicine empowers the teacher within us all to come forth and aid the children of Earth in undertaking the Great Mystery and life."[5] Perhaps as the red wolf continues to thrive in these old mountains their presence will once again restore a power that will result in each of us who live or come here having the *teacher archetype* awakened within ourselves; that our intuition will come alive within us so that we might each share our knowledge and insights and uniqueness with others. "It is the sharing of great truths that the consciousness of humanity will attain new heights."[6] Perhaps the presence of the wolf will help each of us to seek out the power spots and sacred sites within the Blue Ridge and the Smokies that will assist us in discovering our own individual teacher role and the responsibility that comes with it. We must come to respect all life forms with whom we share the planet as our teachers. We must become capable of mustering the courage and willingness it takes to search for teachers who can guide and direct us. We must also come to recognize, as aptly pointed out by Sams and Carson, that there are times when the greatest teacher is our own inner voice. Listening to and trusting this voice is a matter which involves the task of *trust in our own selves* which, for some, is the most difficult task of all. In any case we can be sure that the presence of the wolves on this land *will* affect the overall energy of the land and those who live here.

Another species, this time a powerful bird of prey.....the peregrine falcon....was reintroduced into the Smokies in the summer of 1985. Around the same time, six golden eagles were set free in the Shining Rock Wilderness; two incredibly powerful ambassadors of the animal kingdom. Both are great hunters. Their power of sight, like all birds of prey, is a skill to be envied and that, physically, humans can only imagine. Having these winged hunters return here can not only help bring the balance of Nature closer to restoration, but releases a unique, subtle power into the psychic consciousness of the environment. The effort to reintroduce the peregrine falcons appears to have been successful. But the golden eagle's plight was not so successful. The eagles did not survive. Let's think about this.

The eagle has long been the most powerful of all totems to the Indian peoples. This great bird is believed to embody the power of the Great Spirit......the Creator. For a Native American to have eagle feathers in their possession is an honor. It is said, for example, that to hold an eagle feather in your hand is to be unable to lie! Eagle feathers have also been used since ancient times by the natives of Turtle Island as tools of healing.

When I first met Sun Bear I asked why the eagle was the most revered of all totems to his people. He answered that because the eagle flies higher than any other bird, it is closer to the Great Spirit. I never forgot his words and have since come to realize the implications of them. From its vantage point high in the heavens, the eagle sees more of the expansiveness of what is below. As we go through our daily lives, how often we see only a small part of the truth of a situation (usually our part!), condition, or another person. As the saying goes, we don't see the forest for the trees. We get so caught up in the details of living we often lose sight of the larger vision. Like all birds of prey, eagles possess incredibly keen sight that enables them to look down upon the greater whole in a unique and powerful way. So when viewed as a totem (teacher), it seems to me that the eagle's true gift is *sight* or, better still, *insight*. Without insight we have little hope of truly experiencing our connection to The Great Spirit. While we cannot learn to fly literally, nor hope to have eyes like an eagle, we *can* rise above the pettiness of life and learn to soar above the mundane levels of our individual selves and the world. Only then can be truly be in touch with our connection to the Divine; only then can we become conscious of the power of the mental and emotional levels within our being that can serve to lift us up to realize greater human capabilities, resulting in the broadening of our true sense of Self. The eagle can help us realize that we can become the wind beneath our own wings! By finding the courage to spread our wings we become ready to take greater steps towards becoming all we can be. In short, the eagle is *the* symbol of power. Its "sight" translates, when the eagle is viewed as a totem, to mean the power to see into the darkness of our personality defects and free ourselves from self-imposed limitations. The *Medicine Cards* (Sams and Carson; pg. 41) remind us of our connection to the Creator. How many times we "fail(ed) to recognize the light that is always available for those who seek illumination."[7] The eagle embodies the most potent of all spiritual energies and through this most magnificent of creatures we can consciously participate in the life of the Creator.

Sadly, the eagles did not survive their reintroduction into the Smokies, thus rendering the project unsuccessful. From my perspective this failure has several varied implications, the first being that the timing was premature. Perhaps because the reawakening process was still in its earliest stages, there may not have been enough "power" from the mountains to sustain a fitting home for eagles. Perhaps we humans are not yet ready or spiritually fit to receive the eagle's gifts. After all, when the eagle's presence is lost, anywhere on earth, does it not symbolize our loss of closeness with the Creator? For years the eagle's existence has been threatened. We need only look at the ills of modern society and see that the frantic efforts being made to save the eagle may represent a much deeper struggle than we realize. Surely on some level deep within ourselves, both individually and collectively, we *know* what our relationship with all fellow creatures means and what we lose when those connections are threatened or broken. In any case, we can be certain that the collective eagle consciousness knows precisely what is going on and when the time will be right for the eagle to return to these old mountains. And I do believe that time will come.

The river otters, the object of many Cherokee legends, were already nearly gone from the Smokies by 1934. (Katuah; Fall, 1985) But they too have been brought back. On March 10, 1986, sixteen otters were released in Abrams Creek in Cades Cove; five male and female pairs among them.

Otters are busy and playfully curious creatures. According to a reliable source of totem knowledge, otters are understanding and creative beings; the very embodiment of female energy and sisterhood. (Sams and Carson; pg. 69) And according to Albion, female energy is *pure magnetism* and therefore possesses all magnetic qualities. I often think of the otter as a personification of the child within us all. For many of us the inner child is wounded because of events that happened early in life. For others it is the part of us that suffers from the lack of emotional nourishment and who never grew up. But, more positively, it is the inner child that possesses a sense of wonder and an insatiable curiosity that I, for one, wish never to lose. Otter reminds us that life is to be enjoyed.....that play is necessary if we are to develop into healthy and whole beings. Having the otters and the energy they emit returned to the mountains feeds and accentuates the feminine, magnetic energy that is so profoundly present here to begin with. To have the land and its waters intensified by the otter's presence means that the humans who live and come here will find it a place where it is easier to perceive our feminine selves, experience dreams and visions, develop latent psychic skills and intuition, and our emotional sensitivity in positive and constructive ways so that what we feel is not a source of fear and dishonesty. Think about it. Being in these mountains can help us, both individually and collectively, go into our own inner landscape and find....and heal.....the child within. What a wonderful thought and potential.

Remember: *all is energy.* If the presence of these totems.......the falcon, otter, wolf....and others......has positive affects on the overall balance of Nature, then humans are affected by their presence. Although we may not always behave as if it is so, we are a part of Nature. The powers inherent within each totem mentioned represent qualities which we need to have become more conscious. Perhaps the presence of these animals can help us remember and value that truth.

I learned from reading *Katuah Journal* that the rattlesnake is an ancient totem of the Smokies and Blue Ridge. I have always thought of the serpent as a symbol of wisdom. Sams and Carson tell us in *The Medicine Cards* (pg.61) that "the power of the snake medicine is the power of creation, for it embodies sexuality, psychic energy, alchemy, reproduction, and ascension (or immortality)." When we view each of these attributes as powers, and know that these powers are strong in these ancient mountains, we get some insight as to the energies present here. The very word *immortality*, in and of itself, suggests a knowing of the continuity of life and speaks of the very essence of our divinity. We are universal beings, one and all. Alchemy speaks of transformation; creation and creativity speaks to us of the true nature of life. We are all creators. As we create (reproduce) we come closest to being like The Creator. During my initial conversation with the Cherokee elder, Walker Calhoun, he happened to mention that the deer are coming back. I assumed from his choice of words that the deer population, though not extinct, had dwindled. Deer are such gentle animals and the lesson of gentleness is what they can teach us. (Sams and Carson; pg. 53) Also, if there is one thing that comes across clearly to me as I move about in these mountains, it is the experience of the land's gentleness. I feel it particularly when I walk into the green forests.......when I hear the gentle flowing streams and listen to the soft warm rain through the tree canopy......and when the clouds lift off the mountain slopes and the mists hug the valleys.......the clouds and the mists that form the "smoke" that gives these Old Ones their name. If the increasing deer population does indeed help to endow the region with gentleness, then in this hectic world be it so.

Even though the black bear, which I view as the true embodiment of the collective power of the Great Smoky Mountains, has not become extinct, it's survival is certainly being threatened. Since I was a child, every post card, every advertisement, and every flyer and poster that was/is put out to draw visitors to the Smokies bears a photograph or drawing of the black bear. It is clear to me that the bear has always been like a *logo* of the area; the Smokies' living symbol, if you will. Black bear, it would seem, embodies the *oversoul* of the entire region. By the cards and ads, one would expect to see bears casually crossing the roadways or roaming freely and visibly throughout the area. While this may have been true at one time, it is hardly the case now. I, for one, have driven all through the Smokies numerous times and at all hours of day and night since moving here. I have driven to every one of the power spots and sacred sites mentioned in this book, up and down forest roads and backroads, and not once have I seen a bear.

The black bear was well-known to the early Cherokees, both literally and in legends, one of which tells of its origin and goes something like this. It seems there was once a young boy who delighted in going into the woods. He often invited his people to come with him, citing that there was plenty to eat and drink there and they would not even have to work for it. After holding council the headmen of the village decided to fast for seven days and then follow the boy into the forest. Along the way the men noticed that their bodies were becoming covered with hair and that their nature was changing! They had become bears! They called themselves *yanu* or *yonah*. The men promised the people they would never go hungry, for when they came into the woods hunting, they would give to them of their own flesh. They then taught the humans two bear songs by which they could call the bears to them for food. (Mooney; 1982)

Today Yonah is in trouble. Because of poaching, periodic food shortages, the long hunting season, poor management plans, and dwindling habitats, the black bear is threatened. This possibility is bad enough on the physical level for they are surely among Nature's most noble creatures. But when viewed symbolically and spiritually, and with the black bear embodying the consciousness of the land that is the Smokies and Blue Ridge, then it becomes clear that the *power* or *life force* of the region is being threatened. And this has been going on for a long time now. To save the black bear is to rescue the mountains from the brink of environmental and spiritual ruin, as I see it.

From Sun Bear I learned that the bear brings us the gift of introspection. He is Mudjekeewis, who represents and is the gatekeeper of "the place of the looks within", he would say. It is clear that many of us have forgotten to go within for strength and guidance or that we never learned how or, worse, have never truly realized the value of doing so. It is not easy to go inside in search for truth and faith. We are so accustomed to looking to others and things outside ourselves for answers. But, albeit slowly, this is changing. Today, many teachings, therapies, and meditation techniques exist which are designed to help us with the inner journey. We need only take advantage of them. Turning our thoughts once again to the bear, what with the reawakening of these mountains currently taking place, I have every reason to believe that the black bear's plight will change for the positive. I also believe that the overall human psychological and spiritual condition can and will improve as a result. But none of this will even have the chance to occur unless we come to see the value of not only the black bear but *all* our relations in all kingdoms. Only this will restore balance and harmony between all that lives.

Throughout this writing there has been mention of several places, some of which are sacred sites, that have long been associated with animals, including birds, reptiles, aquatic creatures, and even insects. I encourage readers to go to these places whenever the opportunity arises in order to connect, in consciousness, with our animal relations. To do so is very much a part of learning about ourselves and coming to have a greater understanding of the whole of Nature. When we reach out in this way, they/our totems *will* respond. They will communicate; they will seek harmony with us.

When Albion first gave the information about the reawakening of the mountains, one of the things that excited me perhaps more than any other was his prediction that interest in the Cherokee spiritual tradition would be rekindled among non-Indians and Cherokees alike. As stated earlier, there is evidence that this is already happening. As Sun Bear might say: "Ho! This is good." However I must say that when I first arrived I realized that, for the most part, Cherokees are Christians. While I have no problem with this, per se, I suppose it had simply not occurred to me that this was the case, as my previous experience with native people had been with the Southwestern tribes, particularly the Hopi, and with members and elders of other tribes who are still very much into their traditional religious practices. I had become accustomed to and maybe I had automatically assumed the Cherokees were no different. So I have often wondered if there are enough Cherokee medicine people left and enough knowledge and respect for the old ways for there to be something to be revived! I now realize there is. The knowledge, or certainly a large portion of it, is still very much in existence; the *seed* is still in the soil of the spiritual consciousness of many of the Cherokees and other of the indigenous peoples.

I recently had that truth reinforced while reading a book entitled *The Cherokee Perspective* (edited by Laurence French and Jim Hornbuckle). In an essay by Herbert and Yvonne Wachacha on *Tra-*

*dition and Change*, I became aware of a community in Graham County. Comprised of Cherokees who have managed to maintain a pure bloodline, the Snowbird Community has survived and managed to keep their identity out of sheer pride and determination. These people have warded off the everpressing encroachment of white, modern society and do not depend on the tourist industry for their livelihood. Rather, they have gone to great lengths to raise needed funds and remain self-sustaining.

Snowbird Cherokees have also preserved the native Cherokee language. The elders, in typical Indian manner, are highly respected for both their age and experience. In addition, religion plays a large role in the lives of the Snowbird people. Although Christian, they go once a week to the top of a mountain to pray. And some of the older people still practice herbal doctoring and the old art of conjuring. The medicine men continue to reveal their secrets to the younger generations so the practices of fighting off hexes and evil spirits might be carried on. (Wachacha; 1981) Although this information was written in the early 1980s, I assume that it holds true. If so, then the *seeds* of the past *are* alive and are still being sown here in the mountains. I believe these seeds will sprout again; the traditional ways will survive, though not necessarily exactly as before, and maybe even in stronger and better ways.

As we go through these perilous times of planetary change, predictions have been made that speak of the future fate of North Carolina. And many of them concern geological and climatic changes. In Sun Bear's last book *Black Dawn Bright Day*, he speaks of North Carolina: "This is a state with lots of good places to raise food but try to learn to eat wild plants also. Storms will continue to cause damage, seemingly randomly."[8] Sun Bear also pointed out that in the area of western North Carolina and northeastern Georgia there is the likelihood of possible earthquakes. The storms he predicted were thought to take the form of both hurricanes and tornados. There was no question in Sun Bear's mind, and there are many who agree with him, that "the earth cleansing that we are experiencing now is necessary for the protection of the planet. It is also necessary because the purpose of humanity here on earth is for each of us to go to our highest level of consciousness and power, and then learn how to apply the knowledge we gain in the process."[9] In light of my own books and work concerning earth changes, I couldn't agree more. I have been asked many times if I moved here because I felt it was a safe place to be. My answer is yes. But physical safety was not my first nor most important consideration. You see, I firmly believe that when one is in harmony and balance with the Earth Mother, one has nothing to fear from her. I never concern myself, as a result, with being "safe" from natural events such as earthquakes, flood, drought, or climatic threat. I am here because of Albion's informing us of the reawakening process, which in and of itself is a part of and the result of current major planetary change. We must remember that there is much more involved with earth changes than geological and climatic upheaval. I wanted to understand the purpose of the reawakening process and my role within it (which this book represents). I wanted the opportunity to learn all I could by living in the midst of such a rare physical and spiritual occurrence.

I must make some comment about the storms Sun Bear predicted. First, he suggested that, for the most part, these storms will occur along the coastal areas of the state, even though some will happen statewide. I feel that he is right on. I, in fact, find it very interesting that in March of 1993, the entire Appalachian range was hit be a severe blizzard that, as blizzards go, was touted as the storm of the century! It hasn't snowed like that in western North Carolina for many generations. The storm was actually called a *white hurricane*! And in May, 1993, the first funnel cloud touched down in Asheville! It was the only one sighted since meteorological records have been kept! Without doubt the weather is changing. And it is not just changing in North Carolina. At the time of this writing, people are still recovering both physically and psychologically from the devastating Midwestern floods of the summer of '93. South Florida continues to struggle to rebuild from Hurricane Andrew, the worst hurricane in history! Coastal South Carolina is only now beginning to see light at the end of the tunnel due to the damage done by Hurricane Hugo; two major storms in less than two years. And southern California, while struggling to recover from ravaging fires that left a path of unbelievable destruction, has been rocked less than six months later by a deadly 6.6 earthquake that took 61 lives and wreaked financial havoc that totaled into the tens of millions of dollars. The earth is changing. In a recent Bear Tribe newsletter (January 1994) Wabun Wind, Executive Director, said: "As I sit writing this in my home office, unable for the third day to get the two miles to the Bear Tribe office (eastern office in near Philadelphia, Pennsylvania) I think about Sun Bear and how he would be saying, 'Sister, the earth changes are really getting strong now. You better be prepared."

I have been told by many who have lived in western North Carolina all their lives that it doesn't snow here like it used to. But I believe the snow spirits are now returning. I also feel that the winds will begin to make their presence known, not just along the coast of the state, but in the mountains too. Maybe the winds, who are the *cleansers,* will feel the need to increase their cleansing. I feel that the summers will become hotter and that there will be less rainfall during summer months, with wetter times during the other three seasons.

Whatever happens, we can be sure that it will be a manifestation of the wisdom of Mother Nature. We have no need to flee from place to place in search of safety during these times of change. No. As Sun Bear's 94-year old uncle said....."The earth takes care of her own." We must only be reminded that as long as we are in harmony with the land, the weather spirits, and all our relations, no harm will come to us and, even if it does, it teaches us a lesson about what in Nature we are out of balance with. To be sure, the reawakening of the Great Smoky Mountains is a positive result of the planetary changes and to be here during these times is a privilege indeed.

Evidence of this last statement was reinforced by a short but profound writing by David Wheeler in the Spring 1990 Issue of Katuah Journal. David tells us......"The Appalachians are old, their power is subtle. Their power is strong. Standing over the eastern seaboard of Turtle Island continent, the intangible influences of the Appalachians radiates out over all the lowlands so thickly inhabited by human beings. As surely as that power is invisible and inexplicable, its subtle influence is also vital to maintaining the balance of life of the eastern half of Turtle Island." Wheeler went on to say that "medicine is power. The mountains power is sacred and powerful. The Cherokees plunged into the river that flowed by each village. Thus they partook of the medicine of water and mountains. They ate wild foods and healed the body with roots - roots filled with medicine."[10]

This is the way it will be again for many of us, in spite of modern society. This is my feeling. No. I am not saying that we will, or should, revert back into primitive lifestyles. I am saying, rather, that the old, traditional values held by American Indians regarding the land and our relationships with it and all our relations will be restored. Some of the people who have the knowledge and skills to help this come to pass are already here. And others are being drawn here all the time. Even as I was writing these words I received a card from a young woman who had come here for private study with me. She wrote: "I feel like those Smoky Mountains became my home and I still hear them calling me." Interestingly, this woman is also a teacher, her expertise being herbs, healing, and shamanic journeys. Yes, many are being *called* to these mountains. Some know why and some do not. They seem to be responding to a strong, unconscious urge to be here. Each of us has our own vision; each our own knowledge, experiences, wisdom, and expertise. And each of us will, in our own way and time, make a contribution to the reawakening and will in turn benefit from being a part of this great and unique planetary event.

I invite my readers to go out into these ancient mountains and valleys and forests with the purpose of feeling and experiencing their beauty and majesty. Go with the intent of relating to the minerals, plants, animals, and...yes....the humans that are here with an open mind and heart. Your eyes can see the beauty. Your feet can walk across the soil. Your mind can soak in the grandeur, both its subtleness and its profoundness. But only your *heart* can guide you to a new, more honest relationship with our Mother, the Earth. Enjoy your journeys and know that they are sacred. So be it.

<u>A UTE PRAYER</u>
Earth teach me stillness
as the grasses are stilled with light.
Earth teach me suffering
as old stones suffer with memory.
Earth teach me humility
as blossoms are humble with beginning.
Earth teach me caring
as the mother who secures her young.
Earth teach me courage
as the tree which stands alone.
Earth teach me limitation
as the ant which crawls on the ground.
Earth teach me freedom
as the eagle which soars in the sky.
Earth teach me resignation
as the leaves which die in the fall.
Earth teach me regeneration
as the seed which rises in the spring.
Earth teach me to forget myself
as melted snow forgets its life.
Earth teach me to remember kindness
as dry fields weep with rain.

[1] *Katuah Journal*; Issue 6; Winter 1984-1985
[2] *Katuah Journal*; Issue 1; Fall 1983; page 11.
[3] *Medicine Cards: The Discovery Of Power Through The Ways Of Animals;* Jamie Sams and David Carson; Bear and Company; Santa Fe, New Mexico; 1988.
[4] Ibid
[5] Ibid
[6] Ibid
[7] Ibid
[8] *Black Dawn Bright Day*; Sun Bear and Wabun Wind; Bear Tribe Publishing; Spokane, Washington: 1990.
[9] Ibid
[10] *Katuah Journal*; Spring 1990.

# BIBLIOGRAPHY

Sacred Places; Swan, James; Bear and Company Publishing; Sante Fe, New Mexico: 1990.

Great Smoky Mountains: The Splendor Of The Southern Appalachians; Walker, Steven L.; Camelback Design Group, Inc.; Scottsdale, Arizona: 1991.

Myths Of The Cherokees/Sacred Formulas Of The Cherokees; Mooney, James; Charles and Randy Elder-Booksellers; Nashville, Tennessee: 1982.

Cherokee Plants -their uses: a 400 year history; Paul B. Hamel and Mary V. Chiltoskey

Stories Of The Yunwi Tsunsdi: The Cherokee Little People; Western North Carolina University English 102 Class Project: March, 1991.

The Earth Changes Survival Handbook; Bryant, Page; Sun Publishing; Santa Fe, New Mexico: 1984.

Terravision: A Traveler's Guide To The Living Planet Earth; Bryant, Page; Ballantine Books; New York, New York: 1991.

Where Legends Live: A Pictorial Guide To Cherokee Mythic Places; Rossman, Douglas A.; Cherokee Publications; Cherokee, North Carolina: 1988.

Earth Memory: Sacred Sites-Doorways Into Earth's Mysteries; Devereux, Paul; Llewellyn Publications; St. Paul, Minnesota: 1992.

Indians In North America; South, Stanley A.; State Department of Archives and History; Raleigh, North Carolina: 1962.

The Aquarian Guide To Native American Mythology; Bryant, Page; Aquarian/Thorsons; London, England: 1991.

Touring The Western North Carolina Backroads; Sakowski, Carolyn; John F. Blair, Publishers; Winston-Salem, North Carolina: 1990.

Mountain People, Places, and Ways; Michael and Ruth Joslin; The Overmountain Press; Johnson City, Tennessee: 1991.

Mountain Roads And Quiet Places; Delaughter, Jerry; Great Smoky Mountain Natural History Association; Gatlinburg, Tennessee: 1986.

The Cherokee Perspective; edited by Laurence French and Jim Hornbuckle; Appalachian Consortium Press; Boone, North Carolina: 1981.

Black Dawn Bright Day; Sun Bear and Wabun Wind; Bear Tribe Publishing; Spokane, Washington:

Practical Celtic Magic; Hope, Murry; Aquarian/Thorsons; London, England: 1987.

Medicine Cards: The Discovery Of Power Through The Ways Of Animals; Jamie Sams and David Carson; Bears and Company; Santa Fe, New Mexico:

Treatise On Cosmic Fire; Bailey, Alice A.; Lucis Trust; New York,

New York:

The Celtic Shaman: A Handbook; Matthews, John; Element; Shaftesbury, Dorset, England: 1991.

Jung And The Story Of Our Time; Van Der Post, Laurens; Penguin Books; London, England: 1976.

Memories, Dreams, And Reflections; Jung, C.G.; Vintage Books/Random House; New York, New York: 1989.

Voices Of Our Ancestors; Ywahoo, Dhyani; Shambhala; Boston, Massachusetts: 1987.

# INDEX

ACUPUNCTURE 85
AGAN UNI'TSI 49, 56
AGAWELA 186
SEE THREE SISTERS
AGISIYI 122
AKASHIC RECORDS 67
HALL OF RECORDS 66
ALABAMA 21
ALASKA 110, 213
DENALI 110, 111
ALBION 20, 21, 65-67, 77, 80-82, 143, 147, 148, 167-173, 180, 213, 216, 219, 220, 226, 230
ALLEGHENIES 13
AMERICA 14, 19, 26, 27, 58, 68, 75, 110, 112, 237
AMERICAN INDIAN 27, 166
SEE NATIVE AMERICAN
AMERICAN INDIAN RELIGIOUS FREEDOM ACT 27
AMPHIBIANS 11
ANCIENT ONES 80, 83, 215
ANCIENT RED 60, 61
SEE FIRE
ANGEL
ARCHANGEL 149
ANIMAL LODGE 120, 121
GREGORY BALD 119-121, 177
MATA TIPILA/BEAR LODGE 120, 121
PA-HA-TU/PAH-UK 120, 121
ANWYNN 155, 196
(WORLD OF)
APPALACHIANS 3, 9, 12, 18, 35, 66, 81, 86, 92, 108, 117, 126, 144, 158, 166, 176, 180, 217, 234, 237
SOUTHERN 3, 9, 18, 66, 86, 92, 114, 117, 126, 141, 144, 166, 171, 176, 180, 203, 217, 233, 237
ARCHETYPE 11, 49, 68, 223
ARIZONA 20, 50, 51, 84, 99, 150, 164, 176, 185, 214, 237
FLAGSTAFF 84
GRAND CANYON 14, 104, 196
PHOENIX 25, 91
SAN FRANCISCO PEAKS 84, 185
SEDONA 99, 102, 214
ASHTORETH 186

ASIA 10
ASIAN TRIBES 19
ATLANTIS 45
ATLANTEAN 21, 45, 46, 82, 138
AURA 4, 14, 40, 78, 94, 102, 167
PLANETARY 3-6, 14, 45, 67, 69, 73, 78, 82, 84, 91, 102, 104, 113, 119, 148, 173, 210, 215, 219, 223, 231, 232, 234, 235
AVALON 73, 169, 179, 196
SEE BRITISH ISLES
BAHAMAS 85
BIMINI 85
BALDS 10, 39, 131, 163, 164
GREGORY 119-121, 177
HEATH 10, 39, 163, 164
JOANNA 129
RUMBLING 105, 128, 129
STRATTON 115
BALSAM MOUNTAIN 115
BASKET 22, 182, 187
BEACON VORTEXES 97, 99, 101, 103, 106
BEAVER 8, 54
BELL ROCK 99, 102
SEE ARIZONA/SEDONA
BERING STRAIT 19
BIBLE 62
OLD TESTAMENT 63
BIG DIPPER 65
SEE STARS
BIG HORN MEDICINE WHEEL 75
BIRDS 8, 11, 12, 22, 29, 41, 48, 120, 139, 140, 162-165, 169, 173, 221, 222, 224, 225, 230
CARDINALS 8, 31, 56, 184
FINCHES 12
GEESE 12
GROUSE 12
HUMMINGBIRDS 136
OWLS 29, 165
QUAIL 12, 61
WOODPECKER 159
BLACK BEAR 11, 12, 68, 199, 218, 228-230
YONAH 12, 66, 229
BLACK DOME 82, 108-110, 112-115, 148
SEE MT. MITCHELL

241

BLACK ELK 1, 147
BLACK MOUNTAINS 108, 114, 115
BLACK WITCHCRAFT 44
BLOOD MOUNTAIN 40, 131
BLUE RIDGE 12, 13, 15, 21, 68, 70, 74, 76, 80-83, 86, 91, 92, 104, 107, 110-114, 117, 119, 121, 123, 124, 131, 133, 138, 139, 141, 142, 149, 150, 157, 159, 172, 192, 204, 210, 214, 216, 217, 223, 227, 229
MOUNTAINS 2-16, 19, 21, 23, 25, 28, 29, 36, 39-41, 43, 46, 61-63, 65-68, 70, 71, 73, 74, 76, 78, 80-84, 86, 89-92, 98, 101, 103, 106, 108-112, 114, 115, 117, 121, 123-127, 129-133, 139, 142, 144, 145, 149-152, 157-159, 161-163, 167, 170, 172, 176, 178, 180, 181, 184, 185, 192, 194, 198, 200, 202, 203, 208, 210, 213-216, 218-221, 223, 225-231, 233-235, 237
PARKWAY 107, 114, 124, 138, 142, 149, 152, 172, 204
BLUE RIDGE PARKWAY 107, 114, 124, 138, 142, 149, 172, 204
BOOGER DANCE 53, 62
BOOGERS 54
SEE DANCE
BOTTOMLESS POOLS 85, 209
SEE WATER
BRITISH ISLES 153, 155, 195
AVEBURY 98
ENGLAND 31, 100, 102, 106, 153, 162, 166, 169, 179, 195, 213, 238, 239
GLASTONBURY TOR 100
GREAT BRITAIN 186
SILBURY HILL 98
STONEHENGE 73, 195
BROWN MOUNTAIN 104-106, 218
SEE LIGHTS
BURL, AUBREY 195
CADES COVE 15, 40, 126, 151, 171, 177, 206, 226
CALIFORNIA 56, 84, 110, 120, 233
CAMPBELL, JOSEPH 73
CAMPGROUNDS 114, 115, 153
AMMONS 95, 114
CABLE COVE 115
CATALOOCHEE 114, 127
DEEP CREEK 115, 202, 206
SUNBURST 114

CANADA 89, 99
DREAMER'S ROCK 99
CATAWBA 29, 105, 141, 172, 174
CATLINITE 75
CATSKILLS 12
CAVE 21, 82, 114, 128, 133, 139, 150, 151, 202
CAVERNS 106-108, 150, 151
CAYCE, EDGAR 45
CEASAR'S HEAD 128, 148
CEDAR MOUNTAIN 113
CELTS 66, 96, 131, 154, 165, 179
CENTRAL SUN 66
SEE STARS
CEREMONY/CEREMONIES
RITUAL 184
SACRED RITE 55, 168
CH'I 85
CHAKRA 90
CHERAW 29, 89
CHEROKEE INDIAN RESERVATION 114, 208
CHEROKEE NATION 61, 67, 89
CHEROKEE 1, 2, 4, 8, 9, 19-25, 27-30, 32-35, 41-44, 46-57, 60, 61, 63, 64, 67, 68, 75, 76, 89-91, 95, 105, 114, 115, 117, 122, 123, 129-132, 135, 141, 146, 152, 160, 162, 169, 178, 182-184, 193, 197-201, 204, 206, 208, 209, 214, 220, 226, 227, 230, 231, 237, 238
CHEROKEE PHOENIX 25
CHEROKEE
EASTERN BAND 23, 52, 220
SYLLABARY 25
WESTERN BAND 23, 52
CHICKASAW 89, 146
CHIMNEY TOPS 127
CHRIST 43
CIVIL WAR 25, 100
CLEAN AIR ACT 16
CLIMATE 29, 80, 181, 222
CLINGMAN'S DOME 61, 82, 83, 111, 115, 124-126, 170, 200
COLD MOUNTAIN 93, 94, 114
COLLECTIVE UNCONSCIOUS 48, 81, 123, 171, 221
COLOR 2, 45, 56, 58, 64, 105, 155, 168-172, 179
DIRECTIONS 56, 78, 86, 89, 90, 93, 109,

119, 127, 181, 217, 218
SACRED 2, 4-6, 20-22, 27-30, 32, 33, 35, 39, 44-46, 48-57, 59, 61-66, 68-71, 73-77, 82, 84, 85, 89-91,94-96, 100, 101, 104, 111, 117-126, 129-133, 135, 136, 138-140, 144, 145, 149-151, 154, 157-160, 162, 165, 167-169, 171, 173-176, 178, 179, 181-187, 193-196, 198-201, 205, 207-209, 213, 214, 216, 219-221, 223, 228, 230, 234, 235, 237
CONNECTICUT 12
COUGARS 12
COUNCIL HOUSE 22, 119, 124, 139
COUNTIES 131, 141
BUNCOMBE 114
CHEROKEE 1, 2, 4, 8, 9, 19-25, 27-30, 32-35, 41-44, 46-57, 60, 61, 63, 64, 67, 68, 75, 76, 89-91, 95, 105, 114, 115, 117, 122, 123, 129-132, 135, 141, 146, 152, 160, 162, 169, 178, 182-184, 193, 197-201, 204, 206, 208, 209, 214, 220, 226, 227, 230, 231, 237, 238
GRAHAM 121, 123, 131, 145, 203, 231
HAYWOOD 114, 145
HENDERSON 114
JACKSON 23, 24, 113, 203, 204
MACON 124, 131, 133, 200, 203, 204
OCONEE 113, 204
SWAIN 123, 131, 200
TRANSYLVANIA 113, 114, 139, 202, 203, 205
COVE 10, 15, 17, 39, 40, 60, 63, 115, 126, 133, 151, 163, 164, 170, 171, 177, 203, 206, 226
BIG 35, 40, 60, 63, 65, 74, 75, 120, 157, 202, 204, 206
CADES 15, 40, 126, 151, 171, 177, 206, 226
COWEE VALLEY 150
SEE N.C.
COYOTE 7, 30, 220
CREATION 3, 7, 28, 37, 64, 80, 83, 156, 162, 221, 227
CREATOR 57, 61, 73, 144, 149, 157, 162, 199, 224-227
SEE GREAT SPIRIT
CREEK INDIANS 24
CROPS 21, 25, 55, 116, 163, 195
BEANS 21, 186
CORN 21, 25, 52, 53, 55, 57, 186, 187, 220

CORN DANCE 55, 187
CORNMEAL 32, 186
GOURDS 21, 54
GREENS 63, 181
JILLICO 63
MELONS 21
RAMP 181
SQUASH 21, 186
SUNFLOWERS 21
TOBACCO 21, 136, 145, 181-184, 218
CRYSTAL 7, 45, 46, 57, 93, 94, 118, 123
QUARTZ 22, 46, 75, 92, 93
CULLASAJA 17, 86, 114, 128, 196, 200, 205
CULLASAJA FALLS 205
CULLASAJA RIVER GORGE 128, 196, 200, 205
UPPER CULLASAJA FALLS 205
CULLOWEE MOUNTAINS 114
SEE TENNESSEE
CUMBERLANDS 13
DANCE 12, 38, 53-55, 57, 60-62, 91, 101, 118, 120, 121, 187, 220
BEAR DANCE 54
BEAVER DANCE 54
BOOGER DANCE 53, 62
DANCERS 53-55
EAGLE DANCE 54, 55
FANCY FEATHER DANCE 61
HOOP DANCE 61
STOMP DANCE 62, 91, 220
DEATH 7, 12, 23, 31, 56, 147, 164
DEER 7, 12, 45, 54, 63, 159, 163, 199, 218, 227, 228
WHITE TAIL 12
DEMETER 186
DESOTO 22
DEVA 94, 109, 125, 139, 142, 149, 196, 201, 206
GREAT DEVA 109, 125
MOUNTAIN DEVAS 5, 118
DEVEREUX, PAUL 106
DEVIL'S COURTHOUSE 124, 149
DEVIL'S TOWER 120
SEE WYOMING
DHYANI YWAHOO 46
DIVINATION 77, 165, 193
DOG 24, 32

243

DOWSING 77, 151, 174, 207
DREAM 96, 120, 122, 177, 183, 200
DROWNING BEAR 51
DRUID 165, 167
DRUM 53, 54
EARTHWORKS 33, 75
EARTH MOTHER 1, 3, 7, 14, 28, 42, 43, 52, 83, 84, 86, 93, 104, 108, 111, 117, 118, 126, 128, 129, 132, 144, 147, 148, 150, 157, 160, 208, 210, 213, 216, 218, 219, 223, 232
EGYPT 85, 99, 194, 213
KARNAK TEMPLE 84
ELLICOTT ROCK TRAIL 95
ELLICOTT ROCK WILDERNESS 91, 94, 113
ELVES 11, 35, 40, 92
SEE LITTLE PEOPLE
ENGLAND 31, 100, 102, 106, 153, 162, 166, 169, 179, 195, 213, 238, 239
SEE BRITISH ISLES
ESP 42
EUROPE 10, 155, 194
EVERGLADES 85
FAIRIES 11, 35, 40, 43, 153, 155
SEE LITTLE PEOPLE
FAIRY CROSSES 42, 75
FATHER SKY 64, 65, 68
FEATHER 55, 61, 224
FERN 156
SEE PLANTS
FINDHORN 93
FIRE 13, 36, 44, 45, 60-64, 66, 74, 78, 79, 105, 120, 123, 130, 131, 169, 194, 218, 220, 238
ANCIENT RED 60, 61
FIRE CARRIER 44
FIREKEEPER 130
FIRE CARRIER 44
EVERLASTING FIRE 131
FIREKEEPER 130
SACRED 2, 4-6, 20-22, 27-30, 32, 33, 35, 39, 44-46, 48-57, 59, 61-66, 68-71, 73-77, 82, 84, 85, 89-91, 94-96, 100, 101, 104, 111, 117-126, 129-133, 135, 136, 138-140, 144, 145, 149-151, 154, 157-160, 162, 165, 167-169, 171, 173-176, 178, 179, 181-187, 193-196, 198-201, 205, 207-209, 213, 214, 216, 219-221, 223, 228, 230, 234, 235, 237

FIRST MAN 162
FISHES 11, 21, 44, 163, 221
RAINBOW TROUT 15
FODDERSTACK MOUNTAIN 124
FROG 30, 32, 64
GALUN'LATI 8, 29
SEE MONSTER
GAP 23, 85, 124, 133, 136, 139, 151, 173, 209
HICKORY NUT 85, 124, 136, 151, 209
WALLACE 133
WAYAH 133
GEOMANCY 3, 77, 84, 116, 118
GEORGIA 12, 76, 95, 100, 131, 133, 231
ATLANTA 100
BLOOD MOUNTAIN 40, 131
STONE MOUNTAIN 100, 218
GHOST 105
GINSENG 39, 136, 145, 158, 184, 185, 218
SEE PLANTS
GISEHUN YI 122
GLACIERS 9, 10, 174
GORGE 40, 91, 97, 101, 102, 104-106, 112, 113, 128, 132, 136, 145, 146, 196, 200, 203, 205, 218
CULLASAJA 17, 86, 114, 128, 196, 200, 205
LINVILLE 86, 91, 97, 101-107, 112, 113, 142, 145, 218
NANTAHALA 40, 86, 91, 95, 112, 114, 132, 133, 203, 207
GRANDFATHERS 215
GRANDFATHER MOUNTAIN 39, 82, 83, 105, 107, 142, 144, 145, 166, 218
GRAND CANYON 14, 104, 196
SEE ARIZONA
GREAT CRAGGY MOUNTAINS 114
CRAGGY GARDENS 114
GREAT SMOKY MOUNTAINS 2, 4, 7-9, 11, 12, 14-16, 19, 25, 43, 65-68, 80, 83, 91, 111, 117, 123, 125-127, 130, 131, 139, 151, 152, 163, 167, 170, 172, 176, 180, 184, 192, 194, 198, 200, 202, 203, 208, 213, 216, 218, 220, 228, 234, 237
GREAT BARRIER REEF 85
GREAT FEMALE 122
GREAT ONE 49, 144
GREAT PLAINS 50, 120

GREAT PYRAMID 73
SEE EGYPT
GREAT SERPENT MOUND 75
GREAT SKY BUZZARD 9
SEE MONSTER
GREAT SMOKY MOUNTAIN NATIONAL PARK 14, 16, 26, 34, 61, 91, 115, 126
GREAT SPIRIT 28, 57, 61, 71, 95, 139, 147, 150, 178, 183, 224, 225
GREEN CORN CEREMONY 52, 53, 57, 220
GREEN MOUNTAINS 12
GRID 85, 86, 91-97, 104, 108-112, 114, 115, 118, 125, 126, 132, 133, 136, 150, 151, 202-204, 207, 208
BLACK DOME GRID 108
ELLICOTT ROCK WILDERNESS 91, 94, 111, 113
LINVILLE GORGE 91, 97, 101, 102, 104-106, 112, 113, 145, 218
SHINING ROCK WILDERNESS 91, 93, 94, 114, 224
SLICKROCK WILDERNESS 91, 96, 97, 114, 115, 203
UPPER NANTAHALA WILDERNESS 91, 95
HAWAII 20, 74, 213
HAWKSBILL 97, 100-106, 113
HEALING 21, 23, 30, 55, 56, 68, 70, 75, 80, 83, 92, 104, 106, 109, 110, 116, 123, 124, 126, 133, 139, 142, 149, 150, 158, 159, 162, 167, 177, 178, 183, 185, 187, 192, 193, 198-203, 206, 208, 210, 217-219, 222, 224, 234
HEINTOOGA OVERLOOK 115
HIMALAYAS 21, 106
HOLLIFIELD, CLYDE 35, 36, 38, 105
HONEYCUTT MOUNTAIN RANGE 113
HOPE, MURRY 166, 167, 170, 172, 179
HOPI 20, 44, 47, 51, 57, 185, 186, 197, 230
HORSESHOE BEND 24
HUMPBACK MOUNTAIN 106
INDIAN 1-3, 11, 20, 22-24, 27, 29, 32, 44, 47, 50-52, 57-61, 63, 67, 83, 92, 95, 114, 136, 146, 158, 166, 181-184, 202, 206, 208, 209, 214, 224, 231
SEE NATIVE AMERICAN
INSECTS 11, 15, 44, 47, 158, 162, 187, 230
INTERNATIONAL BIOSPHERE RESERVE 14

IONA 73
IROQUOIS 89
ISHTAR 186
JACKSON, ANDREW 23, 24
JETER MOUNTAIN 113
JOYCE KILMER MEMORIAL FOREST 114
JUNALUSKA 23, 24, 145
GRAVE 19, 145
LAKE JUNALUSKA 145
NICIE 145
JUNG, C.G. 31, 48, 59, 60, 122, 161, 162, 193, 239
KANATI 139
SEE THUNDER BEINGS
KANUGA 131
KATUAH 16, 17, 28, 36, 38-41, 60, 61, 70, 89-91, 105, 117, 136, 158-160, 168, 169, 177, 180-182, 184-188, 192-194, 197, 207, 217-220, 226, 227, 234
KITU'HWA 89, 131, 132
KING ARTHUR 48, 132
FISHER KING 90, 132
KNIGHT 49
ROUND TABLE 48
KNOB 114, 127, 131, 137, 143
AMMONS 95, 114
COLD SPRINGS 127
WOLF 7, 114, 220-223, 227
LAND OF DARKENING 12
LAND OF THE MIDDLE SUN 132
SEE NANTAHALA GORGE
LEBANON 75
LECONTE 82
LEMURIA 20
PACIFICA 20
LEY 84, 86, 99, 103, 109-115, 142, 213
BALSAM LINE 115
BLACK MOUNTAIN LEY 113
CELESTIAL LEYS 99, 102, 103
CHEROKEE LEY 114
DRAGON LINES 84
LEY TERMINALS 84, 86, 111
LINVILLE LINE 113
TRANSYLVANIA LEY 113
LIFE ENERGIES 77, 78, 215, 216
ELECTRIC 98, 99, 102, 115, 148
ELECTRICAL 78, 79, 81, 84, 86, 93, 95, 97, 101, 109, 110, 119, 123-125, 129, 131,

133, 138-140, 146
ELECTROMAGNETIC 80, 81, 84-86, 92-99, 104, 106, 109-111, 113, 115, 116, 124-127, 132, 133, 136, 138, 140, 144-146, 153, 197, 200, 202, 204, 206, 207
ELECTROMAGNETISM 78-80, 84, 109, 110
MAGNETIC 79, 81, 84, 85, 91, 96-99, 102, 104, 106-109, 112, 115, 122, 123, 125, 126, 128, 135, 136, 138, 139, 141, 142, 144, 145, 149-153, 155, 162, 177, 197, 202-204, 206-209, 219, 226
MAGNETISM 78-81, 84, 132, 141, 143, 144, 152, 177, 178, 191, 226
LIGHT 8, 20, 24, 31, 32, 36-38, 44-46, 51, 58, 59, 65, 68, 74, 83, 90, 93, 94, 101, 105, 106, 116, 123-125, 147, 152, 154, 163, 172, 175, 179, 185, 196, 201, 216, 221, 222, 225, 232, 233, 235
BROWN MOUNTAIN LIGHTS 105, 218
EARTH LIGHTS 106
LIGHT CENTERS 68, 116, 221
LIGHT WORKERS 83, 222
ST. ELMO'S FIRE 105
LIGHTNING 30, 64, 78, 95, 96, 127, 145, 147, 159, 169, 175
LINVILLE FALLS 106
LINVILLE GORGE 91, 97, 101, 102, 104-106, 112, 113, 145, 218
LINVILLE 86, 91, 97, 101-107, 112, 113, 142, 145, 218
LITTLE PEOPLE 32-44, 76, 92, 93, 131, 136, 155, 157, 193, 209, 237
DOGWOOD PEOPLE 33
ELEMENTALS 44, 92, 93, 128, 158, 202
FAIRY FOLK 33, 35, 44, 176
IMMORTALS 44, 76, 131
LAUREL PEOPLE 33
NUNE'HI 34, 35, 39, 40
ROCK PEOPLE 33
SUPERNATURALS 36, 44, 122, 196
UNDERGROUND PEOPLE 29, 39-41
YUNWI TSUNDI 32-34
LITTLE SNOWBALL MOUNTAIN 115
LIZARD PLACE 129
LONE PEAK 131
LONG, WILL WEST 51
LONG KENNET BARROW 106

SEE BRITISH ISLES
LOUISIANA 101
SEE MOUNDS
LOURDES 73
MACHU PICCHU 73
MAINE 12
MANSER, ANN 161
SHUSTAH 161
MASK 54
MASSACHUSETTS 12, 27, 239
MATA TIPILA 120, 121
SEE ANIMAL LODGE
MAY DAY 131
MECCA 73, 124
MEDICINE 20, 27, 28, 43, 49, 54-56, 68, 75, 94, 122, 133, 140, 145, 158, 162, 165, 166, 170, 177, 178, 181-184, 186, 193, 199, 213, 221, 223, 225, 227, 230, 231, 234, 238
MEDITATION 79, 96, 108, 123, 126, 132, 138, 142, 150, 197, 198, 202, 206, 229
METEOR/METEORITE 123
MEXICO 5, 47, 74-76, 221, 237, 238
MONACAN 89
MONSTER 44, 47-49, 75, 95, 132, 197
ACHIYALATOPA 44
DOTSI 197
GREAT BUZZARD 44
ICE MAN 47
OGRE 47
SPEAR FINGER 47
UKTENA 44-46, 48, 49, 56, 76, 132
UNCEGILA 44
USTU'TLI 44
WATER MONSTERS 197
MONTANA 75
PIPESTONE NATIONAL MONUMENT 75
MOON 20, 21, 28, 30-32, 37, 38, 64, 65, 94, 98, 99, 141, 142, 162, 168, 179, 193, 196, 210, 219, 221
MOONEY, JAMES 27, 30, 32, 45, 117, 162
MOSS 34, 39, 152-154, 164, 192
SEE PLANTS
MOTHER EARTH 1-3, 5, 14, 15, 58, 68, 77, 83, 118, 153, 216
MOTHER NATURE 10, 93, 157, 192, 220, 233
MOUND 22, 40, 60, 75, 90, 100, 101, 129-132

CAHOKIA 101
NIKWASI 130-132
PEACHTREE MOUND 130
POVERTY POINT 101
SACRED 2, 4-6, 20-22, 27-30, 32, 33, 35, 39, 44-46, 48-57, 59, 61-66, 68-71, 73-77, 82, 84, 85, 89-91, 94-96, 100, 101, 104, 111, 117-126, 129-133, 135, 136,138-140, 144, 145, 149-151, 154, 157-160, 162, 165, 167-169, 171, 173-176, 178, 179, 181-187, 193-196, 198-201, 205, 207-209, 213, 214, 216, 219-221, 223, 228, 230, 234, 235, 237
MOUNT STERLING 127
MT. EVEREST 84
MT. GUYOT 170
MT. MITCHELL 17, 83, 91, 103, 105, 108-115, 139, 141, 148, 218
MT. PISGAH 17, 82, 138, 139, 149, 218
MT. SHASTA 84
SEE CALIFORNIA
MT. ST. HELENS 74
MYSTERY HILL 148
NATIVE 1, 2, 15, 19, 21, 24, 27, 28, 30, 32, 42, 50-52, 55-61, 63, 64, 66-68, 75, 82, 92, 101, 120, 121, 130, 135, 144, 145, 158-162, 165, 167, 168, 181, 186, 195, 197, 221, 222, 224, 230, 231, 238
NATIVE AMERICAN 1, 2, 19, 27, 30, 32, 42, 50, 55, 59-61, 66, 92, 120, 121, 145, 158, 160, 165, 181, 221, 224, 238
NATURAL WORLD NEWS SERVICE 16
NEBRASKA 120
OMAHA 120
PLATTE RIVER 120
NEWGRANGE 98
NEW HAMPSHIRE 12
NEW YORK 12, 76, 101, 191, 237-239
NIKWASI 130-132
SEE MOUNDS
NOLAND DIVIDE 114, 115
NORTH CAROLINA 14, 20, 24, 33, 34, 40, 60, 75, 76, 85, 86, 91, 94, 106, 109, 111, 112, 116, 117, 119, 131, 132, 141, 149, 152, 164, 169, 179, 198-200, 214, 231-233, 237, 238
ASHEVILLE 52, 108, 232
BAKERSVILLE 141
BEECH 10, 114, 172

BLACK MOUNTAIN 113, 114, 139
BREVARD 127, 139, 143, 148, 202, 205
BRYSON CITY 40, 91, 122, 131
CANDLER 114
CATALOOCHEE DIVIDE 114
CAVE CREEK 114
CHEROKEE 1, 2, 4, 8, 9, 19-25, 27-30, 32-35, 41-44, 46-57, 60, 61, 63, 64, 67, 68, 75, 76, 89-91,95, 105, 114, 115, 117, 122, 123, 129-132, 135, 141, 146, 152, 160, 162, 169, 178, 182-184, 193, 197-201, 204, 206, 208, 209, 214, 220, 226, 227, 230, 231, 237, 238
COVE CREEK 115
COWEE VALLEY 150
ELK PARK 202
ENKA 114
FRANKLIN 33, 40, 130, 132, 133, 150
HAYESVILLE 133
HENDERSONVILLE 113, 140
HIGHLANDS 17, 21, 124
LAKE JUNALUSKA 145
LEICESTER 114, 115
MURPHY 43
REEMS FALLS 114
ROLLINSVILLE 97, 122, 123, 145
SAPPHIRE VALLEY 113
SOUTH HOMINY 114
SWANNANOA 113
TUSKEEGEE 114
VALLEYTOWN 122
WAYNESVILLE 6, 181
WEAVERVILLE 114, 115
NORTH AMERICA 19, 27, 58, 68, 75, 110, 112, 237
NUNDA 64
SEE SUN/MOON
OCEAN 8, 79, 81, 192-194
ATLANTIC 81, 193
PACIFIC 79, 110, 153, 197
OCONOLUFTEE 114, 115, 126, 197, 200, 202, 208
OCONOLUFTEE FAULT 114, 126
OCONOLUFTEE RIVER 115, 197, 200, 208
OGLALA 1, 147
OHIO 75
OKEEFEENOKEE SWAMP 85
OKLAHOMA 23, 24, 61

INDIAN TERRITORY 23, 61, 83
OLD NATION 90
OLD ONE 136, 182, 183
OLD WAYS 21, 52, 58-60, 62, 64, 67, 69, 214, 230
OLD WOMAN 186
OREGON 148
OTHERWORLD 29, 145, 154, 193, 196
OTTO, RUDOLPH 74
OWLE, LLOYD 41, 51
OZONE LAYER 14
PENNSYLVANIA 13, 233
PETROGLYPHS 20
CAVE DRAWINGS 21, 82
JUDACULLA ROCK 134, 135
PAINT ROCK 140
ROCK ETCHINGS 21
PIEDMONT 89
EASTERN 10, 12, 14, 21, 23, 29, 40, 50-52, 61-63, 74-76, 89, 93, 96, 110, 112, 116, 117, 119, 125, 131, 132, 146, 152, 164, 167, 168, 174, 194, 204, 220, 233, 234
PILOT MOUNTAIN 40, 139, 140
PINK BEDS 139
PIPE 61, 120, 181
PEACE PIPE 61
PISGAH FOREST 139, 149
FISH HATCHERY 139, 149
PISGAH NATIONAL FOREST 17, 138
PLANT 9, 14-16, 30, 39, 67, 96, 104, 126, 136, 139, 144, 156, 158, 159, 161-163, 165, 176-180, 182-186, 188, 218
BARK 21, 82, 145, 168, 170
BERRIES 7, 40, 179, 188
BROAD LEAF TOOTHWORT 181
CEREMONIAL PLANTS 180
COTTON 40
CUDZU 15
EDIBLE PLANTS 180, 181
EXOTIC PLANTS 15
FERN 156
FLOWERING 10, 141, 164, 172, 173, 176
FRUITS 41, 188
FUNGUS 15
GINSENG 39, 136, 145, 158, 184, 185, 218
GREEN NATION 153, 163
HONEYSUCKLE 15, 22
MISTLETOE 178, 179

MOSS 34, 39, 152-154, 164, 192
NON-FLOWERING 10, 173, 176
NUTS 7, 41
PLANT NATION 161, 163, 178
ROOT 2, 22, 23, 56, 163, 181
RUE ANEMONE 180
SUN ROOT 181
TROUT LILY 180
YELLOW ROOT 22
PLEISTOCENE AGE 9
POINT MISERY 110
POLLUTION 13, 15-17, 110, 218
POTTERY 22
POWHATAN 89
POW WOW 52, 220
PRAYER 28, 79, 85, 96, 104, 111, 118, 132, 140, 142, 144, 150, 175, 176, 197, 198, 200, 203, 217, 235
PRECAMBRIAN AGE 9, 10
QUALLA RESERVATION 40, 41
RABBIT 30, 119, 121
GREAT RABBIT 119
RAINBOW 15, 64, 65, 93, 151, 153, 201, 203, 204, 207, 209
RATTLES 53, 55
RATTLESNAKE MOUNTAIN 123
RAVEN 60, 200-202
CEREMONIAL GROUNDS 60, 219
RAVEN ROCK 60
RED WOLF 7, 220, 223
REPTILES 8, 11, 12, 120, 163, 173, 221, 230
RIDGE 12, 13, 15, 21, 68, 70, 74, 76, 80-83, 86, 91, 92, 104, 105, 107, 110-115, 117, 119, 121-124, 131, 133, 138, 139, 141, 142, 149, 150, 157, 159, 172, 192, 204, 210, 214, 216, 217, 223, 227, 229
FORNEY 115
THOMAS 114, 115
WELCH 115
RING OF FIRE 79
ROANOKE 89
VALLEY 8, 21, 89, 103-105, 113, 147, 150, 217
ROAN MOUNTAIN 141, 142, 172
ROARING FORK 128, 151-154, 204
SEE TENNESSEE
ROCK 7, 8, 11, 21, 33, 35, 39, 40, 42, 60,

248

82, 83, 91, 93-95, 97-104, 106, 113, 114, 117, 120-122, 133-140, 145-149, 151, 154, 156, 164, 192, 205, 206, 224
BELL 99, 102
BLOWING ROCK 83, 146-148
CAIRNS 121, 122
CHIMNEY 82, 83, 127, 136-138, 151
ELLICOTT 91, 94, 95, 113
FLAT 8, 83, 140, 154, 218
JOHN 24, 113, 198, 238
JUDACULLA 44, 93, 124, 134, 135
PAINT 13, 140
SHINING 39, 40, 71, 91, 93, 94, 114, 149, 224
SITTING BEAR 145
SLIDE 139, 203, 205
TABLE 48, 83, 97, 100-104, 106, 113, 145, 167
ROCKS 9, 10, 13, 20, 35, 37, 56, 152, 154, 192, 203, 204, 209
IGNEOUS 10
JUDACULLA 44, 93, 124, 134, 135
METAMORPHIC 10
SEDIMENTARY 10
STANDING INDIAN 95, 114, 209
ROSSMAN, DOUGLAS 132
ROUND TOP 136, 138
RUMBLING BALD MOUNTAIN 128, 129
SAKOWSKI, CAROLYN 149, 198
SCOTLAND 93, 213
SELU 186
SEQUOYA 24
SYLLABARY 25
SHACONAGE 10, 16
SHAMAN 20, 101, 136, 165, 178, 184, 238
SHAPESHIFTER 132, 133
SHAWANO 89
SHENANDOAH VALLEY 217
SHINING ROCK 39, 40, 91, 93, 94, 114, 224
SHINING ROCK MOUNTAIN 93, 94
SHINING ROCK WILDERNESS 91, 93, 94, 114, 224
SILBURY HILL 98
SEE BRITISH ISLES
AVEBURY 98
SIOUX 1, 29, 44, 55, 100, 120, 121, 147
EASTERN 10, 12, 14, 21, 23, 29, 40, 50-52,

61-63, 74-76, 89, 93, 96, 110, 112, 116, 117, 119, 125, 131, 132, 146, 152, 164, 167, 168, 174, 194, 204, 220, 233, 234
SKIDI 120, 124
SKY COUNTRY 8, 11, 140, 173
SKY GODS 101, 140
SNAKE 45, 132, 227
SNOWBIRD MOUNTAINS 129
SNOW BEAR 161, 180, 181
SOHIYI 137
SEE CHIMNEY ROCK
SONG OF CREATION 3, 7, 80, 83
SOUTH CAROLINA 4, 17, 21, 95, 128, 148, 164, 233
RUTHERFORD COUNTY 128
SPHINX 73
SPIRIT FORCES 74, 79, 84, 106, 123, 127
SQUIRREL 63
STANDING INDIAN 95, 114, 209
LEGEND 8, 28, 45, 46, 95, 105, 117, 121, 123, 132, 135, 136, 139, 141, 146, 197
MOUNTAIN 5, 13, 14, 16, 21, 23, 25, 26, 34, 37, 39, 40, 61, 74, 80-83, 86, 91, 93-95, 97, 100, 102-107, 109-111, 113-115, 117-119, 123-129, 131, 133, 138-145, 149, 153, 166, 167, 169, 170, 172, 185, 218, 228, 231, 238
STANDING INDIAN ROCK 95, 114
STAR, HICKORY 61, 62
STARS 30, 32, 36, 37, 65, 68, 70, 99-101, 120, 150, 222
CENTRAL SUN 66
CONSTELLATION 65-67
MILKY WAY 32
ORION 65
PLEIADES 30, 32, 65, 67, 69, 135
SIRIUS 65-67
STAR NATION 65, 124
URSA MAJOR 65, 66
STARWALKING 101, 104
STONEHENGE 73, 195
STUPKA, ARTHUR 167
SUN 9, 13, 28, 30-32, 37, 38, 47, 64-66, 76, 94, 95, 98, 99, 113, 120, 121, 123, 124, 132, 140, 148, 161, 162, 166, 181, 182, 185, 213, 219, 224, 229-233, 237, 238
ECLIPSE 64
NUNDA 64

SUN BEAR 161, 181, 182, 213, 219, 224, 229-233, 238
MEDICINE WHEEL GATHERINGS 166
SWAN, JAMES 5
SWEAT 51, 55, 56, 131, 168, 175, 181
SWEAT BATH 55
SWEAT LODGE 55, 131, 168, 181
TABLE ROCK STATE PARK 113
TENNESSEE 14, 17, 20, 21, 29, 32, 40, 45, 64, 76, 89, 111, 112, 114, 116, 117, 119, 122, 125, 128, 141, 151, 177, 200, 202, 204, 208, 220, 237, 238
CARTER COUNTY 141
EASTERN 10, 12, 14, 21, 23, 29, 40, 50-52, 61-63, 74-76, 89, 93, 96,110, 112, 116, 117, 119, 125, 131, 132, 146, 152, 164, 167, 168, 174, 194, 204, 220, 233, 234
GATLINBURG 128, 151-153, 177, 238
GROTTO FALLS 153, 204
KINGSPORT 17
ROAN MOUNTAIN 141, 142, 172
ROARING FORK 128, 151-154, 204
TENNESSEE RIVER VALLEY 89
TEXAS 106
THOM, CHARLIE 56
CHIEF BOB 62
THUNDER 30, 64, 127, 139, 140, 145, 147, 159, 169, 192
KANATI 139
THUNDER BEINGS 127, 140, 159, 169
THUNDER SPIRITS 145, 159
THUNDERERS 44, 158, 159
THUNDERHEAD MOUNTAIN 127
TIME WARP 148
TOTEM 68, 121, 124, 140, 145, 158, 221, 222, 225-227
TOWNHOUSE 130
TRAIL OF TEARS 23, 24, 51
RELOCATION 20
REMOVAL 23, 30, 51, 61-63, 83
TREES 10-12, 25, 29, 30, 34, 36, 37, 63, 73, 75, 96, 97, 123, 126, 131, 141, 144, 153, 156, 157, 161, 162, 164-169, 171-178, 184, 185, 188, 224
TREES:
ALDER 171
AMERICAN CHESTNUT 15
APPLE 169, 179

ASH 169, 170, 174
BEECH 10, 114, 172
BLACK CHERRY 172
BLACK WALNUT 22
BUCKEYE 53, 54, 170
CEDAR 29, 113, 120, 130, 165, 167, 173, 174, 184
CONIFERS 141
DECIDUOUS 178
DOGWOODS 172
ELDER 1, 20, 29, 32, 45, 53, 54, 60, 64, 158, 161, 171, 184, 185, 200, 201, 215, 227, 237
ELM 170
FIR 10, 15, 109, 164, 167, 170, 174
HACKBERRY 172
HARDWOOD 10, 133, 153, 164, 170
HEMLOCK 164, 167, 170
HICKORY 61, 62, 85, 124, 136, 151, 172, 209
HOLLY 29, 165, 174
IRONWOOD 172
JUNIPER 167, 168
LAUREL 29, 33, 38, 153, 172, 174, 204
MAPLE 164, 170
MULBERRY 172
OAK 22, 96, 97, 164, 170, 171, 174, 175
OLD GROWTH FORESTS 177, 223
PERSIMMON 172
PINE 29, 153, 164, 165, 167, 170
RHODODENDREN 153
ROOT 2, 22, 23, 56, 163, 181
SASSAFRAS 172
SPRUCE 7, 10, 14, 29, 109, 127, 164, 165, 170, 171, 174
SYCAMORE 169
TREE WISDOM 165, 172, 173, 175
TULE TREE 75
TUPELO 170
WALNUT 22, 168, 169
WILLOW 55, 168, 174, 181
WITCH HAZEL 169
YELLOW BIRCH 10, 171
YELLOW POPLAR 10
TRICKSTER, THE 30
TSALI 23
TSULKALA 93
SEE JUDACALLA

TURQUOISE 75, 170, 196
TURTLE ISLAND 1, 27, 52, 67, 68, 89, 117, 176, 215, 224, 234
TUSCARORA 29
UFO 102, 106
UNITED STATES 10, 12, 74, 110, 213
UNTO THESE HILLS 55
VAN DER POST, LAURENS 31, 161, 222
VERMONT 12
VIRGINIA 13, 21, 167
VISION QUEST 55, 133
VOLCANO 74
VORTEX 76, 84, 85, 93, 95, 97, 101-104, 106, 109, 111-115, 119, 123, 125-128, 131, 133, 138-140, 142, 145-149, 201, 202, 204-206, 209
WASHINGTON 196, 231, 238
SNOQUALMIE FALLS 196
WATCHER, THE 143
WATER 8, 10, 13, 17, 33, 35, 36, 38, 41, 44, 53, 55, 76, 79, 81, 92, 110, 112, 116, 120, 122, 132, 137, 148, 149, 154, 157, 168, 169, 174, 176, 188, 191-202, 205, 206, 208, 210, 218, 221, 234
ABRAMS FALLS 127, 206
ARAKA FALLS 201
AVERY CREEK 114
BIG LAUREL FALLS 204
BLACK DOME FALLS 110
BOTTOMLESS POOLS 85, 209
BRIDAL VEIL FALLS 202
CHEOAH RIVER 115
CHEOWA RIVER 121, 131
CONESTEE FALLS 202
COVE CREEK 115
CULLASAJA RIVER 86, 128, 196, 200, 205
DEEP CREEK 115, 202, 206
DRY FALLS 196, 200, 202
EAGLE CREEK 200
ELK FALLS 202
ENLOE CREEK 202
FONTANA DAM 112
FONTANA LAKE 112, 114, 115
FRENCH BROAD RIVER 17, 218
GLENVILLE LAKE 112
GROTTO FALLS 153, 204
HIWASSEE LAKE 112, 130, 133

HORSEPASTURE RIVER 203, 207
HOT SPRINGS 208
INDIAN CREEK FALLS 202, 206
KATHEY FALLS 203
KENTUCKY RIVER 89
LAKE JAMES 112
LAKE JUNALUSKA 145
LAKE LURE 128, 151, 209
LAKE TOXAWAY 113, 125, 204
LINVILLE RIVER 104
LITTLE SNOWBIRD CREEK 123
LITTLE TENNESSEE RIVER 122
LOOKING GLASS FALLS 114, 127, 128, 203
MIDNIGHT HOLE 206
MILL SPRINGS 209
MINGO FALLS 206
MITCHELL FALLS 110
MOODY SPRINGS 209
MOONEY FALLS 204
MOUNT TOXAWAY FALLS 203
NANTAHALA LAKE 112
NANTAHALA RIVER 207
NIAGRA FALLS 85
NICHOLS COVE BRANCH FALLS 203
OCONOLUFTEE RIVER 115, 197, 200, 208
OTTAWA RIVER 89
PEACHTREE CREEK 130
PIGEON RIVER 114, 115, 131, 208
QUEEN FALLS 203
RAINBOW FALLS 203, 204, 207
RAINBOW SPRINGS 209
RAMSAY CASCADES 206
RHINE 193
SANTEELAH 96, 97, 112, 114
SHATLEY SPRINGS 208
SHOOTING CREEK 209
SLICKROCK CREEK 121, 122
SLIDING ROCK 205
SNOQUALMIE FALLS 196
STILL HOUSE FALLS 204
TUCKASEGEE RIVER 89, 122
UPPER CULLASAJA FALLS 205
WHITEWATER FALLS 204
YELLOWSTONE FALLS 204
WATERS, FRANK 57
WATSON, LYALL 191

251

WELLICOTT ROCK WILDERNESS
LINVILLE GORGE 91, 97, 101, 102, 104-106, 112, 113, 145, 218
MIDDLE PRONG 93, 114
SHINING ROCK 39, 40, 91, 93, 94, 114, 224
SLICKROCK 91, 96, 97, 114, 115, 121, 122, 203
UPPER NANTAHALA 91, 95, 114
WHITESIDE MOUNTAIN 133
WHITE MOUNTAINS 12
WILDERNESS 16, 25, 26, 86, 91, 93-97, 104, 106, 112-115, 121, 145-147, 151, 188, 203, 224
WIND 3, 12, 44, 53, 62, 65, 81, 92, 94, 105, 120, 121, 123, 130, 147, 153, 176, 186, 197, 199, 209, 213, 223, 225, 231, 233, 234, 238
WIND SPIRITS 92, 94, 147
WRIGHT, MICHELLE SMALL 101, 108
WYOMING 75, 120
DEVIL'S TOWER 120
YELLOW CREEK MOUNTAINS 115
YONAH 12, 66, 229
SEE BLACK BEAR
ZUNI 44, 197

PAGE BRYANT is recognized throughout the U.S. and England as a teacher, author, psychic counselor, workshop and seminar coordinator, environmental activist, and specialist on earth energies. Page, along with her husband visionary artist, Scott Guynup, travel extensively conducting workshops and seminars on subjects that include Native American spirituality, the psychology of ceremony, planetary consciousness, sacred ecology, archetypal psychology, and personal awareness. Page's books include *The Earth Changes Survival Handbook, Terravision: A Traveler's Guide To The Living Planet Earth, Crystals And Their Use, The Magic Of Minerals, Aquarian Guide To Native American Mythology,* and *Awakening Arthur: His Return In Our Time.* For the past 25 years, Page has helped thousands through her work as a psychic counselor. Page has been a presenter at Sun Bear's Medicine Wheel Gatherings for the past 12 years, and Scott has designed the cover for several Bear Tribe publications, *Wildfire*, and the cover for some of Page's books. Page is the "discoverer" of the seven Sedona vortexes. She and Scott relocated to the Smoky Mountains in 1991 after a decade of residency in Sedona, Arizona.

# PSYCHIC READINGS

Page Bryant is an internationally recognized psychic, author, lecturerer, and teacher in the field of alternative thinking for the past twenty-five years. Her books are popular in the U.S., Europe, and Australia. Page has helped thousands through her psychic readings and counseling, and much of her work is done through the mail. The following readings are available:

TWO-YEAR PERSONAL READING: This reading is designed to look forward into the upcoming two years of one's personal life. Page will define the cycle you are in, how long it will last, and, generally, what you can expect to encounter from it. All major astrological transits and aspects will be pointed out in detail. Page's attunement probes areas of one's life for future conditions and events that concern finances, career, personal and professional relationships, health, and personal change. Questions may be asked. The fee for this reading is $85.00.

IN-DEPTH STUDY: This is a channeled reading by Albion. Page has been the channel for Albion for over twenty years. The In-Depth Study is not a psychic reading, per se, but a "study" which is designed to identify one's *SOUL TYPE*, its nature and qualities, and its purpose for living in physical human form on the Earth. The Study touches upon, in-depth, the following:
* Colors in the aura and how they are operating within your consciousness and life
* Complete health evaluation
* Karmic relationships and personal karmic conditions
* Evaluation of your spiritual path and your progress with same
* Identification of your Spirit Teacher(s)
* Pastel drawing by Scott Guynup of your Guardian Angel
* Personal advice and suggestions for study for greater spiritual awareness

The fee for the In-Depth Study is $250.00. If done in person, the Study takes approximately one and one-half hours. If done through the mail, it ranges from 50-75 typewritten double-spaced pages.

PSYCHIC READING WITH PASTEL DRAWING: This reading is done by Scott Guynup. Scott tunes into your energy and renders for you a psychic drawing and a personal reading explaining the image he has drawn, as well as any personal advice or predictions he intuits for you. The drawing will usually be of your Guardian Angel, Spirit Teacher or Guide, or one of your past lives. The fee for the drawing and reading is $75.00.

**Please provide birth dates for all readings.** All readings done through the mail, by Page, will be typed. Scott Guynup's reading will be sent on cassette tape. Call or write for additional information or to set up an appointment: Mystic Mountains Retreat Center, 707 Brunswick Drive, Waynesville, N.C. 704-456-6714 FAX 704-456-8230. Please enclose check or money order made out to Page Bryant or Scott Guynup for all readings by mail. Please allow 7-10 days for delivery; 30 days for In-Depth Study.

## 3 DAY RETREATS FOR ARTISTS AND SPIRITUAL SEEKERS

1. EXPERIENCING THE REAWAKENING OF THE GREAT SMOKY MOUNTAINS: This retreat is designed to teach participants the location of power spots (vortexes), sacred sites, and ley lines of the Great Smoky Mountains. Each morning there will be a two-hour teaching session with Page Bryant, followed by an excursion into the mountains to visit selected power spots/sacred sites such as Cherokee Indian Reservation, Chimney Rock, Judaculla Rock, Nidawasi Mound, Cullasaja River Gorge, numerous spectacular waterfalls, and Looking Glass Rock, whose summit is pure quartz. Free time may be spent taking hikes or enjoying other wonderful outdoor activities located within a few miles of the Center.

2. CEREMONY AND DAILY LIFE: Each day will begin with a two-hour teaching session with Page about ceremony and its effects upon the physical, emotional, mental, and spiritual levels of the human body, consciousness, and daily life. Topics covered will include setting up and working with a Magic Circle; how to work with an altar; construction and use of solar, lunar, and star shrines; the psychology of ceremony; the nature of sacred objects; the sweat lodge; prosperity and healing rituals. Some ceremonies will be done at various sites in the Great Smoky Mountains. All ceremonial supplies will be provided. Participants are encouraged to bring their own drums, rattles, or other ceremonial/sacred objects.

3. ART AS A TOOL OF SELF-DEVELOPMENT AND SPIRITUAL AWARENESS: This retreat offers the opportunity to study with nationally-recognized visionary artist, Scott Guynup. Scott's work has been featured on the cover of *Wildfire Magazine* and on the covers of several books by various authors. His line of personal greeting cards are found throughout the US and Europe. Scott will share techniques for better self and nature awareness by working in the mediums of oils, pastels, and sculpture. He will also help participants develop greater intuitive skills and how to incorporate these

skills into their personal artwork. Begin perceiving, discovering, and painting "little people", nature spirits and mountain devas. Participants will go into the beauty and splendor of the Smokies for on-site sketching, painting, and meditation.

Seven-day private study programs with Page and her Spirit Teacher, Albion, are also available. Please call or write for information and a free brochure. 704-456-6714

## DAY-LONG TEACHING TOURS IN THE SMOKIES

Mystic Mountains offers day-long teaching tours to some of the power spots and sacred sites located in the Great Smoky Mountains. Page Bryant, or one qualified to teach her information, will personally guide you to selected sacred sites and power spots in western North Carolina.

* Ceremonial Pilgrimage: Experience a guided teaching journey to selected power spots in the Smokies and participate in an earth healing, sacred pipe, and solar ceremony.

* Earth Healing Journey: This excursion into the depth of the Great Smoky Mountains is designed to teach better earth awareness and sacred ecology, the environmental issues facing the Southern Appalachians, and techniques by which you can get in touch with healing energy that comes through trees, mountains and mountain spirits, minerals, and water.

* Spirit Journey: This tour also takes you into the depths of the Smokies to sites where faeries and nature spirits, angels, the legendary little people, and mountains devas reside. Participants will be taught ceremonies and techniques which will assist in developing a closer conscious connection with members of the invisible kingdom. This is also a storytelling journey that will share knowledge of the faery folk of the region.

Page Bryant is available as a guide for large groups, as well as for being a speaker and workshop coordinator for groups and centers on the subject of the psychology of ceremony, earth awareness and sacred ecology, geomancy and earth energies, drawing upon the energy of sacred sites, astronomy of the ancient peoples, and various aspects of personal and spiritual development, and for presenting her teachings on the reawakening of the Great Smoky Mountains. For detailed information about the tours, call or write Mystic Mountains Teaching Center, 707 Brunswick Drive, Waynesville, N.C. 28786; 704-456-6714, FAX 456-8230.